DEPRESSION IN CHILDREN AND ADOLESCENTS

DEPRESSION IN CHILDREN AND ADOLESCENTS

Edited by
Alfred P. French, M.D.
*University of California, Davis
School of Medicine*

Irving N. Berlin, M.D.
*University of California, Davis
School of Medicine*

HUMAN SCIENCES PRESS
72 Fifth Avenue   3 Henrietta Street
NEW YORK, NY 10011 ● LONDON, WC2E 8LU

Copyright © 1979 by Human Sciences Press
72 Fifth Avenue, New York, New York 10011

All rights reserved. No part of this work may be reproduced or utilized in any form or by any means, electronic or mechanical, including photocopying, microfilm and recording, or by any information storage and retrieval system without permission in writing from the publisher

Printed in the United States of America
9 987654321

Library of Congress Cataloging in Publication Data
Main entry under title:

Depression in children and adolescents.

    Papers presented at a conference held in Berkeley, Calif., June 11–12, 1976, sponsored by the Dept. of Psychiatry, Section of Child Psychiatry and Dept. of Postgraduate Medicine of the University of California, Davis, and Extended Programs in Medical Education of the University of California at San Francisco.
    Bibliography: p.
    Includes index.
    1. Depression in children—Congresses. I. French, Alfred P. II. Berlin, Irving Norman, 1917–   III. California. University, Davis. Dept. of Psychiatry. Section of Child Psychiatry. IV. California.

Library of Congress Cataloging in Publication Data

University, Davis. Dept. of Postgraduate Medicine.
V. University of California San Francisco. Extended Programs in Medical Education.
RJ506.D4D46   618.9'28'52   LC79–13481
ISBN 0–87705–390–1

CONTENTS

Preface   7
Acknowledgments   9
Introduction   11
Contributors   13

1. Depression in Children—The Development of an Idea   17
    Alfred P. French, M.D.

2. A Psychobiological View of Depression in Childhood   29
    Melvin Lewis, M.B., B.S., F.R.C., Psych., D.C.H.
    Dorothy Otnow Lewis, M.D., F.A.C.P.

3. Childhood Depression: A Psychodynamic Approach to the Etiology and Treatment of Depression in Children   46
    Elva O. Poznanski, M.D.

4. Childhood Depression: The Mirror of Experience, Interpersonal Interactions, and Depressive Phenomena   69
    Irving Philips, M.D.

5. Some Implications of the Development Processes for Treatment of Depression in Adolescence   87
Irving N. Berlin, M.D.

6. Object Removal and Adolescent Depression   109
Benjamin Kaufman, M.D.

7. Treatment of the Depressed Child   129
Harold Boverman, M.D.
Alfred P. French, M.D.

8. A Longitudinal Study of Two Depressed, Self-Destructive Latency-Age Boys: A Six-Year and Four-Year Follow-up   140
Alfred P. French, M.D.
Margaret Steward, Ph.D.
Thomas Morrison, Ph.D.

9. Psychological Implications of Total Motor Paralysis in a Five-Year-Old Boy   172
J. Allen Miller, M.D.

10. Depression in the Child Abuse Syndrome   184
Charlotte Bible, M.D.
Alfred P. French, M.D.

11. Therapy Vignettes   210
Harold Boverman, M.D.
Alfred P. French, M.D.

12. Annotated Bibliography   218
Alfred P. French, M.D.

Index   291

PREFACE

Development is both continuous and uneven. By definition, "development" refers to a process in which the evolution of new structures from old occurs variably depending on developmental vicissitudes. Developmental processes, like growth spurts, may hurdle impulsively forward or appear to fall to a dead halt, or seek random avenues over apparent obstacles for a new route by which to proceed. As child psychiatrists, we experience joy and anguish as we observe and try to facilitate at close range our patients' developmental strivings toward progress, and, as members of the fledgling profession of child psychiatry, we are excited by our developing field with its energy and variabilities so typical of all young and rapidly developing organisms. We and all child mental health professionals grow with the research in child development, neurophysiology and chemistry, and prevention of early disturbances in childhood. As in the developing child, these phenomena grow unevenly.

"Depression," a powerful current of psychiatric thought long restricted to adult psychiatry, has recently burst with great force into child psychiatry. In this volume, we describe aspects of the flow of "depression" into child and adolescent psychiatry, hoping to harness this energy to further our only goal, the treatment of our patients.

Alfred P. French
Irving N. Berlin

ACKNOWLEDGMENTS

We, the editors, are grateful to Deane Critchley Berlin and the other members of our families for their tolerance during this time-consuming undertaking.

We wish to thank the Department of Psychiatry, Section of Child Psychiatry and Department of Post-graduate Medicine of the School of Medicine of the University of California, Davis, Extension Programs in Medical Education of the University of California at San Francisco, for sponsoring the conference on Depression in Children held in Berkeley, California on June 11 and 12, 1976.

A very special thanks to Ms. Norma Fox of Human Sciences Press for urging us to do this project. We appreciate her foresight, and hope that this volume adequately fulfills her wish to participate in the publication of a book on depression in children.

We wish to express our thanks to Pat Deese, Administrative Assistant to the Section of Child Psychiatry, who coordinated and did much of the typing, and to Karen

Knudsen, Secretary to the Section of Child Psychiatry, who helped her.

We are also grateful for the help from the Child Psychiatry Fund of the Section of Child Psychiatry for funding the final typing.

Alfred P. French
Irving N. Berlin

INTRODUCTION

With publication of this volume, the third book becomes available on depression in children. The first, edited by Anna-Lisa Annell, is a collection of papers presented at a conference in Sweden in 1972. The second, edited by Schulterbrandt and Raskin, 1977, is a collection of papers presented at a conference on depression in children sponsored by the National Institute of Mental Health. Most of the papers in this volume were presented at a conference on depression in children held in Berkeley, California, 1976.

Our objective in this volume is to present a broad view of current clinical thinking regarding depression in children and to facilitate the currently accelerating growth and development of this area. We hope, of course, that this growth and development will be productive and lead in the near future to clinically useful and theoretically sound diagnostic criteria, treatment, and research.

We also included an annotated bibliography to give mental health professionals a sense of the current critical literature on childhood depression.

CONTRIBUTORS

Irving N. Berlin, M.D. is Professor of Psychiatry and Pediatrics, and Head, Section of Child Psychiatry, in the Department of Psychiatry at the School of Medicine, University of California, Davis, and Sacramento Medical Center, Sacramento, California.

Charlotte Bible, M.D. is a Fellow in Child Psychiatry in the Section of Child Psychiatry at the Department of Psychiatry, School of Medicine, University of California, Davis, and Sacramento Medical Center, Sacramento, California.

Harold Boverman, M.D. is Clinical Professor of Psychiatry and Pediatrics and Associate Head, Section of Child Psychiatry in the Department of Psychiatry at the School of Medicine, University of California, Davis, and Sacramento Medical Center, Sacramento, California.

Alfred P. French, M.D. is Assistant Clinical Professor of Child Psychiatry in the Department of Psychiatry at the School of Medicine, University of California, Davis, and Sacramento Medical Center, Sacramento, California.

Benjamin Kaufman, M.D. is Assistant Clinical Professor in the Department of Psychiatry at the School of Medicine, University of California, Davis, and Sacramento Medical Center, Sacramento, California.

Melvin Lewis, M.B., B.S., F.R.C., Psych., D.C.H. is Professor of Psychiatry and Pediatrics at the Yale Child Study Center, School of Medicine, Yale University.

Dorothy Otnow Lewis, M.D., F.A.C.P. is Associate Clinical Professor of Psychiatry at the Yale Child Study Center, School of Medicine, Yale University.

J. Allen Miller, M.D. is Assistant Professor in Residence in the Department of Psychiatry at the School of Medicine, University of California, Davis, and Sacramento Medical Center, Sacramento, California.

Thomas Morrison, Ph.D. is Assistant Professor in Residence in the Department of Psychiatry at the School of Medicine, University of California, Davis, and Sacramento Medical Center, Sacramento, California.

Irving Philips, M.D. is Professor of Psychiatry in the Department of Psychiatry, and Director of Children's Services, University of California, San Francisco.

Elva O. Poznanski, M.D. is Professor of Psychiatry, Department of Psychiatry, School of Medicine, University of Michigan, Ann Arbor.

Margaret Steward, Ph.D. is Associate Clinical Professor in the Department of Psychiatry, University of California, Davis, and Sacramento Medical Center, Sacramento, California.

Chapter 1

"DEPRESSION IN CHILDREN"—THE DEVELOPMENT OF AN IDEA

Alfred P. French

Ideas, like people and families, undergo development, and like people, ideas develop following the four characteristics of epigenetic development outlined by Piaget and Mussen (1970, p. 710): succession in sequential order, progressive integration, necessary developmental sequences each with its individual time-table, and homeorhetic evolutionary regulation that permits selection of the most efficient path of development. Depression in children has a complex and fascinating developmental history.

The objectives of this chapter are to present a brief overview of the literature in this area; an outline of the major areas of discussion, controversy, and conflict; and a

This chapter was originally presented at a conference on depression in children, sponsored by the Departments of Psychiatry (section of Child Psychiatry) and Postgraduate Medicine of the School of Medicine, University of California, Davis and Extension Programs in Medical Education, University of California, San Francisco, June 11, 1976, Berkeley, California.

summary of current concepts, with some discussion about where we might be headed. Occasionally, when giving an overview of an area, one comes across a paper which is such a good summary that most of the job has been done already. Fortunately this is the case here: In *Depression and Human Existence,* edited by Anthony and Benedek (1975) a paper by Anthony, "Childhood Depression" (pp. 231–277) is a beautiful overview of the literature, summary of the essential questions involved, and a discussion of these questions. Let me begin by quoting Anthony: "When two variable terms are brought together in a single diagnostic label, the complexity can be impressive. Both 'childhood' and 'depression' are conceptions that are rapidly outgrowing their original meanings, so specific connotations associated with either of them are continually compounded over time" (p. 231).

In organizing the discussion of this complex area, I have decided to rely heavily on the distinction between boundary conditions, which indicate what *can* happen, and laws, which permit us to predict what *will* happen. The following general points then occur in sequence: the first boundary condition, is there "depression"? The psychiatric community answers affirmatively; some other communities do not. In the second boundary condition, is there a "depressed child"?, the matter becomes immediately complex, as we shall see. In particular, those holding to the *structural* hypothesis, wherein "depression" implies the existence of a superego conflict, hold, as a boundary condition, that the above hypothesis is rejected (Rie, 1974). Others, following Spitz's (1946) analysis of the problem, or Bibring's discussion of depression as an intraego phenomenon (1961, pp. 13–48), take the opposite position and accept the hypothesis.

Such polarities arise easily (Tajfel, 1970), and the discussions that result make and break careers, generate enormous numbers of papers, and are eventually resolved through the development of a point of view that sees each of the prior contesting positions as a special case of a newly clarified general case. In the process, new terms and concepts are generated. It seems that the time is at hand for a new synthesis of observations and concepts concerning depression and childhood.

At this point let me digress somewhat and discuss a bit more the importance of clarifying one's position. Our conceptual base not only determines what we are permitted to think about; it determines our *perceptions*. This point of view, first clearly expressed by Kant who argued for *a priori* knowledge (knowledge which preceeds experience), has received support from recent studies in physiological psychology, which have demonstrated that outflow from the brain to the sensory organs influences perception at the sensory organ level (Pribram, 1971, pp. 85–87). That is, information from the eye or ear is "edited" by information moving *out from* the central nervous system before it ever reaches the brain. We therefore are richly endowed with the wherewithal to be prejudiced.

A very different phenomenon may further the human tendency to cling tightly to a point of view in ways that lead to very different interpretations of the same data. As we are physiologically predisposed to prejudice, so may we be evolutionarily disposed to be highly conforming with respect to our primary social group. Wilson has stated (1975) that "Human beings are absurdly easy to indoctrinate— they *seek* it" (italics original). And how does the indoctrinated individual behave? In an interesting article on personality, Rioch (1972) states: "To be more of a person in a preferred group is the most general reinforcement for humans that has been recognized" (p. 578). Now, if this kind of reinforcement is associated with a particular point of view such as ego psychology or the structural hypothesis, who among us has the courage to abandon a preferred group and wander off in search of another one?

In summary, we seem to assume that "intelligence," a high level of training, or technical expertise will render arguments judgment-free. But this is not at all the case; training and academic clout are often used precisely in the service of the coherence of a primary reference group. The perception of the environment, a process that preceeds obviously by a good margin the collection and analysis of data, may be carried out more with an eye to protection of one's home turf than to a perfectly detached exploration of the issues.

Papers on depression usually begin with a reference to Freud's (1957) and Abraham's (1927, pp. 248–279) early work concerning narcissism, orality, introjection, and ambivalence. Papers on depression in children usually refer to the classic papers of Rene Spitz (1945, 1946), who observed the profound withdrawal of children in a clean but emotionally cold institutional environment. In 1945, in the first volume of *Psychoanalytic Study of the Child*, Spitz described his basic findings, which are well known. The following year, writing in the same annual, Spitz sought to grasp a dangerous nettle. How is the phenomenon of hospitalism best understood? His 1945 paper was titled "Hospitalism—An Inquiry into the Genesis of Psychiatric Conditions in Early Childhood," and defined hospitalism, in the first sentence, as "a vitiated condition of the body due to long confinement in a hospital, or the morbid condition of the atmosphere of a hospital." This is clearly safe ground. In 1946, Spitz titled his paper "Anaclitic Depression: An Inquiry Into the Genesis of Psychiatric Conditions in Early Childhood, II."

Following some case examples, Spitz moves into the eye of the storm on page 316 with the statement, "To this symptomatology should be added the physiognomic expression in these cases, which is difficult to describe. This expression would in an adult be described as depression." On page 320, "The syndrome in question is extremely similar to that which is familiar to us from Abraham's and Freud's classical description of mourning, pathological mourning, and melancholia. The factor which appears to be of decisive etiological significance in our cases is the loss of the love object . . ." and, later, ". . . comes closest to what Fenichel described pre-oedipal infantile depression, called by Abraham 'primal papathymia.'"

Following a specific disavowal of any association with the psychology of Melanie Klein, wherein the depressive position is a universal and normal event, Spitz deals with the question of the superego: "For if anything is certain, then it is that the infant is not ruled by a superego, nor does it dispose of abstractive functions in any way demonstrable before the age of approximately eighteen months." Anaclitic depression is defined clearly as a profound and irreversible deviation in development, the etiology of which involves loss. The core of Spitz's argument is: "In the infant the superego is absent, so that it is impossible to assume destructive hostility of the superego. However, the loss of the love object in itself is equivalent to a hostile deprivation for the infant . . ." (p. 333) and both in melancholia and in anaclitic depression the sadism which threatens the patient with extinction originates from the same source: except that in melancholia the source is an intrapsychic representation, while in anaclitic depression the source is the living original of the later intrapsychic representation." (p. 335)

As we all know, this interesting argument was not to go unchallenged. In 1966, Herbert Rie examined the applicability of "depression" to children and concluded that "the fully differentiated and generalized primary affect characterizing depression, namely, despair or hopelessness, is one of which children—perhaps prior to the end of the latency years—are incapable." He complains that "the failure to specify the criteria (for the diagnosis) is keenly felt when the noted symptoms differ grossly from those of adult depression. The diagnosis is announced *ex cathedra* but one is forced to confess that the term ('depression') has no familiar referent in child psychopathology."

In 1975, Therese Benedek wrote that "Hospitalism, however, is not a depressive illness; it only appears so . . . children suffering from hospitalism do not cry. They are not angry. Their perceptions of their own bodies, and even more of the objects who care for them, are not sufficient to develop object relationships in any meaningful way. Thus what is termed hospitalism is not a mental condition, and is not a depression" (pp. 343–344). Thus the discussion continues, 30 years after Spitz's papers. In summary then, the structural hypothesis excludes, as a boundary condition, the possibility of depression in children.

The evolution of ego psychology, however, cast a whole new light on the matter. If the ego alone is capable of experiencing affective states, "depression" has been redefined, and with this redefinition "childhood depression" can be reconsidered. Ego psychology, in short, changed the boundary conditions in such a way that "childhood depression" is not excluded. We are therefore challenged to develop the *laws* of ego function, in order to determine the conditions under which depression will occur.

Of particular interest here is the Anna Freud-John Bowlby discussion and controversy. Anna Freud utilizes the concepts of "libido," "cathexis" and "narcissism" to organize clinical data; Bowlby argues that ethological concepts, in particular "attachment," are better suited to organize observational data. Bowlby (1960) states his position that "the child's tie is best conceived as the outcome of a number of instinctual response systems, mostly nonoral in character, which are a part of the inherited behavior repertoire of man; when they are activated and the mother figure is available, attachment behavior results" (p. 9). Elsewhere (p. 12) he attacks the "loyalty to the theory of infantile narcissism which remains a feature of the work of many leading analysts" as responsible for the inadequate emphasis on the significance for psychopathology of grief and mourning in early childhood. Immediately following his paper, Anna Freud, Max Schur, and Rene Spitz discuss it with vigor. Anna Freud (1970, p. 56) points to the contrast between "narcissism" and "attachment" as primary organizing concepts; Schur (1960, p. 82) states that Bowlby has felt compelled to "revamp, more or less, some of the fundamental concepts and formulations of psychoanalysis ... (on the basis of) ... *his* application of the instinct concepts of ethology, an application in which he goes far beyond the claims of even Lorenz. His application contradicts also all the evidence accumulated by research on animal behavior and the development of human structure ..." (italics original). Spitz (1960, p. 89) states that the fundamental difference between Bowlby's position and his own is "that Bowlby disregards the difference of developmental levels which obviously exists between infants aged six months and children between three to four years of age." Bowlby's paper is thus not happily received by these three authorities.

As Anthony and Benedek (1975, p. 231) have noted, the definition of depression has evolved enormously. One group of definitions focuses on the basic nature of the relationship between the individual and the environment. Spitz, as we have seen, maintained the structural hypothesis, shifting from intrapsychic to interactional processes; Engel (1962, 1967) and Engel and Schmale (1972), in a well-known and important series of papers, have focused on hopelessness and helplessness and conservation-withdrawal as responses to a nonsupportive environment. French and Steward (1975) have sought to construct a highly general model of depression, based on failure of the organism-environment relationship.

The developmental perspective, obviously crucial to our understanding of depression in children, has not received as much attention as one might hope. In a brief, clear paper Cytryn and McKnew (1974) have proposed that as development proceeds, depressive processes will be manifested successively through fantasy, verbal expression, mood, and behavior, with concomitant evolution of defensive mechanisms.

Anthony (1975, p. 255) similarly proposed primary, secondary, and tertiary manifestations of depression: "the mixture varying with the stage of development, the psychosocial setting, and the severity of the condition." Taking an ego psychology perspective, Anthony speaks to the objections to "child depression" raised by psychodynamic considerations as follows: "all the metapsychological difficulties associated with the operation of classic theory—oral fixation and incorporation, aggression against the self—are here given merely a peripheral or complicating role. The child's depression can assimilate them later when he becomes an adult."

Another group of papers, perhaps the most extensive, has taken a clinical-descriptive approach. This group includes papers by Sandler and Joffe (1965), Poznanski and Zrull (1970), Cytryn and McKnew (1972), Malmquist (1971, 1971, 1975), the GAP report on classification in children (1972), and most of the papers presented in a large symposium on depression in children held in Uppsala, Sweden in 1972 (Annell, 1972). Of particular interest here is a paper by Anna Freud (1970) titled "The Symptomatology of Childhood—A Preliminary Attempt at Classification," wherein she includes (p. 27) "symptoms of bodily neglect, self derogation, inferiority feelings, depressive states, depersonalization (in childhood)" in her fourth major category of "symptoms resulting from changes in the libido economy or direction of cathexis."

Finally we must consider the special problem of the "depressive equivalent." The concept has no doubt been useful clinically in facilitating a more empathetic approach to difficult and obnoxious youngsters. On the theoretical level, it remains insecure. Anthony (1975, p. 262) has argued vigorously: "Toolan carried this idea of depression without depressive affect to such an extreme that the whole concept of equivalents ceased to be clinically credible. His approach has rightfully been criticized by Rie as atheoretical, uncritical, circular, semantically complacent and devoid of any real evidence . . . it both explains too much and explains nothing at all." Clearly, this problem will remain unsolved until underlying problems of definition are solved.

THE OUTLOOK FOR THE FUTURE

First, the concept "depression" is evolving actively, as outlined in a burgeoning recent literature. Of particular interest is a paper by Akiskal and McKinney (1975), seeking to synthesize psychodynamic, biological, and learning theory conceptualizations of depression. Second, "childhood" is being demythologized as a time of innocence and happiness. Third, the concept of development is being extended. The full impact of the epigenetic view of development, articulated by Erikson (1963, pp. 65–67) and Piaget and Mussen (1970, p. 710), is still to be felt. Meanwhile, further theoretical exploration of the concept of development is occurring. For example, Rene Thom, a French mathematician, has developed an extensive and controversial theory, "catastrophe theory" (Thom, 1972; Zeeman, 1976), which promises a rigorous definition of the fundamental processes of physical morphogenesis. In particular, he has demonstrated seven fundamental types of discontinuous processes possible in a four-dimensional space and has applied these "catastrophes" to embryological development. This is the future outlined in such an extensive sweep that we will be mining out the practical implications of

Thom's work for generations, as we currently continue to benefit from the conceptualizations of Newton.

Fourth, we are understanding principles of classification in a profoundly new way. In 1974, Robert Sokal, in a paper titled "Classification: Purposes, Principles, Progress, Prospects" states that "classifications need not be hierarchic and the clusters may overlap. The whole idea of hierarchic nonoverlapping (mutually exclusive) classifications which is so attractive to the human mind is currently undergoing reexamination" (p. 1121). Certainly, we will require decades to integrate such a sweeping and profound change into clinical practice. We are all aware of the intensive efforts to develop better clinical classification (Panzetta, 1974; Strauss, 1975; Spitz, Endicott, Robbins, 1975).

Finally, the concept of the "ego" continues to undergo theoretical and clinical refinement (Friedman, 1973) and our understanding of mental mechanisms is being actively advanced (Vaillant, 1976).

In summary, I hope that we are at a point where we can carefully formulate questions in rich areas, and find reasonable answers to some of them. "Childhood," "depression," and "childhood depression" are coming of age.

REFERENCES

Abraham, K. The first pre-genital stage of the libido. In *Selected papers of Karl Abraham.* New York: Basic Books, 1927.

Akiskal, H. S., & McKinney, W. T. Overview of recent research in depression. Integration of ten conceptual models into a comprehensive clinical frame. *Archives of General Psychiatry,* 1975, *32,* 285.

Annell, A. L. (Ed.) *Depressive states in childhood and adolescence.* Stockholm: Almquist and Wiksell, 1972.

Anthony, E. J. Childhood depression. In E. J. Anthony & T. Benedek (Eds.), *Depression and human existence.* Boston: Little, Brown, 1975.

Benedek, T. Depression during the life cycle. In E. J. Anthony & T. Benedek (Eds.), *Depression and human existence.* Boston: Little, Brown, 1975.

Bibring, E. The mechanism of depression. In P. Greenacre (Ed.), *Affective disorders*. New York: International Universities Press, 1961.

Bowlby, J. Grief and mourning in infancy and early childhood. *Psychoanalytic Study of the Child*, 1960, *15*, 9.

Cytryn, L., & McKnew, D. H. Proposed classification of childhood depression. *American Journal of Psychiatry*, 1972, *129(2)*, 149.

Cytryn, L., & McKnew, D. H. Factors influencing the changing clinical expression of the depressive process in children. *American Journal of Psychiatry*, 1974, *131(8)*, 879.

Engel, G. L. Anxiety and depression withdrawal: The primary affects of unpleasure. *International Journal of Psychoanalysis*, 1962, *113*, 89.

Engel, G. L. Ego development following severe trauma in infancy: A 14-year study of a girl with gastric fistula and depression in infancy. *Bulletin of the Association of Psychoanalytic Medicine*, 1967, *6*, 57.

Engel, G. L., & Schmale, A. H. Conservation-withdrawal: A primary regulatory process or organismis homeostasis. In R. Porter & J. Knight (Eds.), *Physiology, emotion and psychosomatic illness*. Ciba Foundation Symposium 8 (N.S.). Amsterdam: Elsevier-Excerpta Medica, 1972.

Erikson, G. *Childhood and society*. New York: W. W. Norton, 1963.

French, A., & Steward, M. S. Adaptation and affect—toward a synthesis of Piagetian and psychoanalytic psychologies. *Perspectives in Biology and Medicine*, 1975, *18(4)*, 464.

Freud, A. The symptomatology of childhood—a preliminary attempt at classification. *Psychoanalytic Study of the Child*, 1970, *25*, 19.

Freud, S. *Mourning and melancholia*. Standard Edition. London: Hogarth Press, 14:237, 1957.

Friedman, L. F. How real is the realistic ego in psychotherapy? A one-sided review. *Archives of General Psychiatry*, 1973, *28*, 377.

Group for the Advancement of Psychiatry, Report No. 62. *Psychopathological disorder in childhood: Theoretical considerations and a proposed classification*. New York: Mental Health Materials Center, 1972.

Malmquist, C. P. Depressions in childhood and adolescence I. *New England Journal of Medicine*, 1971, *284*, 887.

Malmquist, C. P. Depressions in childhood and adolescence II. *New England Journal of Medicine*, 1971, *284*, 955.

Malmquist, C. P. Depression in childhood. In F. F. Flach & S. C. Draghi (Eds.), *The nature and treatment of depression*. New York: Wiley, 1975.

Panzetta, A. F. Toward a scientific psychiatric nosology. Conceptual and pragmatic issues. *Archives of General Psychiatry*, 1974, *30*, 154.

Piaget, J., & Mussen, P. H. (Eds.), *Carmichael's manual of child psychology*. New York: Wiley, 1970.

Poznanski, G., & Zrull, J. P. Childhood depression. Clinical characteristics of overtly depressed children. *Archives of General Psychiatry*, 1970, *23*, 8.

Pribram, K. H. *Languages of the brain: Experimental paradoxes and principles in neuropsychology.* Englewood Cliffs, N. J.: Prentice-Hall, 1971.

Rie, H. Depression in childhood—a survey of some pertinent contributions. *Journal of the American Academy of Child Psychiatry*, 1966, *5*, 653.

Rioch, D. McK. Personality. *Archives of General Psychiatry*, 1972, *27*, 575.

Sandler, J., & Joffe, W. G. Notes on childhood depression. *International Journal of Psychoanalysis*, 1965, *46*, 88.

Schur, M., Discussion of Dr. John Bowlby's Paper. *Psychoanalytic Study of the Child*, 1960, *15*, 63.

Sokal, R. R. Classification: Purposes, principles, progress, prospects. *Science*, 1974, *185(4157)*, 1115.

Spitz, R. Discussion of Dr. Bowlby's Paper. *Psychoanalytic Study of the Child*, 1960, *15*, 85.

Spitz, R. Hospitalism: An inquiry into the genesis of psychiatric conditions in early childhood I. *Psychoanalytic Study of the Child*, 1945, *1*, 53.

Spitz, R. Anaclitic depression: An inquiry into the genesis of psychiatric conditions in early childhood, II. *Psychoanalytic Study of the Child*, 1946, *2*, 313.

Spitz, R. L., Endicott, J., & Robbins, E. Clinical criteria for psychiatric diagnosis and DSM-III. *American Journal of Psychiatry*, 1975, *132*, 1187.

Strauss, J. S. A comprehensive approach to psychiatric diagnosis. *American Journal of Psychiatry*, 1975, *132*, 1193.

Tajfel, H. Experiments in intergroup discrimination. *Scientific American*, 1970, *223*, 96.

Thom, R. Structural stability and morphogenesis. Reading, Ma.: W. A. Benjamin, 1975.

Vaillant, G. E. Natural history of male psychological health V. The relation of choice of ego mechanisms of defense to adult adjustment. *Archives of General Psychiatry*, 1976, *33*, 535.

Wilson, E. O. *Sociobiology—The new synthesis.* Cambridge, Ma.: Belnap Press, 1975.

Zeeman, E. C. Catastrophe theory. *Scientific American*, 1976, *232*, 65.

Chapter 2

A PSYCHOBIOLOGICAL VIEW OF DEPRESSION IN CHILDHOOD

Melvin Lewis
Dorothy Otnow Lewis

Our purpose here is to review and bring together some basic concepts of depression in childhood. The review is selective and focuses on some recent research on depression in children, including diagnostic criteria, prevalence, classification, etiology, and pharmacological treatment. Finally, we will suggest a psychobiological model for understanding the condition.

DIAGNOSTIC CRITERIA

Numerous lists of symptoms have been compiled (Poznanski & Zrull, 1970; Ling, Oftedal, & Weinberg, 1970; Cytryn & McKnew, 1974). Weinberg et al. (1973), following criteria developed by Feighner et al. (1972) for use in psychiatric research with adults, noted the following ten major categories of symptoms of childhood depression: dysphoric mood, self-deprecatory ideation, aggressive behavior (agitation), sleep disturbance, changes in school performance, diminished socialization, changes in attitudes toward school, somatic complaints, loss of usual energy, and unusual change in appetite and/or weight. Such lists fall short of their purpose in defining a clinical entity by virtue of their: 1) failure to select and demarcate the essential, cardinal symptoms; 2) a tendency to overinclusiveness; 3) failure to recognize less obvious manifestations of depression; and 4) failure to delineate those particularly characteristic symptom clusters that are seen in childhood exclusively.

Depression in children can, of course, exist without the classical unhappy, withdrawn picture that makes the diagnosis easy. Toolan (1962) underscored this with his use of the term "depressive equivalents"; he astutely observed that a teenager "may deliberately mask his own feelings by a pretence of happiness and exhibit the picture of a smiling depression" (p. 407). Other symptoms that may mask a depression include enuresis, headache, school failure, school phobia (Agras, 1958; Watts, 1966), hyperactivity, and antisocial behavior. Renshaw (1972) has recently drawn attention to promiscuity, academic failure, and drug abuse as depressive equivalents. Lewis et al. (1973) reported underlying depression to exist in many of the pregnant teenagers referred to a psychiatrist. Delinquent acts are sometimes an expression of a depression and are often accompanied by hostile and self-punitive behaviors. Kaufman, Makkay, and Zilbach (1959) has described a "depressive core" in children with antisocial aggressive behaviors. Burks and Harrison (1962) also cite aggressive behavior as a symptom of "masked depression," in which the aggressive behavior is used to ward off depression.

Lists that only include sadness, withdrawal, decreased energy, and decreased work productivity cannot really be taken as definitive, since depressed children and adolescents may or may not become members of gangs, compulsively strive to overachieve at school and overimmerse themselves in work, refuse to work at all, lose weight, gorge themselves or starve themselves, boast of their achievements or deprecate themselves. In fact, the degree of what looks like reaction formation in depressed children is quite striking. Furthermore, the interpretation of these behaviors is subjective; one man's "depression" being another's "sociopathy." Thus diagnostic criteria for depression in childhood are not universally agreed upon.

PREVALENCE

Estimates of the prevalence of childhood depression, variously defined, have ranged from less than 1 percent to more than 50 percent depending on the criteria and setting. At one end of the spectrum, Poznanski and Zrull (1970), in a review of 1,788 children evaluated in the outpatient department of Children's Psychiatric Hospital at the University of Michigan Medical Center, found only 14 children who were said to be overtly depressed: 11 boys and 3 girls; 4 were under 6 years of age, and 10 were between 7 and 12 years of age. Rutter (1966) found that the rate of "pure" depression (i.e., disorders characterized predominantly by sadness and misery) was only one to two per 1,000 (three in a total population of 2,199) in his Isle of Wight study of children aged 10 and 11. Frommer et al. (1972) reviewed 210 preschool children (average age 2.9 years) seen in a child psychiatry department. The ratio of boys and girls was 1.5 to 1; 58 percent were rated as depressed, which was defined as excessive weepiness and persistent misery. Weinberg et al. (1973), at the other end of the spectrum from Rutter, found depression to be present in 65.6 percent (45 out of 72) of the children seen for school and behavior problems. From the above studies, little can be concluded about actual prevalence rates, since different investigators used different diagnostic criteria, and the distinction between unhappiness and clinical depression was often unclear.

Classification and Typologies

The difficulty in arriving at an operational definition or universally agreed upon set of symptom criteria, accounts to some extent for some of the difficulty in classifying depression in childhood. The added problems of uncertain etiology and developmental considerations only compound the difficulty. Many typologies have been offered. For example, Frommer (1968) attempted to classify sad children into three groups: 1) enuretic and encopretic depressives, 2) pure depressives, and 3) phobic depressives.

Cytryn and McKnew (1972) took a group of 37 so-called neurotic depressive reactions of mid-childhood (aged 6 to 12 years), and subdivided them into three groups: 1) masked depressive reaction of childhood, 2) acute depressive reaction of childhood, and 3) chronic depressive reaction of childhood.

Others (e.g., Ossofsky, 1974) have attempted a developmental classification. Such classifications usually start with anaclitic depression of infancy described by Spitz (1946), followed by affectionless character (Bowlby, 1951), then neurotic depression of childhood and adolescence. However, such classifications, while attractive, are also deceptive, since, among other problems, they do not really distinguish between primary depression and depression secondary to chronic illness occurring at any age, or between depression and manic-depressive illness in children. Nor can one really infer differences in etiology, treatment, or prognosis from what is otherwise an appealing arrangement. They are, in short, more often linear classifications rather than true developmental classifications.

Malmquist (1971) tried to overcome this by proposing a tentative classification in which he tried to combine several criteria, including descriptive features, age, and etiology. The common principle in his classification was the predominance of depressive affect, which, of course, may not be present at all, either as a conscious affect or as a perceivable external sign in certain depressed children.

The fact of the matter is that none of the above classification systems works well because they are not consistently etiological, prognostic, or treatment oriented. It would seem that little is gained by placing a child in any one of the proposed categories.

Etiology

Research on the etiology of childhood depression is scarce, and plagued with obvious methodological difficulties. In general, there are four common research strategies: 1) a search for antecedent factors from histories given by current patients, 2) so-called follow-back studies, in which an attempt is made to search for antecedent factors from old records, 3) regular follow-up studies, and 4) so-called follow-through studies, in which children are studied continuously, along with various controls, over a period of time.

We have chosen to discuss briefly certain studies emanating from a variety of different research strategies that contribute to our understanding of depression in childhood. For present purposes, we have classified the etiological data into three areas: 1) psychological, 2) genetic, and 3) biochemical.

Psychological

The classical psychoanalytic views of depression pertaining to adults and children, include the following concepts:

1. self-reproach against an internalized love object (Freud, 1917),
2. internalizing hostility and ambivalence (Abraham, 1927),
3. loss of self esteem (Bibring, 1953).

While research methodology on the psychodynamics of depression has remained essentially unchanged since Freud, various refinements of these concepts have been expressed.

For example, Sandler and Joffe (1965) reviewed 100 cases of children treated psychoanalytically at the Hampstead Child Therapy Clinic in London. On the basis of this review (there were no comparison groups), they described a depressive reaction in which the children appeared sad, bored, and discontented. In addition, there was withdrawal, and a sense of the child feeling rejected and unloved. The children turned away from disappointing love objects and refused to accept help or comfort. Further, the children regressed to oral passivity, and sleep disturbances and autoerotic behavior occurred. Sandler and Joffe believed that the children seemed to feel they had lost or were unable to acquire something that was essential to their well-being. In a word, the children felt helpless. Sandler and Joffe further believed the children were experiencing psychic pain as a result of the child's perceived discrepancy between the actual self and an ideal state of well-being. Depression, then, was one manifestation of this psychic pain, the depression consisting essentially of a persistent sense of helplessness and/or passive resignation. Whether this was true persistent depression or transitory unhappiness was not made entirely clear.

Laufer (1976) reported a psychoanalytic study of eight adolescents, four males and four females, aged fourteen to nineteen years, who attempted suicide—a symptom often associated with depression. The criteria for inclusion in the study was that there had to be a conscious intention of being dead, and that the adolescent was not psychotic. Each adolescent who agreed to be studied was seen five times a week by a psychoanalyst. The length of treatment ranged from 1 year to 18 months. The parents were informed of the treatment, and the adolescent was required to live in a protected setting, i.e., not alone. The method of study consisted of weekly reports in which the analyst was simply asked to write what he thought was most salient in the previous five hours of analysis. The reports were then reviewed, with paricular reference to antecedent factors and precipitating events. The findings that have emerged so far are:

1. The adolescent sees his or her body as dangerous (i.e., as an instrument for aggression) and intends suicide as a means of controlling aggressive feelings towards the mother. The girl is afraid of killing her mother; the boy, of committing some aggressive sexual act. This constitutes what Laufer calls the "perverse fantasy."
2. There is a fear of being abandoned. This is conceptualized by Laufer as abandonment by the superego rather than the mother, although at the same time there is a feeling of actual psychological abandonment by the mother.
3. There is an inability to change the relationship to the mother. This is experienced in association with the experience of being rejected by another person.
4. All the mothers were experienced as dominating, controlling, and intrusive.
5. The fathers were seen as the weaker parents.

The study suffers, of course, from the lack of a control group and possible observer bias. Other observers might, of course, make different inferences from the same data. Stanley and Barker (1970), for example, in a well-controlled study comparing 38 suicidal and 38 nonsuicidal youths, found no distinguishing psychiatric features between the two groups. Observer bias might be overcome if this material were made available to others.

The psychodynamic findings are still of interest because they tend to point to the importance of early experience of loss and abandonment and ungratified longing.

Loss and deprivation, of course, have long been held to be important in the etiology of depression. Jacobson, Fasman, and DiMascio (1975) studied 461 depressed women (347 inpatients and 114 outpatients) aged 18 to 60 years, and compared them with a control group of 198 normal women. Suprisingly, their findings "revealed no association of adult depression with overt childhood loss events, but did provide evidence to support an association of depriving childrearing processes with adult depression. The findings also suggested that a relationship existed between the degree of depriving childrearing experience with the severity of the adult illness as measured by hospital status" (p. 5).

What was surprising, of course, was that the loss events that were not significant included death, or separation from parents. However, what was important was the greater incidence of "separation of parents, more frequent psychiatric illness of parents, and a more deprived childrearing milieu...." (p. 12), deprivation being defined as "the lack, loss or absence of an emotionally sustaining relationship prior to adolescence" (p. 6).

This study is a useful one because it did have a control group, and did try to examine some of the more subtle, experiential forms of deprivation that occur without the more obvious events of death or separation. However, the problem in the study remains that of defining precisely what constitutes the "depriving childrearing processes," and how exactly these processes set in motion a serious mood disorder. Furthermore, the association of parental psychiatric illness and subsequent depression in a child may be a result, in part, of an inherited predisposition to depression.

Deprivation can occur in at least four major ways (Langmeir & Matejack, 1975):

1. Stimulus deprivation, in which there is a lack of sensory and motor stimulation, particularly at the earliest stages of life.
2. Cognitive deprivation, in which the environment fails to provide sufficient structure, organization, and reasonable predictability of events making it difficult for the child to make sense out of his or her experience, particularly in terms of his or her behavior and the responses from the environment.
3. Attachment deprivation, in which there is a failure of the reliable presence and responsiveness of a person to whom the child can focus his perceptual, cognitive, and affective activities—this failure leading to a failure to become attached.
4. Social deprivation, in which the absence of adequate socialization experiences give rise to a series of impairments, including learning difficulties, a deformed value system, and impaired facilty for the performance of social functions and roles.

Interestingly, Akisal and McKinney (1973), using a learning theory model, proposed that the loss of significant reinforcers is an important factor in producing depression. Such a conceptualization brings together issues of stimulus, cognitive, attachment, and socialization deprivation and will be discussed later.

Genetic

Numerous studies have pointed to a genetic factor in adult depression, particularly in bipolar depression. For example, Mendlewicz and Fleis (1974) studied 60 unipolar patients and 125 bipolar patients, and their spouses and available first-, second-, and third-degree relatives on both sides. The diagnostic criteria were similar to those of Winokur, Clayton, and Reich (1969) and to the concept of "primary affective disorders" (Robins & Guze, 1972). The Current and Past Psychopathology Scales of Endicott and Spitzer (1972) were used along with a clinical, semistructured interview, for the evaluation of all relatives. In short, it was a detailed and meticulous study which demonstrated that "within the families described in this study, a dominant x-linked gene is involved in the transmission of bipolar illness while x-linked inheritance can be ruled out as a mode of transmission in unipolar illness" (p. 261).

Unfortunately, a lower age limit of 20 was taken for unipolar illness in order to avoid confounding depression with childhood and adolescent disorders. In fact, little is known about genetic factors in childhood depressive illness. Manic-depressive illness (i.e., bipolar affective illness) is thought to be a rare condition (Anthony & Scott, 1969; Feinstein & Wolpert, 1973), however its rarity may reflect our own inability to recognize its characteristics.

Rutter (1966) has stated that as yet there is no convincing evidence that sadness and misery in middle childhood have any genetic link with adult depression.

Indeed, Rutter (1966) did not find any particular relationship between depression in parents and any single disorder in children, or vice versa (i.e., no relationship was found between sadness in children and any single disorder in parents) although he did find that physical as well as psychiatric disorders in parents had adverse effects on the psychological well-being of children. Frommer et al. (1972), however, in their review of 210 preschool children, of whom 58 percent were rated as depressed, found that 72 percent of the mothers of these children were mentally ill (schizophrenia, treated depressed illness, alcoholism, or other severe psychopathology), even though specific etiological factors for each group could not be determined. In the Frommer study there was considerable overlap between children who were rated as aggressive, depressed, or anxious, depending on their main symptomatology. This raises the further question of whether these different symptoms represent different depressive manifestations or styles.

Biochemical

Few studies comparable to the biogenic amine studies of adult unipolar and bipolar depression have been carried out in children. One reported biochemical study of a single case of depression in childhood is of interest (McKnew, Cytryn, & White, 1974).

This study was performed on an 8-year-old boy who exhibited manic behavior following the amputation of his left forearm (required because of a serious electrical burn). As the child approached adolescence, the hypomanic picture began to alternate with a "typical" picture of chronic depressive reaction. A wide range of biochemical studies were performed during of manic behavior, revealing two findings: 1) an increased secretion of 17-hydroxycorticosteroids, and 2) a decreased excretion of 3 methoxy-4-hydroxphenylethyl glycol. McKnew et al. (1974) point out that these findings run counter to the findings in manic adults. As noted, this was a single case study and remains to be repeated on a larger sample of children. It is important also to note in this case a background of frequent object losses, ambivalence and covert rejection on the part of important parenting figures, as well as an episode of physical abuse. In addition, the boy's mother was depressed.

Studies of the biochemical component of depression in childhood are too few and incomplete at present to allow anything beyond speculation by extrapolation from adult studies.

In short, there is insufficient evidence to draw any conclusions regarding a genetic factor in childhood depression, strong evidence that psychological loss is an important factor, and tentative but incomplete evidence for a biochemical disturbance in some childhood depressions.

Psychopharmacological Treatment

Research in the use of drugs in the treatment of depression in children is rare. Conners (1972) noted, "the antidepressant drugs have little or no background of carefully controlled investigation...," and this still holds true. The few studies that are available suggest the need for further research (Annel, 1969; Campbell et al., 1972; Dyson & Barcai, 1970; Frommer, 1967, 1968; Gram & Rafaelson, 1972; Lucas et al., 1965). Recently, Rapoport (1976) reviewed antidepressant drug use in children and could provide no conclusion about drug efficacy. Little, therefore, can be concluded from the available studies in children.

Discussion

The psychoanalytic, psychological, and even biological points of view discussed have certain commonalities. Almost all call attention to issues of insufficient "input," be it in the nature of maternal abandonment, a lack of reinforcers, or cognitive, attachment, social, or sensory deprivation. Even in the case of the manic depressive child, described by McKnew et al. (1974), who had demonstrable biochemical abnormalities, there was strong evidence of psychic trauma and maternal deprivation. It would seem therefore that many childhood depressions are associated with the history of apparent insufficient human contact.

Were the effects of insufficient positive human interaction exclusively psychological, one might expect depressions to yield to replacement therapy in the form of an ongoing psychotherapeutic relationship. Indeed, many depressions do resolve with psychotherapy alone. These depressions we retrospectively tend to call "reactive" depressions and find an immediate psychological precursor to which to attribute the disorder.

Unfortunately, many depressions continue even after the psychodynamic issues of loss, anger, low self-esteem, etc. have been well analyzed and understood. Such ongoing intense depressive states often yield quite dramatically to antidepressant medication when psychotherapeutic intervention alone has been ineffective. In cases where there is no family history of depression to suggest a genetic predisposition, the question arises whether certain kinds of cognitive, emotional, or sensory deprivation at particular times of development, or whether ongoing deprivation of a particular quality or intensity may permanently alter the biochemical functions of the human organism and result in a chronic or recurrent dysphoric state recalcitrant to psychotherapy alone.

This hypothesis is consonant with Mandell's (1976) biochemical theory explaining the persistence of depressive affect even after the neurotic conflict related to the depression has been worked through. Mandell hypothesizes a psychologically induced altered biochemical state. He suggests that this condition could conceivably arise because the developing nervous system of the young infant is particularly vulnerable to impingement on its biochemical balance. Thus, if a depletion of monoamine transmitters occurs in response, say, to an early and persistent psychological loss, that altered biochemical state may then become the "normal" permanent biochemical state for that individual throughout his life. Any subsequent return to a more gratifying or stimulating environment would then be perceived as though that were the deviant and temporary state of mind, in the sense that the prevailing tendency of the biochemical response would remain in the direction of returning to the previously acquired and permanent "depressive" baseline state.

Depressed children and adults often feel better during the course of psychotherapy, and there is a tendency among therapists to ascribe this to the resolution of unconscious conflict. It may be, however, that improvement is not so much a result of what is discussed or analyzed but is rather the result of the central nervous system stimulation engendered during the therapeutic encounter.

It may be that psychotherapy of almost any theoretical variety as long as it involves genuine, caring, human interaction stimulates those neurotransmitters that diminish the subjective feeling of depression and enhance feelings of well being. The long- and short-term effectiveness of such therapy may be related more to the biological state of the patient than to the therapist's orientation. That empathy is a sine qua non of many therapies and may be a reflection of our empirical recognition that empathic rapport literally stimulates cure. For example, in our clinical experience, two young patients with well-documented recurrent depressions, who have responded well to trycyclic medication, have reported a need for less medication on days when they saw their therapists.

We are inclined, therefore, to look more closely at the bridge between psychological mechanisms and biochemical events, in which a psychobiological interplay occurs. The effect of psychodynamic factors on biological functioning and of biological factors on alterations of mood is an especially promising and exciting direction for future research in depressive illness in children.

References

Abraham, K. A short study of the development of the libido, viewed in the light of mental disorders (1924). In: *Selected Papers of Karl Abraham, M.D.* 1927, pp. 418–502. Translated by Douglas Bryan & Alix Strachey. London: Hogarth Press.

Agras, S. The relationship of school phobia to childhood depression. *American Journal of Psychiatry,* 1959, *116,* 533.

Akisal, H., & McKinney, W. T. Jr. Depressive disorders: Toward a unified hypothesis. *Science,* 1973, *182,* 20.

Annel, A. L. Manic-depressive illness in children and the effect of treatment with lithium carbonate. *Acta Paedopsychiatrica,* 1969, *36,* 292.

Anthony, J., & Scott, P. Manic depressive psychosis in childhood. *Journal of the American Academy of Child Psychiatry,* 1960, *1,* 53.

Bibring, E. The mechanism of depression. In P. Greenacre (Ed.): *Affective Disorders.* New York: International Universities Press, 1953.

Bowlby, J. (1951), *Maternal Care and Mental Health,* Ed. 2. Geneva: World Health Organization Monogr. Series No. 2.

Burks, H., & Harrison, S. Aggressive behavior as a means of avoiding depression. *American Journal of Orthopsychiatry,* 1962, *32,* 416.

Campbell, M., Fish, B., Korein, J., Shapiro, T., Collnis, P., & Koh, C. Lithium and clorpromazine: A controlled crossover study of hyperactive, severly disturbed young children. *Journal of Autism and Childhood Schizophrenia,* 1972, *2(3),* 234.

Conners, C. K. Pharmacotherapy of psychopathology in children. In Quay, H. C., & Werry, J. S. (Eds.): *Psychopathological Disorders of Childhood.* New York: Wiley, 1972, pp. 316–347.

Cytryn, L., & McKnew, D. H. Jr. Factors influencing the changing clinical expression of the depressive process in children. *American Journal of Psychiatry,* 1974, *131(8),* 879.

Dyson, W. L., & Barcai, A. Treatment of children of lithium responding parents. *Current Therapeutic Research,* 1970, *12,* 286.

Endicott, J., & Spitzer, R. L. Current and past psychopathology scales: Rationale, reliability and validity. *Archives of General Psychiatry,* 1972, *27,* 687.

Feighner, J. P., Robins, E., Guze, S. B., Woodruff, R. A., Winokur, G., & Munoz, R. Diagnostic criteria for use in psychiatric research. *Archives of General Psychiatry,* 1972, *26,* 57.

Feinstein, S. C., & Wolpert, E. A. Juvenile manic-depressive illness: clinical and therapeutic considerations. *Journal of American Academy of Child Psychiatry,* 1973, *12(1),* 123.

Freud, S. Mourning and melancholia. *Standard Edition*, 1917, *14*, 243. London: Hogarth Press, 1957.

Frommer, E. A. Treatment of childhood depression with antidepressant drugs. *British Medical Journal*, 1967, *1*, 729.

Frommer, E. A. Depressive illness in childhood. *British Journal of Psychiatry*, 1968, *2*, 117.

Frommer, E. A., Mendelson, W. B., & Reid, M. A. Differential diagnosis of psychiatric disturbance in pre-school children. *British Journal of Psychiatry*, 1972, *121*, 71.

Gram, L. F., & Rafaelsen, O. J. Lithium treatment of psychotic children and adolescents. A controlled clinical trial. *Acta Psychiatrica Scandinavica*, 1972, *48(3)*, 253.

Jacobson, S., Fasman, J., & DiMascio, A. Deprivation in the childhood of depressed women. *Journal of Nervous and Mental Disease*, 1975, *160(1)*, 5.

Kaufman, I., Makkay, E., & Zilbach, J. The impact of adolescence on girls with delinquent character formation. *American Journal of Orthopsychiatry*, 1959, *29*, 130.

Langmeir, J., & Matejeck, Z. *Psychological deprivation in childhood*, 3rd ed. Translated by P. Anger. New York: Halsted Press, 1975, p. 489.

Laufer, M. Attempted suicide in adolescence. Presentation at the Yale Child Study Center, May 4, 1976.

Lewis, D. O., Klerman, L., Jekel, J., & Curry, J. Experiences with Psychiatric Services in a Program for Pregnant Teenage Girls. *Social Psychiatry*, 1973, *8*, 16.

Ling, W., Oftedal, G., & Weinberg, W. Depressive illness in childhood presenting as severe headache. *American Journal of Diseases of Children*, 1970, *120*, 122.

Lucas, A. R., Lockett, H. J., & Gruin, F. Amitriptyline in childhood depression. *Diseases of the Nervous System*, 1965, *26*, 105.

McKnew, D. H. Jr., Cytryn, L., & White, I. Clinical and biochemical correlates of hypomania in a child. *Journal of the American Academy of Child Psychiatry*, 1974, *13(3)*, 576.

Malmquist, C. P. Depression in childhood and adolescence. *New England Journal of Medicine*, 1971, *284*, 887, 955.

Mandell, A. J. Neurobiological mechanism of adaptation in relation to models of psychobiological development. In Schopler, E., & Reichler, R. J. (Eds.): *Psychopathology and Child Development*. New York: Plenum Press, 1976, pp. 21–22.

Mendlewicz, J., & Fleis, J. C. Linkage studies with x-chromosome markers in bipolar (manic-depressive) and unipolar (depressive) illness. *Biological Psychiat*, 1974, *9(3)*, 261.

Ossofsky, H. J. Endogenous depression in infancy and childhood. *Comprehensive Psychiatry,* 1974, *15(1),* 19.

Poznanski, E., & Zrull, J. P. Childhood depression: Clinical characteristics of overtly depressed women. *Archives of General Psychiatry,* 1970, *23,* 8.

Poznanski, E., Krahenbuhl, V., & Zrull, J. P. Childhood depression: A longitudinal perspective. *Journal of the American Academy of Child Psychiatry,* 1976, 15(3):491.

Renshaw, D. C. Depression of the 70's. *Diseases of the Nervous System,* 1972, *35(5),* 241.

Rapoport, J. Psychopharmacology of childhood depression. In Klein, D. F., & Gittelman-Klein, R. (Eds.): *Progress in psychiatric drug treatment,* Vol 2. 1976, New York: Brunner/Mazel, 1976, pp. 493–503.

Robins, E., & Guze, S. B. Classification of affective disorders; the primary-secondary, the endogenous-reactive, and the neurotic-psychotic concepts. In Williams, T. A., Katz, M. M., & Shield, J. A. (Eds.): *Recent advances in psychobiology of the depressive illness.* Washington, D.C.: DHEW Publication No. (HSM) 70–9053, 1972.

Rutter, M. *Children of sick parents.* London: Oxford University Press, 1966.

Sandler, J., & Joffe, W. S. Notes on childhood depression. *International Journal of Psychoanalysis,* 1965, *46,* 88.

Schildkraut, J. J. Biogenic amine metabolism in depressive illness. In Williams, T. A., Katz, M. M., & Shield, J. A. (Eds.): *Recent advances in the psychobiology of the depressive illness.* Washington, D.C.: DHEW Publication No. (HSM) 70–9053, 1972, pp. 11–23.

Spitz, R. A. Anaclitic depression. *Psychoanalytic Study of the Child,* 1946, *2,* 313.

Stanley, E. J., & Barker, J. T. Adolescent suicidal behavior. *American Journal of Orthopsychiatry,* 1970, *40,* 87.

Toolan, J. M. Depression in children and adolescents. *American Journal of Orthopsychiatry,* 1962, *32,* 404.

Watts, C. A. H. *Depressive disorders in the community.* Bristol: John Wright, 1966.

Weinberg, W., Rutman, J., Sullivan, L., Renick, E., & Dietz, S. The ten symptoms of childhood depression and the characteristic behavior for each symptom. *Journal of Pediatrics,* 1973, *83,* 1072.

Winokur, G., Clayton, P. J., & Reich, T. *Manic-depressive illness.* St. Louis: C. V. Mosby, 1969.

Chapter 3

CHILDHOOD DEPRESSION: A PSYCHODYNAMIC APPROACH TO THE ETIOLOGY OF DEPRESSION IN CHILDREN

Elva O. Poznanski

The Development of the Concept of Clinical Depressions in Children

Prior to the 1970's children were, for the most part, regarded as incapable of experiencing depression. The myth of childhood being a happy, carefree state (despite literary giants who described it differently) apparently prejudiced the observations of the psychiatrist. Thus, prior to 1970 children were felt to be incapable of having depression, and professions thought that the "familiar manifestations of adult, nonpsychotic depression" are virtually nonexistent in childhood. The rationale for this viewpoint was derived from the basic assumptions that children lacked an adequate superego development, that they were unable to tolerate painful affects for any length of time, and they lacked experience with separations until the end of adolescence.

From the Department of Psychiatry, University of Michigan Medical School, Ann Arbor.

In the 1960's the concept of masked depressions or depressive equivalents was put forth. This concept held that the depressive affect was not directly expressed except for possibly short periods of time and that a variety of behavioral problems were alternate ways of expressing depressions in childhood and adolescence. While depressive equivalents may, in fact, be a valid concept there are at least three difficulties with accepting this idea as a predominant view of depression in childhood: 1) it assumes that depressive affect is only rarely observable in children; 2) the behaviors cited as expressing "equivalents" to depression are so diverse as to encompass most of the nonpsychotic psychopathologies in children and adolescents; and 3) the linkage of such conditions to depressive affect is frequently tenuous or nonexistent. Clearly from clinical and research experience the concept of depressive equivalents as the mode of expressing depression in childhood is unacceptable.

An exception to the general trend in the 60's was the work of Sandler and Jaffe of Hampstead Clinic who examined the psychoanalytic records of 100 children and set forth the features they felt were commonly associated with depressive affect. Their paper was concerned primarily with theoretical formulations of the depressive reaction and its relationship to loss, pain, aggression, the role of defenses and issues of individuation. While these are important concerns, it would have been more helpful clinically if the behavior and duration of the depressed state had been more sharply described. Despite these limitations, this article constituted an important step forward because the authors were very clear in stating that depressive affect *is* seen in children.

The early 1970's produced a dramatic shift in the thinking about childhood depression in this country and in Europe. In 1970 Poznanski and Zrull published a clinical study of 14 children who showed recognizably overt depression. In 1971 Malmquist wrote an extensive review of the literature of childhood depression well-integrated with his own theoretical concepts. There was the implicit and at times uncomfortable inference that children can become depressed. Also in 1971 the Fourth Congress of the Union of European Pedopsychiatrists convened in Sweden and took as its theme, "Depressive States in Childhood and Adolescence." Cytryn and McKnew published two articles on childhood depression, one on classification and a second on possible biochemical correlates. Again in 1972 the GAP Committee on Child Psychiatry included for the first time a category of childhood depression under psychoneurotic disorders in a proposal for a diagnostic nomenclature suitable for children and adolescents. At last childhood depression was admitted to exist, and it was possible to find it listed in at least one system of diagnostic nomenclature for children.

Diagnostic Criteria in Childhood Depression Studies

Since the concept of childhood depression has only very recently been accepted, there are no uniform diagnostic criteria. At the time of this writing the section for children and adolescents in DSM III is still not finalized. As of now it does not include a category of childhood depression. Implicit is the assumption that if childhood depression does emerge as a diagnostic entity, it will clinically resemble the affective disorders of adults. In DSM's II's childhood disorders the word "depression" is found only in "Adjustment Disorder with Depressed Mood."

Sandler and Joffe, drawing from children seen in analysis at the Hampstead Clinic, stated that any combination of the following symptoms were seen with depressed affect. Although not directly stated, the assumption from reading their paper would be that all children had a sad, unhappy or depressed mood. There is no indication of the frequency of Items 2 through 9, nor is there indication of how long the child remained sad, unhappy or depressed. Those symptoms were: 1) Child recorded as sad, unhappy or depressed (therapist observation); 2) Withdrawal, including boredom; 3) Feels rejected or unloved; 4) Does not ask for help or comfort or if did still disappointed and discontented; 5) Tendency to regress to oral passivity; 6) Insomnia or sleep disturbances; 7) Discontented, not readily satisfied. Little capacity for pleasure; 8) Autoerotic or other repetitive activities; 9) Therapist had difficulty sustaining contact.

Former, also in England, did a retrospective study of children in the outpatient pediatric clinic of a teaching hospital. She attempted to distinguish the "depressed child" from the "neurotic child," however the latter also included some children with depressive features. The distinction has not been replicated.

Poznanski and Zrull used patients from the outpatient clinic of a children's psychiatric hospital. Poznanski and Zrull's group included children who were described as being sad, unhappy and/or depressed as an affective reaction to the content of the interview or who could describe similar affective states within self. Poznanski and Zrull noted that the following additional symptoms were often present: 1) excessive self-criticism; 2) feelings of inadequacy; 3) difficulty in sleeping; 4) excessive concerns about death; and 5) withdrawal.

Connell's study of childhood depression took children from a pediatric outpatient clinic. Those children were taken into the study whose parents described them as persistently unhappy or depressed. The most frequent behavioral items were social withdrawal, feelings of rejection, irritability, behavioral change and negative self-concept.

Cytryn and McKnew felt that they could identify a group of latency-aged children with a clearly identifiable depressive syndrome. The symptoms which they listed include persistent sad affect, social withdrawal, hopelessness, helplessness, psychomotor retardation, anxiety, school and social failure, sleep and feeding disturbances, and suicidal ideas and threats.

Weinberg, et al, working in an educational diagnostic setting, set forth his criteria for the diagnosis of childhood depression as follows. Required: 1) dysphoric mood; 2) self-deprecatory ideation. Two or more of the following: 1) aggressive behavior; 2) sleep disturbance; 3) change in school performance; 4) diminished socialization; 5) change in attitude toward school; 6) somatic complaints; 7) loss of usual energy; 8) unusual change in appetite or weight. He further stated that the symptoms had to have been present for one month or more.

There appears to be some compounding of symptoms since two of the items in Weinberg's criteria (change in school performance and change in attitude toward school) are likely overlapping behavioral items. Generally speaking, children who are not doing well in school dislike school for obvious reasons.

While Weinberg's study is to be commended for the clarity with which his diagnostic criteria are described, he failed to provide a measure of the severity of the observed disorder in terms of the degree of impairment in overall functioning. This is particularly to be regretted since Weinberg's study was described to test the efficacy of antidepressant medication. In addition, there was no indication on whether the behavioral measures were based on parent report or direct observation of the child.

These studies highlight the need for careful diagnostic criteria—criteria which could be acceptable to experienced child psychiatrists as well as items which represent clearly differentiated aspects of behavior.

In clinical practice the issue regarding the duration of a mood change as a basis for classifying it as pathological has been based primarily on the intuition of the clinician.

Thus, the length of time a child may be sad and still be considered to be within normal limits is a highly debatable issue. Generally, children are thought of as having more lability of mood than adults. Yet the Research Diagnostic Criteria defines adults as "probably" depressed if a depressed mood lasts two weeks. Most experienced child psychiatrists are unwilling to accept these short time spans, feeling more comfortable accepting changes which last a month or more.

Etiology Factors in Childhood Depression

Since even the phenomenology of childhood depression has yet to be fully described, it is difficult to discuss etiological factors. Therefore, the focus will be on those factors which are suspected to have some relationship to depression in childhood.

Loss

Historically, the concept of loss in the etiology of depression was initiated by Freud's classic work "Mourning and Melancholia." In that paper Freud compared two situations —grief and depression—and found them clinically similar except that the decrease in self-esteem was greater in depression. He proposed that the loss was conscious in grief and unconscious in depression. Freud was primarily concerned with comparing the acute state of grief with the depressive syndrome but there was the implicit assumption that grief eventually ended or became "abnormal."

The concept of loss in some form is often viewed as a central dynamic feature of adult depression. In a recent review of conceptual models of depression in adults, the majority of non-biological models were found to postulate some sort of loss, i.e. "loss of self-esteem, object loss, loss of reinforcement, loss of role status and loss of the meaning of existence."

Confirmation of the loss model of depression comes from another source, namely, the primate laboratories. The work with monkeys pioneered by Harlow has special significance to child psychiatry and the study of childhood depression, which is produced by separating young monkeys from their mothers. These studies indicate that with monkeys the age at which separation takes place and any prior experience with separation can be important factors in determining the behavioral reaction to separation. In these respects the primate reaction is very similar to that of human children.

One of the earliest descriptions of depression in infants came from Spitz's work and what he termed "anaclitic depression." Spitz described how separation from the mother in the second half of the first year of the infant's life could lead to a definitive reaction involving the infant's becoming sad, weepy, apathetic with an immobile face. The babies reacted slowly to stimuli and moved slowly and had poor appetite and sleep patterns with little movement. Spitz concluded the children were exhibiting distinct "depression." A strong mother/child bond increased the chances of an infant becoming depressed after separation from the mother. It is noteworthy, however, that *only 15 percent of the infants* separated from their mothers suffered this syndrome. Therefore, other factors were apparently operating—perhaps "constitutional" or genetic components or perhaps the quality of mothering.

Spitz's study of anaclitic depression was conducted in a prison nursery. Hence the environment for the infants was unusual in terms of cultural norms prior to separation. Furthermore, after separation the infants had the sort of institutional care typical of that era. Anaclitic depression has been classified as a deprivational syndrome. Spitz's study did not determine the time at which the attachment to the mother becomes a specific response to her. Undoubtedly, the cognitive and affective development of the child is of critical importance in determining the response to separation. The older the child is, the more advanced the cognitive and affective development and the more likely it will be that separation from the primary caretaker (usually the mother) will constitute the loss of an important attachment to a *specific* individual which cannot be substituted for by another warm, nurturing adult. It is not clear, however, whether the "anaclitic" depressions of infancy are the prototypes of depression in the preschool or school-age child.

The next significant step was to describe the effects of separation from mother in early childhood. However, the hypothesis that a young child separated from his/her mother suffers a good deal of distress was not generally accepted at the time these studies were done. Bowlby has written extensively on loss and attachment in childhood; his work is primarily anecdotal, however, and does not provide a strong empirical case for his theoretical formulations.

Heinicke and Westheimer did a rigorous study of 10 young children (15–30 months) who were separated from their mothers for brief periods of time—usually while the mother had another child. The immediate reaction to separation was that the child spent considerable time crying and fretting. Initially, this constituted 5 percent of the child's total activity; by the end of two weeks, it had decreased to 0.5 percent of the child's total activity time. In the first few days the children had sleep disturbances and a variety of other behavioral disturbances, including an increased expression of hostility. This phenomena behaviorally resembles bereavement, but it is not known whether or how it may be related to depressive states in childhood and adulthood. Five of the ten children were followed for over a year.

At a one year follow-up interview, none of the children had any obvious or overt after-effects from the previous separation.

One of the difficulties in the "loss" model of depression is the complex situation it postulates, and the resultant necessity of looking carefully at multiple parameters. Some significant considerations in need of incorporation into this model are: 1) The object from whom the child is separated. Generally, the literature has focused on parent loss or separation, and its meaning and effect on the child. There has been somewhat less emphasis on sibling loss or separation. 2) The nature of the relationship before separation. For this feature, retrospective studies are limited in their ability to distinguish satisfactorily the fantasies of the child and his family at an earlier historical moment. 3) The nature of the loss or separation experience which the child endures, i.e. the manner in which it occurs, the conceptualization of the experience by the child, the length of the separation and the type of post-separation environment provided for the child. In addition, it must be kept in mind that separation may be beneficial for children who are physically and/or emotionally abused and neglected usually improve when they are separated from their parents. 4) The effects of the child's age—obviously in a general way younger children are more likely vulnerable to separations—even of brief duration. The question becomes how young and whether children are relatively invulnerable prior to second half of the first year as Spitz postulated. The concept of an eight-month separation anxiety in infants is in question since younger infants, i.e. three-month infants, have been noted to pay selective attention to their mothers. Another issue is whether previous brief separations sensitize a child—one animal study suggests this possibility. Older children are thought to be less vulnerable to separation and loss but systematic studies are still needed. 5) If reunion occurs, the behavior of the child at the time of reunion.

The gap between the descriptive studies of early childhood, loss and separation and the subsequent development of depression in adults has been bridged partially by a number of empirical studies. These studies have indicated that the childhood loss of a parent is significantly more frequent in adult depressives than adults with other psychiatric disorders. Unfortunately, these studies have all the limitations of retrospective research. In addition, they tend to relate the loss of important objects in childhood as being statistically significant (and not all authors agree on this) but clinically not helpful with the depressed child.

d'Elia and Perris, studying adult depressive with unipolar, bipolar and reactive depression, found the highest incidence of childhood bereavement in the "neurotic-reactive depression group." They also concluded that unipolar depressives were more likely to have suffered parental loss before the age of six than bipolar depressives. The latter conclusion was based on a very small sample and obviously needs to be confirmed. The exciting prospect offered by their study is the possibility of linking childhood bereavement with a more specific form of depression in adult life.

While a link is provided by such studies, they do not explain why some children who suffer a loss in childhood develop depressions in adulthood while many others do not. There are many possibilities including: 1) Genetic factors; 2) Abnormal resolutions of grief. Some of these are described in an antedotal way by Wolfenstein; 3) The degree of emotional deprivation (an emotionally depriving environment likely occurs to some extent in all families at least during the phase of acute grief in the remaining parent).

Caplan and Douglas' study of children with depressed moods also appears to correlate childhood depression with parent loss. Loss in their study was globally defined as separation from the parent for any reason, e.g. death, divorce, illness or desertion. The authors studied, for a period of one year, all children on a waiting list for psychotherapy. They divided them into two groups—a group of 71 children with depressed mood and another group of 185 children which they labeled "nondepressed neurotic group." The latter acted as a control for the first group. They found that one-half of the depressed children and one-fourth of the control children had suffered some form of parental loss lasting six months or more before the age of eight.

The relationship between loss and bereavement, loss and subsequent depression, and bereavement and depression continues to intrigue clinicians but the mechanisms need further clarification.

Bereavement in adults is better studied and more clearly defined than in children. Bereavement in adults is characterized by the painful and gradual withdrawal of emotions from the loved person. Sadness and expressions of grief are characteristic of the adult mourner. The adult expresses anger and grief over the missing person as he gradually reconstructs his life for an existence which no longer includes the presence of that dead person.

The normal reactions of children to bereavement are less clear-cut than those of adults. Children have been universally described as generally expressing less affective grief than adults. Wolfenstein speaks of the "short sadness span" of children, referring to the inability of children to tolerate prolonged states of sadness and anger. Furthermore, Wolfenstein comments that for bereavement in children, the depressive affect is isolated from thoughts of death. A similar state in adults, namely, the absence of an affective grief state when it is normally expected to occur, is felt to be indicative of a pathological type of bereavement. Since this situation is common in children, there arises the problem of whether "normal" bereavement can occur in childhood.

Another unresolved difficulty with the theoretical concepts of grief reactions in adults when these are applied to children is the relationship between anger and aggression in both grief states and depressions. Bowlby feels that anger is an integral part of grief for both adults and children and that its expression is a necessary component for healthy mourning. Furman has suggested that a child's difficulty with mourning may be a manifestation of the difficulty in the mastery of aggression.

At any rate, children in response to the death of a parent or sibling, do demonstrate periods of sadness, though of shorter duration than is characteristic of the adult. Children are likely to show evidence of a disturbance in their behavior for a much longer period of time than of affective expressions of grief. A wide variety of behavioral disturbances may appear such as temper tantrums, disobedience, truancy, running away from home, and accident proneness. Thus, the idea that children show "depressive equivalents" rather than demonstrating open depressive affect was the first conceptualization of depression in children. While the focus in the literature now is more on overt depressions in children, the meaning of "depressive equivalents" still needs further clarification.

The reaction of children to the death of a sibling would appear to provide the opportunity to study bereavement issues more clearly than in the case of the death of a parent. In reality, sibling loss frequently brings three complicating emotional issues for the child: 1) a preceding state of parent deprivation if the sibling loss was preceded by a chronic illness; 2) sibling rivalry—which is an issue for adults as well but is much more acute for the child; 3) the parental state of grief again affecting the ability of the parents to relate to the remaining children during the period of their own bereavement.

The knowledge of bereavement behavior in children is based on a limited number of case studies of children who either were in psychotherapy or entered psychotherapy shortly after a death in the family. Bereavement in children needs to be studied by direct observation of diverse groups of children by an adult who is not grieving him/herself. Such studies are not available because of the difficulty in achieving the latter situation. Most of the observations on bereaved children over long periods of time have been reported by parents or parent surrogates. The inadequacy of these reports in states of bereavement is obvious. The older studies of bereavement in children lump together loss due to death or divorce. While death and divorce within a family unit have the common denominator of loss, the resulting reality situation for the child is different and more recent studies have looked at these situations separately.

Many studies have focused on children's reactions to divorce. Obviously, children's reactions to divorce is a complicated situation for the child usually involving the partial loss of one parent and frequently causing distortions in the relationship with the custodial parent. Kelly and Wallerstein's studies are uniquely valuable because they were done prospectively, i.e. the children were interviewed both at the time of divorce and one year later. The children's behavior was subdivided by logical age divisions, thus providing a developmental perspective. The preschool children usually showed global disruptions of their usual behavior patterns to the immediate divorce situations. A few of the preschool children at the one year follow-up showed a "depressive reaction" among several behavioral outcomes. The latency-aged child was more likely to initially react to the divorce with sadness; again one of several outcomes was continued depression.

It is difficult to determine from these studies whether the child's depressive reaction occurs in response to a parental depression or independent of the affective reaction of the parents. It must be emphasized that divorce does not always produce depression in children.

Deprivation

One of the more difficult tasks in the near future is to assess whether there is a deprivational syndrome which is distinguishable from the depressive syndrome. This is an area where definitions become important because of the possible overlapping uses of the terms.

A deprivational state is usually assumed if the child experiences physical and/or emotional neglect of his/her well-being. Physical neglect is easier to prove than emotional neglect and is the one most recognized by our judicial system. Emotional neglect is probably more devastating to the child and also there are some standard measures of what constitutes adequate physical and emotional nurturance in childhood. Since there are no such norms, society tends to recognize only the gross and extreme deviations from its own standards of "normality."

Another problem with the word "deprivation" is that it can overlap with the term "loss." Loss and deprivation often co-exist. Loss for a child, e.g. death of a parent, usually brings about a state of relative affectual deprivation. It is probably easier to identify pure states of deprivation where there has been a continuous state of inadequate affectual supplies and inadequate physical nurturance than situations of loss which may have elements of both deprivation and loss.

Theoretically, deprivational issues in infancy and early childhood should be cleared in the "psychosocial dwarfs." This group of children rarely are reported in their case histories to have sustained a loss of a parent or sibling. The child has not experienced a change from a previous better state of well-being but has always had a chronic state of inadequate physical and emotional supplies. Unfortunately, there are no studies comparing the affect of this group of infants with that of infants whose environment has provided for adequate to superior growth and development. In fact, the entire area of how affective development occurs in infancy is virtually uncharted. Grossly deprived infants are usually retarded in all areas of development, but language and the development of object relationships appear to be especially vulnerable to deprivation. Predictably, these infants and young children test low on IQ tests. Their physical development may show rapid gains if they are put in a good environment, i.e. "rebound growth." Likewise, the psychological development may show rapid gains—a good development if the child is under four years. Whether total reversibility of delayed development is possible in the very young is unknown, however, after four years the rapid gains of the younger child are not reported.

Another type of possible deprivation syndrome is the so-called "affectionless" character frequently seen in adolescence. Most group placements for delinquent or "quasi" delinquent youth have many teenagers whose major inadequacy is their limited ability to relate to other people. These adolescents have rather shallow personalities with a distinct depressive tone. Inevitably, these youngsters have had a very impoverished and nonrewarding environment in their childhood. Not only have they lacked long-term intimate relationships within their families, but their peer relationships are not an adequate substitute for the lack of parental relationships. Hence, these youngsters constitute a group who possibly have experienced a deprivation syndrome.

Parental Factors

The most consistent finding in studies of childhood depression is a *high incidence of parental depression*. However, the possible etiological significance of parental depression relative to childhood depression is as yet unclear. It is not known if parental depression facilitates childhood depression by a psychodynamic mechanism, such as parental identification. On the other hand, the occurrence of childhood depression and adult depression within the same family may simply express a hereditary or genetic vulnerability. Studies which have outside observers looking at the duration of the child's depression and comparing it with parental depression, as well as adoption studies, will allow some clarification of these issues.

An attitude frequently found in parents of children who are depressed is *overt rejection*. Parental rejection may be another possible mechanism by which children lose self-confidence and self-esteem.

DEPENDENCY

Dependency is an issue that is particularly important in working clinically with children because children are realistically dependent on their caretakers until mid or late adolescence. Exactly how dependency may fit into childhood depression is not clear, but the possibility of a relationship between dependency and depression needs to be kept in mind.

Bemporad, who worked with adult depressives, feels that dependency is a central issue in the psychodynamics of the depressive character. He describes the adult depressive as excessively emotionally dependent on a "dominant other" who provides the depressive with his only source of self-esteem. The study of overtly depressed school-aged children by Poznanski, et al did not describe such children as excessively dependent as assessed by evidence of their clinging to their parents or wanting their parents nearby. When these same children were followed longitudinally into adulthood, however, signs of excessive dependency similar to that reported by Bemporad in his adult depressives were observed. In fact, the older adolescents and young adults typically remained at home, despite very ambivalent relationships with their parents and could not separate or emancipate at ages at which it would seem appropriate (e.g. 19, 20, and 21 years). This suggests several possibilities: 1) overtly depressed children may be pathologically emotionally dependent on their parents as children but demonstrate it in other ways than by showing a desire for physical proximity; 2) overtly depressed children have had sufficient dependency gratification in childhood yet fail to develop the normal autonomy characteristic of adolescence; 3) dependency is a secondary manifestation of duration of depression.

Organic Factors

The possibility of an organic component contributing to primary depression in childhood should be kept in mind. There are several possibilities including: 1) a genetic factor predisposing certain infants and children to depression; 2) biochemical factors becoming apparent during infancy and childhood which make the infant or child vulnerable to depression; 3) biochemical factors expressing an alteration in the body secondary to either a continued depressive state or antecedents of a depressive state.

A genetic component to depression has been most clearly demonstrated in manic-depressive illness. Manic-depressive illness can express itself in adolescence, but the descriptions of this illness in children have so far been too meager to allow general acceptance of its occurrence at younger ages.

Manic-Depressive Illness

There is considerable controversy surrounding the question of whether manic-depressive illness exists in childhood. Among those who believe it does, there is controversy over whether it is an early onset of the adult disorder or whether there exists a distinctly juvenile form. Many of the case descriptions in the literature do not give enough information for a definitive diagnosis of a manic-depressive disorder by observation of the child alone. Heavy reliance is placed on the existence of affective illness in the family. Anthony and Scott take the position that in order for a child to be labeled manic-depressive, the following criteria need to be met: 1) Presence of an abnormal psychiatric state approximating the classical clinical descriptions; 2) A "positive" family history suggesting a manic-depressive diathesis; 3) Early tendency to manic-depressive reactions manifested in cyclothymic tendency with gradually increasing length and amplitude of mood swings, and delirious manic or depressive outbursts during pyrexical illness; 4) Evidence of recurrent or periodic illness. There should be at least two episodes lasting months or years; 5) Evidence of diphasic illness; 6) Evidence of endogenous illness, i.e. minimal reference to environmental events; 7) Evidence of severe illness, i.e. need for inpatient, heavy sedation or ECT; 8) An abnormal underlying personality of an extroverted type; 9) Absence of features that might indicate schizophrenia or organic states; 10) Current, not retrospective, judgments.

Anthony and Scott found three cases in literature which met the above requirements and presented a fourth case of their own. All the cases were 11 years or older at the time of onset. Another case, published in 1972 by Varsamus and MacDonald, began age 10 years, 7 months. This patient was followed to age 26. Typical behavior of manic-depressive illness was observed in adolescence and adulthood.

A major difficulty with the concept of a manic-depressive illness in childhood hinges on the concept of a manic state in childhood. The clinical characteristics of mania in adults have been fairly well delineated. The classical symptoms of mania in adults are increased speed of thought, anger, poor judgment, and increased social contact. Beigel and Murphy have refined their clinical appraisal of the manic state and have found 11 of 26 items of the Manic State Rating Scale particularly useful in assessing the severity of mania. These are: is talking; moves from one place to another; has poor judgment; is distractible; is irritable; is active; is argumentative; is angry; has diminished impulse control; demands contact with others; jumps from one subject to another.

The above scheme of clinical symptomatology cannot be directly transposed to children. A major problem is the overlap between the adult manic symptomatology and the hyperactivity syndrome in children. The hyperactive child who is characteristically moving all the time, distractible, active, has poor impulse control, and may have poor judgment, is far too common to be considered equivalent to a manic state in adults, although a subgroup of hyperactive children may be delineated which are the equivalent of mania in childhood. Further clinical descriptive clarification is needed.

Weinberg and Brumback contend that a juvenile form of manic-depressive illness exists. This criteria for mania in childhood includes either euphoria or irritability and agitation, plus three of the following six items: hyperactivity, push of speech, flight of ideas, grandiosity, sleep disturbance, and distractibility. The problem with this criteria is that a hyperactive child is always distractible (hence these are not separate items) and frequently irritable. Thus, any additional symptom such as grandiosity would then label the child manic. They described a four year old who acted out the fantasy of flying in her home, and called this "delusional grandiosity." Likely not all child psychiatrists would agree.

McKnew, et al, as a part of a rating scale devised for the study of the offspring of patients with affective disorder, gave a fuller description of grandiosity, i.e. "grandiose, talks of great length, wealth, power, talks of being able to kill or maim." This definition of grandiosity would likely be considered as outside the limits of normalcy by most clinicians if applied to school-aged children.

Weinberg, in three of his five cases, describes a "push of speech." McHarg has also described a pressure of speech. McKnew did not include this symptom in his rating scale. Generally, this term is not frequently used by child psychiatrists and may be of considerable diagnostic value.

All of Weinberg's cases had a marked sleep disturbance in contrast to the usual hyperactive child who sleeps well. The other "manic" symptoms of belligerence, aggression, and denial of any problems described by Weinberg are so common in child psychiatry as to make them useless as specific diagnostic criteria. McKnew, et al, in his study of the offspring of parents with an affective disorder found "a striking absence of hypomanic features."

The most convincing arguments with Weinberg's cases of mania as well as Feinstein and Wolpert's case, will come if these youngsters are followed into adolescence and adulthood and show classic manic-depressive illness.

References

Rie, H. E. Depression in childhood. *J Amer Acad Child Psychiat* 5:653–685, 1966.
Rochlin, G. *Griefs and Discontents*. Boston, Little Brown & Co, 1965.
Wolfenstein, M. How is mourning possible. *Psychoanal Study Child* 21:93–123, 1966.
Glaser, K. Masked depression in children and adolescents. *Amer J Psychother* 21:565–574, 1967.

Toolan, J. M. Depression in children and adolescents. *Amer J Orthopsychiat* 32:404–414, 1962.

Sandler, J., Joffe, W. G. Notes on childhood depression. *Internat J Psychoanal* 46:88–96, 1965.

Poznanski, E., Zrull, J. Childhood depression: clinical characteristics of overtly depressed children. *Arch Gen Psychiat* 23:8–15, 1970.

Malmquist, C. P. Depressions in childhood and adolescence. *New England J Med* 284:887–893, 1971.

Catryn, L., McKnew, D. H. Proposed classification of childhood depression. *Amer J Psychiat* 129:149–155, 1972.

Catryn, L., McKnew, D. H., Logue, M., Brennan, M. Biochemical correlates of affective disorders in children. *Arch Gen Psychiat* 31:659–661, 1974.

Group for the Advancement of Psychiatry: *Psychopathological Disorders in Childhood,* Report No. 62, New York, GAP, 1966.

Frommer, E. A. Depressive illness in childhood. *Brit J Psychiat* 1–5:117–136, Special edition, 1967–70.

Connell, H. M. Depression in childhood. *Child Psychiat Human Development* 4:71–85, 1972.

Cytryn, L., McKnew, D. H. Proposed classification of child depression. *Amer J Psychiat* 129:63–69, 1972.

Weinberg, W. A., Rutman, J., Sullivan, L., Perrick, E. C., Dietz, S. G. Depression in children referred to an educational diagnostic center: diagnosis and treatment. *J Pediat* 83:1064–1072, 1973.

Research Diagnostic Criteria, developed collaboratively by Psychobiology Branch of NIMH with Drs. Spitzer, Endicot and Eli Robbins.

Annell, A-L (ed): *Depressive States in Childhood and Adolescence.* Stockholm, Sweden, Almqvist and Wiksell, 1972.

Anthony, E. J. Childhood depression, in Anthony J., Benedek T. (eds): *Depression and Human Existence.* Boston, Little Brown & Co, 1975, pp. 231–278.

Freud, S. (1917): Mourning and melancholia, in Jones S: *Collected Papers IV.* New York, Basic Books, 1959, pp. 152–173.

Akiskal, H., McKinney, W. Overview of recent research in depression. *Arch Gen Psychiat* 32:285–303, 1975.

McKinney, W., Suomi, S., Harlow H. Depression in primates. *Amer J Psychiat* 127:49–55, 1971.

Spitz, R. A. Anaclitic depression. *Psychoanal Study Child* 11:313–342, 1946.

Bowlby, J. *Attachment and Loss. Vol. I Attachment.* New York, Basic Books, 1969.

Bowlby, J. *Attachment and Loss. Vol II Separation.* New York, Basic Books, 1973.
Heinicke, C., Westheimer, I. *Brief Separations.* New York, International Universities Press, 1965.
Bruhn, J., McCulloch, W. Parental deprivation among attempted suicides. *Brit J Psychiat Soc Wk* 6:186–191, 1962.
Greer, S. The relationship between parental loss and attempted suicide. *Brit J Psychiat* 110:698–705, 1964.
Greer, S. Parental loss and attempted suicide: a further report. *Brit J Psychiat* 112:465–470, 1966.
d'Elia, G., Perris, C. Childhood environment and bipolar and unipolar recurrent depressive psychosis, in Annell A-L (ed): *Depressive States in Childhood and Adolescence.* Stockholm, Sweden, Almqvist and Wiksell, 1972.
Wolfenstein M. Loss, rage and repetition. *Psychoanal Study Child* 24:432–463, 1969.
Caplan, M. S., Douglas, V. I. Incidence of parental loss in children with depressed mood. *J Child Psychol Psychiat Allied Disciplines* 10:225–232, 1969.
Bowlby, J. Childhood mourning and its implications for psychiatry. *Amer J Psychiat* 118:481–498, 1961.
Furman, R. Death and the young child. *Psychoanal Study Child* 19:321–333, 1964.
Kelly, J., Wallerstein, J. The effects of parental divorce: experiences of the child in early latency. *Amer J Orthopsychiat* 46:20–32, 1976.
Wallerstein, J., Kelly, J. The effects of parental divorce: experiences of the child in later latency. *Amer J Orthopsychiat* 46:256–269, 1976.
Wallerstein, J., Kelly, J. The effects of divorce on the preschool child. *J Amer Acad Child Psychiat* 14:600–616, 1975.
Wallerstein, J., Kelly, J. in Anthony J., Kaupernik C. (eds). *The Child and His Family.* New York, John Wiley, 1974.
Bemporad, J. R. New views on the psychodynamics of depressive character, in Arieti S. (ed): *World Biennial of Psychiatry and Psychotherapy.* New York, Basic Books, 1971.
Poznanski, E., Zrull, J., Krahenbuhl, V. Childhood depression: a longitudinal perspective. *J Amer Acad Child Psychiat* 15:491–501, 1976.
Zrull, J. P., McDermott, J. F., Poznanski, E. The hyperkinetic syndrome: the role of depression. *Child Psychiat Human Development* 1:33–40, 1970.
Cantwell, D. Genetics of hyperactivity. *J Child Psychol Psychiat Allied Disciplines* 16:261–264, 1975.

Annell A-L. Manic depressive illness in children and effect of treatment with lithium carboniate. *Acta Paedopsychiat* 36:292–301, 1969.

Dyson, W, Barcai A. Treatment of children of lithium-responding parents. *Cur Ther Res* 12:286–290, 1970.

Anthony, J., Scott, P. Manic-depressive psychosis in childhood. *J Child Psychol Psychiat Allied Disciplines* 1:53–72, 1960.

Varsamis, J., MacDonald, S. M. Manic depressive disease in childhood. *Canad Psychiat Assn J* 17:279–281, 1972.

Janowsky, D., El-Youself, M. K., Davis J. Interpersonal maneuvers of manic patients. *Amer J Psychiat* 131:250–255, 1974.

Beigel, A., Murphy, D, Assessing clinical characteristics of the manic state, *Amer J Psychiat* 128:688–694, 1971.

Weinberg, W., Brumback, R. Mania in childhood, *Amer J Dis Child* 130:280–385, 1976.

McKnew, D.H., Jr., Cytryn, L., Efron, A.M., Gershon, E.S., Bunney, W.E. Offspring of patients with affective disorders. Brit. J. of Psychiat., Vol. 134: p. 148–152, 1979.

McHarg, J. F. Mania in childhood: report of a case. *Arch Neurol Psychiat* 72:531–539, 1954.

Feinstein, S. C., Wolpert, E. A. Juvenile manic-depressive illness: clinical and therapeutic considerations. *J Amer Acad Child Psychiat* 12:123–136, 1973.

Chapter 4

CHILDHOOD DEPRESSION: THE MIRROR OF EXPERIENCE, INTERPERSONAL INTERACTIONS, AND DEPRESSIVE PHENOMENA

Irving Philips

In *Jude the Obscure* by Thomas Hardy, Arabella deserts her husband and has his baby. She sends the baby boy away to live with relatives who treat the youngster harshly. The father learns of the boy and brings him to live with him and his mistress. The boy reflects on his plight and tells her, "I think that whenever children be born that are not wanted, they should be killed directly before their souls come to 'em and not be allowed to grow big and walk about." The mistress informs the youngster there will be another born in the family. The boy, despondent, reacts with despair. He hangs himself and in his hand he carries a note, "Done because we are too menny."*

To elaborate the effects of parental behavior on child development speaks to the obvious. Parental depression interferes with the ability of a parent to best meet the needs of the child, and the result may be subsequent psychopa-

---

*From Thomas Hardy, *Jude the Obscure*. New York: The Modern Library. Random House, 1967, pp. 357–358.

thology in the child, in the form of depression or its equivalents. The following case is an example.

> As Mrs. W described the behavior of her 6-year-old son, Michael, she remarked that she was alarmed by his cold and calculating manner as he threatened to find his hunting knife and chop his mother and sister to bits. When she tried to talk to him, he responded that she should not leave him again by going to work the next morning. Following this episode, he became contrite and somewhat withdrawn. She reported that he would have frequent temper outbursts on the slightest provocation. She described an incident when he was thwarted by his sister and "accidentally" threw a rock hitting her in the head and inflicting a wound that required four stitches. He pleaded that she not go to visit his father or go to school the following day so that no one would know that he had injured her. Later that evening he told his mother that he had thought sometimes about pushing her off the top of the stairs. He confided that he had thoughts that he wanted to kill himself by running in front of a car or in some other way. He often expressed anger at his mother for having divorced his father and for having allowed the remarriage of his father to a strange woman. He demanded frequently to know whether his mother loved him and went to extremes to please her. In school, his teachers were concerned with his hyperactivity and with his need to please those around him. They remarked that he had severe separation anxiety when he left his mother, and it was often difficult for him to settle down and do his work. This had been a recurrent complaint since the time he was three and was first placed in day care. When his mother would leave him, he became severely upset and screamed. At school, it was noted that his writing had deteriorated, especially the writing of his name. He remarked that he did not like his name and would never write it well. He often appeared sad and withdrawn and tried to buy friends with gifts of candy or some of his lunch money. The school noticed that he vacillated between being an extremely aggressive child, hurting himself and his peers, and being hurt by older boys whom he challenged or the other extreme of remaining by himself, seeming terribly sad, and sometimes crying in a corner.
>
> Michael's development since birth had been erratic. At

the time, the parents' marriage was beginning to fail and the father became more abusive toward his wife. When Michael was 17 months, his mother went to the hospital for surgery and then remained in a body cast for four months. During that time, Michael lived with his grandparents, often remaining with the maternal grandparents for a few weeks and then with the paternal grandparents. His severe separation anxiety developed soon after this. Although he was described as a happy baby up until the time of his mother's surgery, thereafter his behavior became more and more difficult.

The mother was a depressed woman, whose childhood had been chaotic. Her alcoholic parents were abusive to her, and she was always reprimanded and referred to as a "bad" girl. When she was 8, her parents divorced and she was placed first in an orphanage and then in a series of foster homes. She met her husband when she was 19 and after a brief courtship she married him in order to escape her sad life situation. He had no job, and it was necessary for her to work to support the family. She described herself as sad and lonely all of her life, with many self-deprecatory feelings and periods in which she felt very "blue" and had difficulty functioning. Her divorce occurred when Michael was three. Although she was excellent at her work, she had few outlets to find satisfaction for herself. The only happy time in her life was the birth of her two children and she reveled in her newly found happiness. This period was short lived because of the failure of her marriage and even more because of the months of separation from her family because of her difficult surgery and subsequent incapacitation. She found herself less attentive to her children as her marriage failed and her depression became more acute.

Bowlby (1973), in a classic description of attachment behavior and the consequences of separation and loss on the developing child, widened our horizons regarding the influence of normal and anxious attachment on child development. Attachment behavior is the close ties children form with their mother during the first year. The availability of responsive and helpful persons to the child is basic to the development of self-reliance. When such a figure is available, the individual will learn that he can deal with alarming situations, feelings of anguish or humiliation, and he can seek help when necessary without hesitation. When the attachment figures are not available and responsive enough in a warm and consistent manner to allow such learning to take place, the result is what Bowlby called "anxious attachment." Children who are reared without an attachment figure, or in an environment in which they are threatened with abandonment for disciplinary reasons or where there are frequent family quarrels associated with threats of a parental figure leaving, may become insecure individuals or may demonstrate distorted personality development.

To quote Bowlby (1973):

> Yet a further difficulty turns on the fact that a mother can be physically present but 'emotionally' absent. What this means, of course, is that although present in body, mother may be unresponsive to her child's desire for mothering. Such unresponsiveness can be due to many conditions—depression, rejection, preoccupation with other matters—but, whatever its cause, so far as her child is concerned she is no better than half present. Then again, a mother can use threats to abandon a child as a means of disciplining him, a tactic that probably has an immeasurably greater pathogenic effect than is yet recognized.... Whether a child or an adult is in a state of security, anxiety, or distress is determined in large part by the accessibility and responsiveness of his principle attachment figure (p. 23).

A child confronted with such a situation goes through a typical sequence: *Protest* whereby he tries to recover his mother; *despair,* when he remains preoccupied with her and vigilant for her return; and, finally, *detachment,* when he becomes emotionally uninterested in her as a defense against painful feelings. The period of protest is related to his anxiety about separation and the period of despair to grief and mourning.

Ainsworth (1973) and her students have portrayed vividly how brief separations of young toddlers from their mothers produce immediate response by the child. In an experiment a child and his mother are placed in a room with an examiner. The mother leaves the room. The affective response is immediate. The child with normal attachment pursues, protests, searches, and is saddened. The child with anxious attachment withdraws and demonstrates little responsiveness, either in the absence or on the return of the mother. The affective sadness is apparent. Szurek (1973) has described mothers who were unresponsive or severely ambivalent toward their children. The earliest expressions of these children's sensual impulses were thwarted and repressed when met by the conflicted tension of the person on whom the child depended for the satisfaction of his needs. A parent often will find it difficult to help his child experience basic needs if his own needs were thwarted during his development; thwarting of such impulses leads to frustration and inevitable rage. Repression of impulses in the child undergoes transformation and expresses the parental psychopathology that influenced the initial behavior in a distorted and often caricaturized fashion.

Although the occurrence of depression in childhood has been debated, clinicians have recognized significant affective disturbance in the developing child of sufficient severity to indicate, if not frank depression, at least the precursors of adult psychopathology. Anna Freud (1965) noted, "It was known in psychoanalysis long before such infant observations that depressive moods of the mother during the first two years after birth create in the child a tendency to depression (although this may not manifest itself until many years later). What happens is that such infants achieve their sense of unity and harmony with the depressed mother not by means of their developmental achievements but by producing the mother's mood in themselves" (p. 87).

Retrospective analysis has contributed to our understanding of parental loss through death or abandonment and its effects on subsequent development, as well as on adult behavior. Such losses are apparent and obvious. The need for major realignment occurs. Anthony (1975) noted that "there is a profound difference between the parents being present and not present. Interaction with a living parent is an ongoing process in which the demands on the adaptive capacity of the parent are minutely and incessantly balanced against the demands on the developmental potential of the child. Thus, every conflict is fought out on both the intrapsychic and interpersonal level and has its own outcome. When the parent dies or otherwise disappears irrevocably from the everyday life of a child, this ongoing give and take is brought to a standstill and a new type of process termed mourning enters the picture" (p. 225). A more common occurrence is partial loss, when the caretaker, because of whatever neuroticisms are awakened by life events, cannot be emotionally available as much as he would like or as the infant needs. The parent may threaten desertion or abandonment or may shame the child sufficiently that he is afraid to seek expression of his wishes and impulses.

We are dealing with those interpersonal elements between parent and child that result in aberrations of development and the onset of depression in childhood, not transitory moments of affective sadness or disappointment, but rather to a frank disorder that affects development and interferes with the fullest realization of innate potential. It is obvious, as Malmquist (1971) has noted, that "the response is contingent upon the child's developmental stage. The reactions to a depressed mother in an infant will vary from those in the child during the height of oedipal feelings as well as in the child during middle latency" (p. 956). Not only the psychic structure but also the cognitive level of the child and his ability to express painful affect by language or symbolic representations are significant. "If one accepts this close relationship between cognitive and affective development as advocated by Piaget, it would stand to reason that the experience of depression in late childhood will be radically different from the earlier experience. It is possible to go further and suggest that depression itself undergoes development throughout the child's development and that its characteristics are determined by parallel developments in symbolism, representation, language, and logical operations. The question whether depression does or does not occur during childhood, therefore, can no longer stand by itself" (Anthony, 1975, p. 235).

The following clinical experiences encountered in the treatment of children and families reveal incidents in which the child and a caretaker were experiencing similar affect that was expressed in different modes because of different maturity in the psychic structure of each.

>At a pediatric well-baby clinic, a consultation was requested for a 17-year-old young mother and her 9-month-old infant, who had failed to thrive. In a brief history, the mother, self-deprecatory, with frequent crying spells and suicidal ideas, indicated she had little time for herself or the infant. The infant was unresponsive and quite difficult to arouse. His face had a withdrawn and distant look, he was undernourished, and his growth rate was retarded.
>
>Bill, a 4-year-old, was abandoned by his father at birth. He was one of three children. His 32-year-old mother frequently spanked him (sometimes a bit too hard) to control difficult behavior. The mother's life pattern was punctuated by frequent depressive episodes and one hospitalization soon after Bill's birth. Bill was a problem in nursery school, alternating between aggressive outbursts and hurting other children smaller and younger and passively remaining by himself, refusing to enter into activities.
>
>George, an 8-year-old, was referred because of symptoms of encopresis. On entering the office, the psychiatrist's

pinched nose evidenced the symptoms. George remarked, "Doctor, I have troubles. I stink inside and out." His mother had had repeated hospitalizations for psychotic depression ever since his birth and his father was a chronic alcoholic. George was a highly intelligent youngster who was failing in school because of daydreaming. He remained by himself most of the school day. His teacher remarked that she had never known a sadder youngster: When barely scolded he broke into tears.

June, a 7-year-old, refused to go to school because of overwhelming fear. Her mother felt incapable of helping her attend. When June was 7 months of age, the mother had had a severe depression that necessitated hospitalization for a three-month period. Her father, with whom she felt unusually close, was an immature underachiever who had frequent job changes and dreams of great success that was soon to appear on the horizon.

Jean, a 10-year-old, was devasted by the sudden death of her father when she was nine. After two days, she rarely mentioned him again. Nevertheless, she wore his oversized parka wherever she went. When asked about him, she responded with little emotion. Her mother, an ambitious, successful attorney, denied her grief and ambivalent feelings toward her departed husband. She lamented her new role in life. She was highly critical of her daughter, demanding high scholastic performance, a full social life, and after-school work. The daughter responded with compliant behavior but alternated between obesity and anorexia, elation and depression. Soon after the daughter entered treatment and began to rebel against her mother's unrealistic demands, the mother sought psychiatric help for herself because of behavior that was progressively deteriorating due to severe depression.

These five examples of childhood disorder are merely paradigms of the expression of depression at various developmental levels. The symptoms of failure to thrive, passive aggression, frank sadness, school avoidance, and psychosomatic expression were related to the developmental levels of the child in the expression of a pervasive, depressive affect and clinical depression.

A further review for this study was undertaken by the author of clinical experiences at the Langley Porter Institute, University of California at San Francisco. In the evaluation of all children studied at the Institute, work with each parent is part of the diagnostic process. The understanding of the family through an evaluation of both the parents and of the child with the presenting complaints gives a fuller perspective on the disorder of the child. A review of records revealed a number of depressive parents who sought treatment for their children and the relationship of these parents and the subsequent development of their children was recorded. Eleven cases are summarized in Table 1.

In all these cases, it was maternal depression that was reported. There were eight males and three females in this series and adolescents with depression were not included. The predominant response to caretaker depression was related to aggression, whether passive or active. The response to caretaker disability was related to aggression directed outward or to inner passivity and withdrawal. The underlying themes seem related to efforts at compensation, an expression of bereavement by whatever means is available to the child. In these cases, the experiences were continuous, the bereavement unresolved, and the result was frank disorder—in these examples, depression. The sample is small and certainly is not completely representative, but it indicates the great number of children that might be identified by clinicians if they were more aware of parental distress and its influence on the child.

In this series, the clinical depression of the mother was the significant variable. In each case, the past history of the mother influenced her care of the child. It was evident that what she had not received in her childhood she could not give to her child. The attachment behavior of the child was distorted. It is likely that other disorders than parental depression may result in anxious attachment with subsequent manifestations of depression in childhood. An in-

Table 1 Caretaker Depression and Childhood Disorders

Family	Sex	Age (yrs)	Diagnosis	Significant events and symptoms
1. Child	M	10	Depressive reaction	Lonely, no friends, unhappy, enuretic, once set a fire.
Mother		34	Depressive reaction	Divorce at birth of son. Remarried age 3. Divorce at 5. Chronic fatigue, remorseful, isolated from friends. Maternal father died when she was 6.
2. Child	M	9	Passive-aggressive reaction	Poor learner, physical attacks on others, emotional outbursts in school. A "loner."
Mother		51	Depressive reaction	Father deserted family at son's birth and died 3 years later. Mother moved to new city; lost job, friends. Clinically depressed.
3. Child	M	8	Withdrawing reaction	Physical abuse by father. Insecure, withdraws when threatened. Underachiever, gives up easily.
Child	M	5	Passive-aggressive reaction	Physical abuse by father. Enuretic, aggressive and hurtful to younger children. Negativistic.
Mother		34	Depressive reaction	Abused by husband. Masochistic relationship. Divorced when children 5 and 2. Father kidnapped children, returned under stress. Depressed since adolescence. Spends days in bed. Lonely and isolated.
4. Child	M	5	Withdrawing reaction	Shy, withdrawn, speech deteriorating. History of neglect by mother. Sleep problems, chewed on crib (pica), many babysitters.
Mother		25	Depressive reaction	Deserted by mother at age 5. Lived with relatives. Lonely childhood. Depressed since adolescence. Guilt-ridden in everything she does.
5. Child	F	9 (mo.)	Failure to thrive	Unresponsive. Difficult to arouse. Undernourished. Poor feeder. Father deserted before birth.
Mother		17	Depressive reaction	Suicidal ideas, crying spells. Apathetic, self-depreciatory ideas. Lives alone with child.

6. Child	M	4	Passive-aggressive reaction	Hurtful to other children. Remains by self. Aggressive outbursts. Refuses to participate in school activities. Physical abuse.
Mother		32	Depressive reaction	Frequent depressive episodes (1 hospitalization). Often unable to work because of mood.
7. Child	M	8	Depressive reaction	Encopresis. School failure. Isolating behaviors. Daydreamer. Would cry when scolded by teachers.
Mother		28	Depressive reaction	Frequent hospitalizations for psychotic depressions. Difficulty caring for son. Husband chronic alcoholic which interfered with professional career.
8. Child	F	7	Refusal to go to school	Recurrent school absences for "bellyaches" and minor U.R.I.'s. Easily frightened, night terrors.
Mother		32	Depressive reaction	Postpartum depression (3 month hospitalization). Overly concerned about family. Hard worker, husband immature underachiever.
9. Child	F	10	Depressive reaction	Loss of father at age 9, no grief. Overinvolvement in activities, anorexia, and obesity. Elation and depression.
Mother		46	Depressive reaction	Successful professional but chronically unsatisfied in career and successes. Father died at age 7. Hard to please. Two previous unsuccessful marriages.
10. Child	M	6	Passive-aggressive reaction	Divorce age 3. Temper, outbursts, threats to kill mother and sister with knife. Needs constant reassurance. Severe separation anxiety. Difficult at school. Self-depreciation.
Mother		28	Depressive reaction	Alcoholic parents. Always told she was "bad." Parents divorced when 6, sent to series of foster homes. Married at 19 to unstable husband. Chronically depressed.

creasingly frequent situation is the discharge of a mother from a psychiatric hospital after an acute illness and heavily dosed with psychoactive drugs. Obviously this will interfere with the ability of the parent to best provide for optimal development of young children and will interfere with their attachment behavior. The parent not only is separated from the child through hospitalization, but on return finds it difficult to care for him.

A variety of symptoms may result, depending on the nature of attachment between parent and child, the developmental level of the child, and current life events. A survey of phases of the growth cycle indicates various manifestations of response to interpersonal experience.

INFANCY

The classic study of Spitz (1947) called attention to the institutionalized child who receives little attention from personnel with resultant anaclitic depression. In these situations, the maternal figure is not present and there are no other opportunities for attachment. The infant fails to thrive, withdraws, becomes apathetic, and in some cases dies. It became clear from a number of studies that similar effects occur in infants who remain in their own homes and fail to thrive because of maternal depression. Mothers who experience severe depression, disinterest, or apathy react to their infants in a distorted fashion. The descriptions of Fischhoff (1975) and those of Fraiberg et al. (1975) in the classic "Ghosts in the Nursery" emphasized this. The infants in these series were little different from those described by Spitz. Both caretaker and infant were depressed, each expressing the disorder consistent with his own developmental level. Fischhoff wrote that deprivation may not be the only factor in failure of development, that there exists a multitude of factors. He noted, "Recently Cravioto

(1973) reported an ongoing study, now in its seventh year, of 300 children in a Mexican village where malnutrition of some degree is prevalent among all the children because of 'low socioeconomic and cultural backgrounds,' but severe malnutrition is a 'seemingly random occurrence.' The investigators concluded that the development of severe 'third degree' malnutrition is strongly associated with the lack of social, emotional, and cognitive stimulation within the home" (p. 223).

The separation and resultant despair that reflect caretaker disability may be the infantile expression of depression. Szurek reported that "only one child among 264 psychotic children . . . seen at Langley Porter between 1946 and 1961 was in any appreciable degree malnourished and definitely physically underdeveloped. This patient, at age three years, presented a picture of a severe agitated depression, restless, wringing her hands with an extremely tense facial expression and speaking little and often not at all, and showed little sign of attachment to any staff member" (p. 255). The history of the family was not presented.

A similar patient was admitted to the Langley Porter Institute Children's Ward. The child, at age 3, was severely undernourished, refused to eat, and was cachectic in appearance. She wrung her hands so severely that she had caused tissue damage to her wrists. She refused to speak but had good eye contact. Her posture and gait were stiff and awkward. Repeated results of neurological examinations were within normal limits. After 3 years of residential treatment her condition changed very little. She was below the first percentile in height and weight. Her early years had been chaotic, with her mother so constantly frightened and under threat from a paranoid husband that she had little time for her daughter. Early normal development receded into the more pathological picture described above.

Are these two examples of what may be called psychotic depression expressions of the vagaries of the depressive phenomena in infancy? It is intriguing to speculate whether the most severe disorders of childhood, such as the psychotic maldevelopments, may not be prototypes of severe depressive episodes occurring early in the child's development.

Preschool (2–6 years)

In the preschool period, the child's language increases considerably. With his cognitive development, he gains the capacity for observational learning with increased emphasis on mental representations through imitation, but he is still quite egocentric and tends toward direct action. The structuralization of his mental process becomes more formal, but his ability for conceptual thinking is not achieved until he moves closer to 6 or 7 years of age. He is able only partially to conceptualize ideas such as death. It is in this period that the child is vulnerable to his quest for autonomy and initiative and may identify with a depressed mother. The manifestations of depression may be varied. The reactions of children to parental disability are frequently observed as regressive reactions: severe separation anxieties, hyperactivity, learning disorders, somatizations, and others. Depression in childhood may be best diagnosed by the analysis of the caretaker-child dyad and their reactions to each other.

School Age (6–11 years)

In the child's cognitive development, the beginning of operational thinking is a major turning point. The child now learns how to organize the facts of reality to those in the immediate situation. In the structural sense, this is the time of the forming of the panoply of defenses, together with the consolidation of the superego. The loss of a parent is now understood in conceptual form, although understanding of death in the abstract sense must wait a few more years. The symptoms of depression take more nearly the form of adult depressive reaction and mirror the depression of the caretaker. The child is overly sensitive and easily hurt. Self-deprecatory feelings begin to emerge. He seeks relationships but fears them; the threat of abandonment remains in the air. Consequently, his relationships are tenuous or tentative. He vacillates between harsh self-criticism and blaming others for their faults. Observation reveals a sense of sadness and an unhappy child who may complain chronically about physical or psychological hurts. In school, he may daydream or be the class clown and in his effort to seek acceptance and reward he is scolded and sometimes punished. Seldom is he recognized as needing consolation; rather, his acting out behavior is annoying and results in further reinforcement of his negative feelings. His suffering is unrecognized by teacher or parent and he may go unnoticed, never receiving the attention he craves and so desperately needs. Malmquist (1971, p. 955), listing symptoms of depression in middle childhood, described this child very well. The child's symptoms are more focused but they mirror those of his parent.

Finally, separation through divorce, an ever-increasing phenomenon in contemporary society, must be mentioned. The work of Wallerstein and Kelly (1975) indicated the acute effects on children of such an event. Their descriptions are of depressed children, although they are not diagnosed as such. Their findings are consistent with those of clinicians who work with such families. The affect of such children is obvious and mirrors further the affects of each of the separated parents now attempting a new life apart. In divorce, the family continues though the marriage has died. Table 2 summarizes the disorder of depression as it appears in the developing child.

Table 2 Depression in Childhood

Age	Psychosocial	Cognitive	Mode	Symptoms	Caretaker problems and life events
Infancy	Trust vs. mistrust Normal vs. "anxious" attachment	Sensorimotor phase	Autonomic nervous system, distorted ego differentiation	Anaclitic depression, failure to thrive, psychophysiologic manifestations	Parental depression Rejection, abuse-neglect (physical and psychological, incapacity and inability
Preschool (2–6 yrs)	Autonomy vs. shame and doubt	Preoperational thought	Premature superego development, autonomic nervous system	Depressive equivalents, passive aggression, psychophysiologic manifestations, separation anxiety, etc.	Separation Death, hospitalization, divorce Chronic illness
Early school-age (6–8 yrs)	Initiative vs. guilt	Stage of concrete operations	Organization of defenses	Refusal to go to school, psychophysiologic manifestations, variety of affective symptoms, aggression, learning problems, hyperactivity, etc.	
Late school (8–11 yrs)	Industry vs. inferiority	Stage of concrete operations	Superego consolidation	Depression similar to adult picture	

Conclusion

Childhood depression probably is underdiagnosed in clinical practice. Its manifestations depend on age, psychosocial development, cognitive integration, and attachment behavior. All are significant factors in the expression of symptomatology. If the clinician considers the child as a miniature adult and his expectations are that symptoms will be similar to those seen in adult depression, many children will be misdiagnosed and their problem neglected. This chapter has attempted to delineate those life events that have significance for the development of this disorder in a child. He may be a victim of the unexpected and unplanned and mirror the experience of those who care for him. Interpersonal transactions and developmental level influence both the development of disorder and the varied manifestations of its occurrence. Parental disability, whatever its origin, but especially if it is related to depression, interferes with the parent's capacity to provide the relationship needed by the child. The child, in turn, is inhibited from achieving his innate potential. A close study by the clinician of the dyad of child (with attention to his developmental level) and caretaker will increase the accuracy of diagnosis and make possible a greater understanding of the manifestations of depression in childhood.

References

Bowlby, J. *Attachment and loss, volume II, separation.* New York: Basic Books, 1973.

Ainsworth, M. D. S. The development of infant mother attachment. In B. M. Caldwell & H. N. Ricciuti (Eds.), *Child development research, volume 3.* Chicago: The University of Chicago Press, 1973.

Freud, A. *Normality and pathology in childhood.* New York: International University Press, 1965.

Anthony, E. J. Childhood depression. In E. J. Anthony & T. Benedek (Eds.), *Depression and human existence.* Boston: Little, Brown, 1975.

Malmquist, C. P. Depressions in childhood and adolescence, II. *New England Journal of Medicine,* 1971, *284,* 955.

Spitz, R. Anaclitic depression: An inquiry into the genesis of psychiatric conditions of early childhood. *Psychoanalytic Study of the Child,* 1947, *2,* 313.

Fraiberg, S., Edelson, E., & Schapiro, V. Ghosts in the nursery. *Journal of the American Academy of Child Psychiatry,* 1975, *14,* 387.

Fischhoff, J. Failure to thrive and maternal deprivation. In E. J. Anthony (Ed.), *Explorations in child psychiatry.* New York: Plenum Press, 1975.

Szurek, S. A. Attachment and psychotic detachment. In S. A. Szurek & I. N. Berlin (Eds.), *Studies in childhood psychoses.* New York: Brunner/Mazel, 1973.

Wallerstein, J. S., & Kelly, J. B. The effects of parental divorce: Experiences of the preschool child. *Journal of the American Academy of Child Psychiatry,* 1975, *14,* 600.

Chapter 5

SOME IMPLICATIONS OF THE DEVELOPMENT PROCESSES FOR TREATMENT OF DEPRESSION IN ADOLESCENCE

Irving N. Berlin

In recent years the work of child and adolescent psychiatrists and mental health professionals who work with adolescents in a variety of settings have begun to document some of the normal developmental patterns of adolescence. Erikson (1963) identified the developmental tasks of adolescence which, if not successfully achieved, result in pathology. These tasks are described as identity versus role diffusion and intimacy versus isolation. Barger (1962), from his work with college students, tends to agree. Hamburg and Hamburg (1961), Offer and Sabshin (1966), Offer and Offer (1968), Offer (1969), Offer, Marcus, and Offer (1970), Offer and Offer 1971), Offer and Offer (1973), Silber (1961), and others have emphasized the more normative developmental issues in contrast to the issues usually found in the literature of maldevelopment which are reflected in psychopathology, dysfunction, and alienation.

The major developmental tasks of adolescence can be stated as individuation from the family, the establishment of independence, and a work or professional role as well as a capacity for achieving intimacy with individuals of the opposite sex. In this process, the development of meaningful social relations occurs first with peers of the same sex then developmentally there evolves a capacity for intimacy with adolescents of the opposite sex. The evolution of a healthy sexual identity permits loving and relating to others and becoming appropriately intimate with women or men in a nonfearful, close, and satisfying relationship. Independence cannot be achieved unless an occupational or professional role is worked out. Blos (1967), Berlin (1977), Blos (1962), Caplan & Leborici (1969), Gutman (1973).

As Ravenscroft (1974) has described in a recent paper that regression in both the adolescent and family are normal developmental phenomenae in adolescence. Regression occurs when the normal preadolescent, who has been self-motivated, learning well, enjoying peer relations, and no great problem to parents at home, becomes rebellious, apathetic, demanding, ignores school work, and is at constant odds with parents, siblings, and schoolteachers. The regression is related to the adolescent's increased needs for firm limit-setting on the one hand and greater independence on the other. Thus, the young person's dependence on his parents for direction, modeling behavior, and assistance paradoxically increases.

Not unlike the 2-to-3-year-old's search for autonomy, the constant negativism is a request for firm and consistent discipline which sets limits to aggression and to destructive or self-destructive aspects of the search for autonomy. Both the firmness and support encourages and facilitates autonomy, exploration, and learning. In adolescence, the adult's clarity about being both firm in areas of potential danger to the adolescent or others without experiencing feelings of conflict or retaliation and being equally encouraging about independence and self-assertion is critical for the adolescent's optimal development. In White's (1960) terms, the achievement of competence is an adolescent goal. Parental anxiety and retaliation responsive to efforts toward independence causes circular conflict, mutual anxiety, and retaliation. If severe repression occurs, there may be rebellion and flight from the home or abdication of autonomous strivings and regression into submissive, passive-aggressive behavior. Anthony (1969).

Many workers like Offer (1966–1973), Block (1971), Barger (1962), and others who see large numbers of adolescents in school and work situations remark about how little overt conflict is evident. It appears that in many instances the transition to a more independent status is not seriously interfered with by parents. That is, the rebellion, or efforts at self-assertion and independence, are not countered seriously by repression. There is, therefore, growth of mutual respect of the adolescent and parent as their conflicts are openly, and even angrily, debated. Such debate leads not to rupture of relationships but to negotiations as age makes independence and reliable self-care and capacity to responsibly take care of others manifest for the adult. The epidemiologic data here is not great and the samples studied at present are relatively small, especially in lower, middle, and working class and poverty populations (We know more about the upper middle-class college population.)

Many clinicians who treat young adults have some sense that although there were no major signs of stress in adolescence, in fact, both the conflicts about achieving the goals and of independence and intimacy were not resolved in some adolescents. The adolescent was able to repress and sublimate those conflicts in the work and study routine and to use previously effective defenses from school and college without dealing with major developmental issues.

The opportunities presented in adolescence to resolve residual conflicts from previous developmental periods often do not occur. The conflicts often become manifest in young adult life around efforts to establish intimacy with the opposite sex and to achieve independence through developing the capacity to earn a living.

Adult Models—Effective and Ineffective

Education in our society began primarily to provide an upper class and upper middle class with the tools for professional and management occupations. However, education for the masses in the early 1900s was first designed to take child labor off the street. Later it was to provide the basic skills for reading, writing, and arithmetic to a large immigrant population. At no time has education been viewed as a way of helping young people learn to solve problems of increasing complexity so that they could cope more effectively with the problems that affect their lives. Only recently, and in very few places, has there been a beginning at assessing societal needs, the marketable skills and talents of adolescents, and providing vocational, paraprofessional, and professional training in the needed areas. Such efforts are still only fragmentary. One of the major areas of disequilibrium for young people is that the problems facing our world are overwhelming. The issues of pollution and of nuclear warfare with their threat to survival, the issue of world hunger, overpopulation, and, in this country, of fewer employed and employable, and of an energy crisis that no one can find answers to makes it clear to adolescents that the adults are helpless and unable to provide approaches to solutions to these critical problems. Thus, the adult, as model for the adolescent in terms of work roles, paternal-maternal roles, and the bearer of societal traditions becomes less tenable and increases the burdens on the adolescent during development. Masterson (1967).

THE NEED FOR CHALLENGE AND LEARNING TO SOLVE PROBLEMS

The critical issue of recognizing the cognitive capacities and the variety of talents and needs of the preadolescents for challenge are not met. The universal needs of adolescents to learn how to think in terms of the problem-solving process is avoided. Their need to learn to assess problems, to find out where the data can be found, and to be able to gather the data is provided rarely. To learn data evaluation and from it how one can establish hypotheses to be tested as one explores various possible solutions to problems is critical to learning to solve problems as a way of life. Thus, the schools who could provide rites of passage rarely do. Coles (1976), Haan, et al. (1968), Piaget (1969), White (1966, 1973).

Several experimental efforts reveal the hunger of adolescents for relevant learning. In one ghetto high school, a university professor of physics volunteered to teach a class of dropouts. Not being a high school teacher and with experience primarily with graduate students, he had no preconceived ideas about teaching. He turned to the eight students who had come to test out this nutty professor and said essentially, "All I know is how to help you find information about anything you want to learn. What do you want to learn?" The five boys and three girls, some of whom were black, with much smirking agreed that they wanted to learn about sex. Further exploration revealed they knew practically nothing about their own anatomy and physiology, which are necessary to learn about sex. Most of these high school students were poor readers. Given some help with where to find materials on simple anatomy, physiology, and sex manuals, and with help from several tutors in reading, they began to read and to discuss. The learning was rapid and very exciting to the physics professor who also learned. In short order the experimental, voluntary dropout class size increased from eight dropouts to twenty. In that year, they also studied embryology, child development, and family relationships. For the professor and his students, the enthusiasm made for an exciting experience.

Mary Kohler (1971) and the projects of the National Commission for Youth in helping adolescents learn child care by working in a day-care center and participating in child development seminars also report that both young men and women want to understand development, sexuality, and human relationships, if given facilitating teachers. Adolescents' observations of children in the day-care center led to explorations about parenting, discussions of the problems of their own parents, and their own problems. These adolescents were especially concerned about the kinds of experiences that might cause the behavioral problems of some of the small children with whom they work in the day-care centers. The readiness of adolescents to learn about real issues of life is great. The readiness of adults to teach about them is limited.

Other experimental efforts at work experiences for adolescents that might lead to viable work opportunities also reveal the readiness of many adolescents to discover their own talents and to try to find out how they might be used gainfully. The lower Harlem experiment reveals that a large hospital complex can provide work-learning opportunities in human services in every aspect of maintenance and repairs, dietary and cooking skills, outreach social service skills as well as nursing aide skills. This nation faces a serious question with most adolescents. Will society recognize their right to become self-respecting, employed, and productive adults? Mt. Saini Community Project (1976).

TALENT DEVELOPMENT

The discovery and development of talent so necessary for a civilized and highly industrialized country is still largely accidental or the result of parents' or teachers' perceptions and pushing. In early Greece, talent was recognized and promoted by the society as a sign of a favor bestowed by the gods (Aires, 1962). Bronfenbrenner (1973) and others have described how in the Soviet Union talent in the arts, sciences, medicine, etc. is searched out and developed as an investment for the nation, and all education is paid for by the nation. Or, as is true in some European countries and Australia, those who compete for college and have the talents are paid stipends to develop their skills and talents. In this, the most industrialized and the richest nation in the world, there is *no* systematic effort to discover, or even when discovered, to support talented young people in the arts, sciences, and human services. Such complete disregard for the potential of our youth and neglect of our resources clearly spells out the nation's lack of concern for the development and creativity of its children and youth. How can our adolescents develop normally with a sense of being valued and important in a society that makes no place for them?

ADOLESCENT SEXUALITY—ITS DEVELOPMENTAL IMPLICATIONS

The onset of puberty and flooding of sex hormones with subsequent awareness of one's own sexual feelings creates confusion for most adolescents. Since there presently are no effective, formal ways to teach the adolescent what is occurring, despite more high school classes in hygiene, the adolescent turns primarily to his or her peers for information and mutual understanding. Community education efforts by health and mental health professionals to provide sex information to high school and junior high school students make it clear that peer information as it is conveyed and understood is distorted and highly inaccurate.

Learning to deal with sexual feelings is a primary task for adolescents. They reduce their anxieties about sexual thoughts and feelings through peer group discussions. The more adventurous members share their experiences or fantasies with the less adventuresome. There is still little in our society to help adolescents understand and deal with their own sexual urges, to understand their physiology, and acquire knowledge and experience about what makes for tender and mutually satisfying relationships. Masterson (1967), Blos (1967).

Too often—still especially for girls but for boys too—sex becomes the only means of hopefully experiencing closeness with someone else. A good deal of research shows that many unwed young mothers and fathers engaged in sex not only for sexual pleasure but to experience closeness and a feeling of being loved.

Perhaps of significance today is the information that comes from various organized peer discussion groups that some adolescents of all classes are involved in. These experiences demonstrate that there is a clear identification by the adolescent with the sexist attitudes of society, especially of their parents. However, what does emerge from some well-planned, open and honest school, church, and social group discussions with open and honest teachers is a greater sense of equality between sexes and less fearful feelings about closeness. For most adolescents, these nonexploitative aspects of sexual relationships as well as the close, tender aspects of sexuality are never explored.

Problems About Intimacy in Development

The development of a capacity for intimacy, closeness of feeling, capacity for empathy and sharing of feelings is a major developmental goal in adolescence. In a society where intimacy and sharing of feelings often do not occur in most families and there are not other models of such behavior in the education system, it becomes an important developmental problem. The search of today's youth for a variety of experience, with and without drugs, that will lead to greater capacity for experiencing and expressing feelings and ability to share feelings is indicative of the need to find ways of helping young people learn to become aware of and to express affect.

Of some interest to many clinicians are those experiments in a few high schools and in some college dormatories where models for free expression of feeling are provided. Both the female and male group leaders are chosen for their capacity to express their own feelings easily and openly. The leader's lack of anxiety about open disagreement with their fellow group leaders and their openness to discuss feelings or any topic of concern to their younger colleagues is identified with. The impact of such models on young people is evidently great. It is heartening from some reports to recognize how great the changes are that can occur in adolescence and how much these changes seem to alter the capacity of the young person to function more effectively in that setting. What is especially noted is the reduction of depression in adolescents who learn to express themselves freely, to feel more easily, and therefore to relate more easily to others and become less isolated. One of the evident by-products is a greater capacity to work and to express their own talents more openly. Barger (1962), Halleck (1967), Farnsworth (1966).

How one begins to help young people who will be the parents of the next generation to more universally experience freedom of feeling and greater intimacy with others is still a major developmental problem.

THE ROLE OF SELF-ASSERTION IN INDIVIDUATION

Perhaps one of the most important developmental issues is how the adolescent learns to become an authoritative rather than authoritarian adult. In this process, young persons must be permitted to assert their knowledge. They need to have their current information, logic, understanding, etc. seriously considered, and their very frequent superior knowledge in some areas not only acknowledged but praised and rewarded by the parent attention. Adults must provide overt recognition of the individual's real competence and knowledge base in certain areas. The developmental-cognitive capacities for creative and abstract thinking occur approximately at the time of puberty unless previous conflicts have interfered with cognitive, social, and psychological development. Opportunity to use these new cognitive capacities must be found. Unless there are opportunities for expression and development in these cognitive areas, there is some evidence that they do not develop. Such adolescents appear to be permanently handicapped in their thinking. Problems of the world and society, present and past, must be posed and attacked by young thinkers without preconceived biases. The use of logic, models, and problem-solving methods are best understood and most effectively and creatively used during this period of adolescence. It is no accident that the late adolescents and young adults in colleges have been in the forefront of both scientific and social revolutions.

The affirmation of adolescent competence and knowledge and a lack of competitiveness with the adolescent requires that the parents and teachers are themselves fairly secure and unafraid of challenge. Since most middle class adolescents have acquired newer knowledge in a rapidly changing technical society, that knowledge may pose a serious threat to the parent, teacher, or other adult involved with the adolescent.

For individuation to occur, such acknowledgment and encouragement of competence becomes an important part of the developmental process.

Some Implications of the Developmental Processes for the Treatment of Depression in Adolescence

Some Varieties of Adolescent Depression

The literature suggests that depression in adolescence may be masked by other symptoms and disguised as other disorders (DeYoung, 1976; Glaser, 1967; Masterson, 1967). Thus, hostile, antisocial behavior has been described as masking severe depression. Fear of failure and inability to see any way of becoming an effective, valued adult "worth something to someone" in a society where there is mass unemployment of young adults especially affects the poor and racial minorities. Some of the antisocial, hostile behavior has been ascribed to feelings of helplessness and confusion about establishing one's sex role and being able to form a stable sexual relationship as well as the need to assert oneself aggressively in a stereotyped sex role. While much aggressive antisocial behavior is influenced by environmental factors, the need to appear assertive, effective, and competent in youth that feel helpless and are developmentally stunted may be defended against by violent behavior. Despite desiring close intimate relationships, efforts in those directions are usually shortlived sexual liaisons. It is likely in many instances that development of very early object relations has been interfered with to a marked degree. A very angry, depressed young mother or father abuses their child. The parents need the child to provide them with gratification and the child demands of them the nurturance they do not have to give.

A few studies indicate that over 50 percent of the hospitalizations for serious antisocial delinquent behavior with psychotic behavioral episodes have severe depressions. One may use the usual behavior criteria for depression: Characteristic sleeping patterns, feelings of sadness and being slowed down, history of previous such depressions, and a family history of depression which is then consonant with family data from unipolor and bipolar manic depression psychoses. (Personal communication 1974). Some of these adolescents have done well on lithium and tricyclic antidepressants.

Several kinds of depressions among college students have been described by college mental health services. In large campuses, the students in their first year from small towns who feel alone without anyone to turn to and find the work very difficult are serious suicidal risks (Barger, 1962; Shore, 1977).

Students who have done well in high school and find college competition overwhelming feel terribly inadequate. The poor first exam grades confirm their sense of failure and they become seriously depressed. Thus, due to a variety of poor adaptations to college life, students who previously felt they were effective students, popular, well-liked, important to peers and family and had friends to relate to seem to be candidates for serious depressions, and some become suicidal.

The sense of aloneness, lack of counsel and concern from others, feelings of failure, and inability to face family and friends are frequent causes of depression and suicide not only in college populations, but in boarding schools, especially Indian boarding schools. In Indian boarding schools, depression and suicide are related to lack of expressed concern for the youngsters' cultural background, their needs for academic help, and their sense of loneliness. Usually no one relates to these adolescents with understanding and concern for their problems. Most male adolescent Indian suicides occur in jail where they are alone and despondent about whatever minor crime or incident (often with alcoholism) has landed them there. They are in fear of family and tribal judgment. Shore (1972), Shore (1977).

Sexual anxieties, especially first awareness of homosexual feelings, lead to isolation, estrangement from former friends, sometimes overt panic or withdrawal and seem to be important factors in yet other depressions. Among the most depressed adolescents are those who have had recurrent troubles in school, at home, and with peers, or those who have very tenuous family relationships and then suffer the trauma of severe family disintegration from divorce or death of a parent.

The extent to which drugs are used to mask depression and feelings of worthlessness and loneliness can only be guessed at from the frequency with which young addicts describe their feelings of desperation that precede their hunger for relief.

In many instances of severe depression in adolescence, there have been antecedent episodes of behavioral disturbances, school problems, school refusal, and anxiety episodes for which some symptomatic help is sought from school counselors, physicians, and others. Settlage (1978).

The middle-class adolescent who has been a good student and relatively secure with his peers seems less likely to become as severely depressed as the adolescent who, though a good student, has never learned to make friends and who has few social and coping skills. Such a youngster appears to have not felt secure enough in relations with both parents to express his feelings openly. He has not learned that he is loved sufficiently by both parents so that there is little risk of retaliation for opposing behavior or debate and that his rebellious independent behavior will not cause disruption of a fragile parental relationship.

THE DIAGNOSTIC IMPLICATIONS OF DEVELOPMENTAL DATA FOR TREATMENT PROGRAMS

The Feelings of Failure and Depression

Recent work of Shore (1977) and other workers has revealed that depression and suicide of Indian adolescents is reduced markedly in the boarding homes if there are some counselors from the same tribes as the students. Counselors need to learn how to spot beginning depression, especially to attend to beginning isolation and falling off of school work. They must reach out and spend time talking to these young people and helping them sympathetically, but firmly, to master their academic work. In an effort to reduce suicide in jail on several reservations, elders from the tribe volunteered to spend days and nights in the cell with the youths talking to them in their native tongue and helping them to recognize their role as carriers of tribal tradition. They also act as the adolescents' advocates with the family. Drastic reduction in suicide rates have occurred as well as in subsequent depression with need for hospitalization.

Barger (1962) and others have described the vicissitudes of the first year of college and especially the impact of first midterm exams on students. To reduce isolation, loneliness, feelings of alienation in several dormatories, there were mandatory group meetings led by upper classmen and young male and female faculty members. Leaders had been trained to open discussions about the freshman syndrome, to help work out a buddy system with older students, and to provide help on how to study for exams. Group and individual coaching sessions were available.

Their open discussions and their freedom to talk about problems of making friends, feeling adequate, satisfying folks at home, sexual anxieties, etc. decreased the number of dropouts in the freshman year and vastly decreased the number of depressed and suicidal students in the experimental dorms.

Developmental Issues

The hospital assessment of adaptive functioning by close scrutiny of premorbid data about cognitive, social, psychological, and sensorimotor development gives one a clearer sense of the strengths of the depressed patients and where and how they can begin to be helped. At the same time, an effort to assess the family relationships through direct interviews with the family and careful historical data from the patient gives one a sense of the previous relational deficiencies and resultant adaptive behaviors, and how understanding these may make it easier for staff to deal with the depressed patient who may also be demanding, helpless, manipulative, and hostile.

A clear sense of the unachieved developmental goals gives one ideas about how the milieu could be programmed to enhance the sense of effectiveness of the depressed adolescent by efforts to help in the achievement of the next developmental steps.

Most often, therapeutic work, especially in the milieu and with the family, while attending to some issues of individuation and independence, seems to ignore the issues of authority and competence and the issues of intimacy and freedom to feel and express warm and tender feelings. There is frequently a concentration on helping the adolescent more freely express hostile, angry feelings without the recognition that close and warm feelings and openness are even harder to express and that hostile feelings may indeed by a cover for the great need to experience tender, close feelings. The efforts to help the adolescent find areas in which he can feel authoritative and competent are usually not approached with a structured plan in mind. The general issues of talent, capacity, and competence are especially important to those adolescents who have done well in their living, studying, and working and have suddenly decompensated under a variety of stresses.

The very depressed, middle-class adolescent has usually achieved a large measure of effectiveness that he currently discredits. Unless these areas of competence are understood and evaluated, the antidepressants will help the adolescent feel less depressed, but his sense of self-worth will depend on the reacquisition of former skills and abilities which require a great deal of support and need to be spelled out clearly. Graded expectations which are geared to actual capacities to perform need to be defined. In addition, the other developmental goals, especially social competencies, which are not yet achieved and may be factors in the etiology of the illness, need to be approached as part of the therapeutic process both with the adolescent and with the family.

Case Example

> A suicidal, seriously depressed 21-year-old physics major on tricyclic antidepressants began to feel somewhat better. He took part in more activities, enjoyed athletics, and visits from friends. When this became apparent, discussions with him led to his disclosure of a vague anxiety that since his illness and previous inability to concentrate, he could not recall or concentrate on physics. It was clear he had no problems when it came to reading novels and nonfiction. It was made clear that he really could begin to study physics but would probably experience initial anxiety. One of his friends brought in an early assignment that he had completed successfully before he became ill. With the friend, he slowly went over the reading material and the lab notebook. To his great surprise and obvious delight, he had not forgotten

how to solve the physics problems, and his understanding of physics had not deteriorated. His gradual return to functioning in physics was an important part of his full recovery. It also led in his psychotherapy to a clearer view of some of the reactivation of competitive issues with his father that his success in physics had brought to a head and may have been an etiological factor in his illness.

Case Example

A 15-year-old suicidal young woman, F., posed many problems for the staff and her therapist. On the one hand, she could be charming and seductive, bright, involved with the milieu group meetings as a leader, very cheerful and helpful. On the other hand, she could appear very regressed, seriously depressed, threatening suicide and demanding constant attention, especially from her therapist or the occupational therapist (O.T.) with whom she had grown close. Several suicidal gestures kept her therapist and staff very jumpy.

Her history revealed that chronic allergies and asthma, now not difficult to manage, were at least partly responsible for learning to manipulate her family. She was especially able to manipulate her mother, whose depression and anger at the birth of her daughter had prevented early nurturance on the one hand and later firmness on the other about her need to function in school and not use asthmatic attacks as ways to avoid exams and as explanations for poor performance. Her father was a much more authoritative person and more attentive and helpful around academic work when he was at home. He was a construction engineer and often not at home. It was noted by both parents that the young woman rarely, if ever, had an asthmatic episode when father was at home.

She had few friends in school. Since she was rarely there, her social world centered around the treatment of her asthma. The depression and suicidal effort that resulted in hospitalization was related to being invited by a new boyfriend to a dance at school. At the last moment he cancelled their date because he had to work. F. had been able to manipulate him by several other threats of suicide; he had no alternative this time but to work overtime on his after-school job. Since he did not respond, she swallowed a bottle of her mother's tranquilizers; she told her sister and was hospitalized.

In the hospital, as she learned grooming skills and felt she looked prettier, she seemed better able to socialize more. Both the male therapist and the female O.T., who were able to be firm with her and expect her to work and learn in school, in occupational therapy and physical therapy, were respected but constantly tested. The other staff members whom she could manipulate were held in contempt and thus she evoked retaliatory anger.

Since her developmental assessment was shared with the staff, she was rewarded for progress. Failures to try in any areas were explored without any rancor or blame but also without any excusing for her lack of effort.

One of the schoolteachers, a very bright young man with a congenital hip deformity that required the use of crutches, finally became a mainstay in her school work. He insisted she begin to read history and elementary philosophy. He spent extra time with her when she had done her homework and listened briefly to excuses when she had not. He said he would talk to her next time after she had done her reading.

Her increased competence in school was also reflected in increased social effectiveness with other adolescents on the ward and a gradual decrease in manipulative behavior.

In family sessions, there were efforts to work on more forthright relations with the mother, and the father uniting in efforts to clarify home problems rather than joining F. as her champion. He believed he was the only one who could get to her and thus he denigrated mother. As the developmental tasks of adolescence were spelled out and a tentative agreement made about how they would be worked on by family members and ward personnel with F., she began to make some strides. She then suddenly began to look depressed, regressed, refused to get out of bed and again made threats of suicide if anyone tried to force her. Her therapist, the O.T., teacher, and ward personnel paid her brief visits, but made no efforts to persuade her to get out of bed. The hypothesis was that having experienced the satisfaction of more integrative behavior, this regression could be accepted without the old battles reestablishing old patterns. After four days, she appeared at the evening meal very nonchalant and was accepted in a friendly way without fuss.

Over an eight-month period, her behavior in a number of areas was altered; she was able to negotiate more privileges from her mother and related better with her peers. In her therapy she was able to reconstruct her methods of manipulating her environment and recognize, in the transference, what she really wanted for herself in terms of unlimited nurturance.

She left the hospital a much more effective and competent and insightful young woman than on entry.

A clearer view of the entire process of development of the child and adolescent may help during this period of reconstructive opportunities to utilize the reconstructive ego capacities of the adolescent to help disturbed young people.

Summary and Conclusions

The developmental tasks of adolescence and of individuation and separation from family, developing a capacity for intimate relationships with others, especially persons of the opposite sex, and discovering one's capacities or talents for specific work or professions may push some adolescents into a depression as they face separation, individuation, and the unknown. As one of the investigators in adolescent development has described, no one can really fear death until he has experienced the real trauma of separation from family, the final separation necessary for independence. For many vulnerable adolescents, the conflicts so engendered lead to depression. This is in addition to Anthony and Kiells' description of the "vast sorrow for the unrealizable and indefinable which overhangs adolescence."

Teicher's (1973) recent statistics of a several hundred percent increase in adolescent suicide attempts in Los Angeles is reflected in the experience of many other clinicians. The increased suicide rate may well reflect the general problems of adolescents in industrial societies where they have no clear function or clear place, and where adolescence is interminably prolonged.

It is clear that in certain settings such as college, fear of failure, sense of isolation, and general sense of worthlessness seem to result from the new stresses of not being able to cope effectively with a new situation. This is a severe blow to the ego. Other writers have noted that drugs, alcholism, promiscuous behavior, and delinquent behavior may be depressive equivalents (Brandes, 1971).

A general increase in adolescent depression is difficult to document, but Henderson, McCulloch, and Phillip (1967) and Evans and Action (1972) in studying adolescents in Edinburgh, find that 64 percent of those who come for psychiatric help have clinical depressions.

REFERENCES

Aires, P. *A social history of family life.* New York: Vintage, 1962.
Anthony, E. J. The reactions of adults to adolescents and their behavior. In G. Caplan & S. Lebovici (Eds.), *Adolescence.* New York: Basic Books, 1969.
Barger, B. The University of Florida mental health program. In B. Barger & E. E. Hall, (Eds.), *Higher education and mental health.* Gainesville: University of Florida, Mental Health Project, 1962.
Berlin, I. N. Some implications of the developmental process for treatment of depression in adolescence. Association for the Psychiatric Study of Adolescence. Proceedings of International Conference on Adolescence, Edinburgh, 1977. Evan (Ed.)
Block, J. *Mastery learning: Theory and Practice.* New York: Holt, Rinehart and Winston, 1971.
Blos, P. Second individuation process of adolescent. In *Psychoanalytic study of the child* (Vol. 22). New York: International Universities Press, 1967. Eissler R. et al (Eds.)
Blos, P. *On adolescence: A psychoanalytic interpretation.* New York: Free Press, 1962.

Brandes, N. S. A discussion of depression in children and adolescents. *Clinical Pediatrics,* 1971, *10(8),* 470.
Bronfenbrenner, U. *Two worlds of childhood: U.S. and U.S.S.R.* New York: Basic Books, 1973.
Caplan, G., & Lebovici, S. *Adolescence: Psychosocial perspectives.* New York: Basic Books, 1969.
Coles, R. *Children of crisis: A study of courage and fear.* Boston: Little, Brown, 1967.
DeYoung, H. Homicide, children's division. *Human Behavior,* 1976, *5,* 16.
Erikson, E. *Childhood and society.* New York: W. W. Norton, 1963.
Evans, J., & Action, W. P. A psychiatric service for the disturbed adolescent. *American Journal of Psychiatry,* 1972, *120,* 429.
Farnsworth, D. L. *Psychiatry, education and the young adult.* Springfield, Ill.: Charles C Thomas, 1966.
Glaser, K. Masked depression in children and adolescents. *American Journal of Psychotherapy,* 1967, *21,* 565.
Gutmann, D. The vicissitudes of ego identity: Some consequences of the new morality. In J. C. Schoolar, (Ed.), *Current issues in adolescent psychiatry.* New York: Brunner/Mazel, 1973.
Hamburg, B. A. and Hamburg, D. A. Stressful transitions of adolescence: Endocrine and psychosocial aspects. In L. Levi (Ed.), *Security, Stress, Disease.* London: Oxford University Press, 1974.
Haan, N., Smith, M. B., & Block, J. Moral reasoning of young adults: Political-social behavior, family background and personality correlates. *Journal of Personality and Social Psychology,* 1968, *10(3),* 183.
Halleck, S. Psychiatric treatment of the alienated college student. *American Journal of Psychiatry,* 1967, *124,* 642.
Henderson, A. S., McCulloch, J. W., & Philip, A. E. Survey of mental illness in adolescence. *British Medical Journal,* 1967, *1,* 83.
Kohler, M. The rights of children: An unexplored constituency. *Social Policy,* 1971 *1,* 36.
Masterson, J. R., Jr. *The psychiatric dilemma of adolescence.* Boston: Little, Brown, 1967.
Mt. Sinai Community Project. *Secondary education through health (SETH) program.* Published by Department of Community Medicine, Mount Sinai School of Medicine, N.Y., for internal use, 1976.
Offer, D., & Sabshin, M. *Normality: Theoretical and clinical concepts of mental health.* New York: Basic Books, 1966.
Offer, D., & Offer, J. L. Profiles of normal adolescent girls. *Archives of General Psychiatry,* 1968, *19,* 513.
Offer, D. *The psychological world of the teenager: A study of normal adolescent boys.* New York: Basic Books, 1969.

Offer, D., Marcus, D., & Offer, J. L. A longitudinal study of normal adolescent boys. *American Journal of Psychiatry,* 1970, *126,* 917.

Offer, D., & Offer, J. Four issues in the developmental psychology of adolescents. In J. G. Howells, (Ed.), *Modern perspectives in adolescent psychiatry.* Edinburgh: Oliver and Boyd, 1971.

Offer, D., & Offer, J. Normal adolescence in perspective. In J. C. Schoolar, (Ed.), *Current issues in adolescent psychiatry.* New York: Brunner/Mazel, 1973.

Piaget, J., & Inhelder, B. *The psychology of the child.* New York: Basic Books, 1969.

Ravenscroft, K., Jr. Normal family regression at adolescence. *American Journal of Psychiatry,* 1974, *131,* 31.

Settlage, C. F. The psychoanalytic understanding of narcissistic and borderline personality disorders: Advances in developmental theory. 1978. In Press. *int. Journal of Psychoanalysis:* 1977, *5,* 805.

Shore, J. H. Suicide and suicide attempts among American Indians of the Pacific Northwest. *International Journal of Social Psychiatry,* 1977, *18(2),* 00.

Shore, J. H., Bopp, J. F., Waller, T. R., & Dawes, J. W. A suicide prevention center on an Indian reservation. *American Journal of Psychiatry,* 1972, *128,* 1086.

Silber, E., Coelho, G. V., Murphey, E. G., Hamburg, D. A., Pearlin, L. I., & Rosenberg, M. Competent adolescents coping with college decisions. *Archives of General Psychiatry,* 1961, *5,* 517.

Teicher, J. D. A solution to the chronic problem of living: Adolescent attempted suicide. In J. C. Schoolar, (Ed.), *Current issues in adolescent psychiatry.* New York: Brunner/Mazel, 1973.

University of Washington Pilot Study, 1974, personal communication from Robert Friedel, M.D., Director, Psychopharmacology Research.

White, R. T. Adolescent identity crisis. In J. C. Schoolar (Ed.), *Current issues in adolescent psychiatry.* New York: Brunner/Mazel, 1973.

White, R. W. Competence and the psychosexual stages of development. *Nebraska Symposium on Motivation,* 1960, *9,* 97.

Chapter 6

OBJECT REMOVAL AND ADOLESCENT DEPRESSION

Benjamin Kaufman

INTRODUCTION

The central thesis of this chapter is that those affects that are aroused during any phase of development in which anaclitic or early nurturant figures are removed have lasting consequences on the still-developing psychic structure. In adolescence, therefore, the process of separation of the self from the parents—though a developmental advance—is not only to be celebrated but also to be viewed as a regular, normal, and potential contributor to adolescent depression.

During adolescent psychic growth, the momentous alteration in the reciprocal relationship of the human environment for the youngster is congruent with the drive surges of puberty and a new set of environmental expectations for social growth. Internally, there are enormously increased and persistent stresses on the psychic structures, most importantly, the ego.

As discussed by Erikson (1968), "The ego must safeguard a sense of cohesive existence, and a positive and negative identity." The ego accomplishes this task by automatically screening and synthesizing in any series of moments all the impressions, emotions, memories, and impulses which try to enter one's thoughts and demand action. He described "counterplayers" of the individual ego. One "counterplayer" is made up of the community of significantly related egos. While undergoing object removal of parental figures, the adolescent individual must change from the passive modes of childhood life and increasingly use active modes in communication and internal regulation to approach issues of mutual affirmation and reciprocal negation as part of individuation within the community of significant others.

Erikson sees all egos as inherently social. He feels the degree of "hospitality" that the individual ego and the community of significant egos offers to each other is measured by the degree they include each other in the ordering of their respective worlds. This process of reciprocal "hospitality" is crucial to facilitating the formation of identity and the knowledge of where each individual stands in relation to the other.

Levitt and Rubenstein (1959) view the ego in adolescence as being primarily under the sway of primary process in problem solving and communication. The mode of the ego in adolescence is impulse expression in various forms of acting out of roles and fantasies; most importantly, there is trial action. This must be understood as a significant communication of special importance to therapy. The authors provide clinical material to support their suggestion that acting out must be viewed not as a regressive and valueless feature of adolescence but as an attempt to communicate in the direction of problem solving. Levitt and Rubenstein view the change in adolescence as representing transformations in the forward growth of the ego spurred by pubescence. "In other words," they write, "the mind (in adolescence) has undergone a transformation which really constitutes its intellectual, moral, and ethical development in a very nearly complete sense."

Other stresses on the ego in adolescence include the growth in harshness of the superego and the persistent anxieties of falling short of aspirations contained in the ideal self. Lionel Trilling (1972) has described the ascendency in importance and harshness of the superego demands as far outweighing the demands contained in reality itself.

Theoretical Review

Those who have written about the adolescent experience refer frequently to early developmental prototypes in conceptualizing and clarifying what takes place in the adolescent psychic life and to the concurrent multiple tasks of this period. Winnicott (1967) cited as "crucially important" that transitional object play in infancy must be *in company* with the primary love object. He recognized this joint play as the first vital establishment of internal objects. He regarded transitional phenomena and transitional play as leading toward relating to the "not-me" object world. Winnicott felt failures and successes of this development in the mother-infant relationship had immense consequences for vital social and personal skills needed for survival in society. Winnicott (1971) gave clinical examples of disturbances in adolescent relatedness, creativity, incapacity to symbolize and fantasize, and failure to establish other than dyadic need-fulfilling relationships as attributable to failures in transitional play.

Settlage (1972) adds that reexternalization, as well as internalization, of fantasy and illusions are psychic capabilities which are established in the earliest transitional object periods. Further, failures in these capabilities influence ontogenetic development of qualities in the ego-ideal and the superego of late adolescence. He suggests that cultural and familial values are, by internalization and externalization, functionally and permanently recorded in earliest images, symbols, and fantasies. In this way, they become structuralized in the ego and superego. Familial traditions absorbed all along during childhood must subsequently survive modifications by the psyche during the adolescent days of growth in order for the adolescent to establish basic purposeful attachments and union with the outside adult world. "These values and ideals must remain meaningful in the experience of the individual in his own . . . sociocultural times" (Settlage, 1972).

Vital intrapsychic processes leading to psychic structuring can be characterized from the beginning as being intertwined with equally vital cultural and familial ties in a reciprocally enriching fashion. Failures in this linkage process will result in faulty psychic structure manifested by the blunting of development and creativity and a heightened vulnerability to many psychic disturbances.

Blos (1972) used Mahler's (1968) terminology to describe a second separation-individuation process in adolescence. He recapitulated the individuation process by describing the fate of internalized and externalized objects. In this way, Blos attributes to adolescence the similar valence of importance in psychic growth and etiological significance as psychic events in the infantile oedipal and latency periods. Edith Jacobson (1964) views adolescent depression as "pathology in self-esteem." She proposed that "optimum narcissistic balance" is an essential precondition to regulating self-esteem to conform with the reality principle of mental functioning, e.g., actual experiences should alter self-esteem normally.

Jacobson (1964) referred to the balanced libidinal investment of the self which is not at the expense of object ties. Jacobson also proposed the development of a mental agency for critical self-judgment. This contributes positively to sound self-esteem when one's general assets and accomplishments are concordant with inner standards arising out of stable identification of earlier periods of development. Implicit in the foregoing is that advances in the sublimation of drives is essential to healthy stability and self-esteem.

The continued need for a satisfying reciprocal relationship with society remains crucial while psychic structuralization proceeds in adolescence. This makes it seem paradoxical that object removal is such an exceedingly important measure of development in the adolescent period of growth. Integration and mental functioning in adolescence takes place without the former sense of reliability on the primary mirroring object (Mahler, 1968) or an idealizing self-object (Kohut, 1971). In adolescence, there is normally a movement away from symbiotic ties to those people who had, more or less, harmoniously provided judgment, security, and empathy as well as other mental functions lacking in preadolescent life. Optimally, there is substitution of other idealized adults and peers who provide a continuity of relationships. This favorably enhances loosening of exclusive familial ties and establishment of new objects in place of the old.

The occurrence of negativism and rebellious states is so regular in adolescence that it is referred to as "normal regression". The pursuit of a stable and adaptive sense of self that persists in time and space seems to require antagonistic rebelliousness. This represents deidealization in the object removal phase of growth and the rebelliousness is a dysphoric affective state in the ego connected to object loss. These affects are painful; the unpleasant behavior of this period should be viewed as "signalling" in the same fashion that the crying of infancy is the ego's signal of internal distress. Recognition and responsiveness to the painful affect which are the rebelliousness and the aggression that drive it are tasks which require empathy from the parenting figures and society in general. Deidealization signals not only a change in direction of the child's vital interests, but also imposes a complex reciprocal change in the lives of parents and society, a change which is resisted by significant adults in the environment.

Deidealization of internal and external objects is an imperative of adolescent growth and, in reality, is consistent with the further ascendency of the reality principal of mental functioning. However, the affects associated with deidealization are difficult for parents to tolerate and they often cannot support meandering extremes of ego growth. It becomes a therapeutic task of substantial magnitude to help youngsters and parents alike to accept haughty arrogance as being in any way a painful affective state connected to object loss and forward movement in problem solving.

Erikson (1968) has referred to this development as a negative identity, i.e., an identity perversely based on all those identifications and roles which, at *critical* stages of development, had been presented to them as most undesirable and dangerous and yet also as *most real*. The "negative" identity can be more real than natural attempts at being good ... "In some cases, the negative identity is dictated by the necessity of finding and defending a niche of one's own against the excessive ideals either demanded by morbidly ambitious parents or indeed actualized by superior ones." The choices of negative identity are attempts at gaining mastery in which positive identity efforts are insufficient. In those adolescents who come to treatment, the patient insists on acceptance of his negativity "without concluding that ... this negative identity is all there is to him" (Erikson, 1968 p. 175).

Developmental Issues

Sexual tension is ever persistent and the young teenager is perplexed. He is often fearful of remaining autoerotic without appropriate aims or objects for his drives. He worries about being homosexual, heterosexual, or being sexual at all. Sexual promiscuity and/or urgent masturbatory activity may be attempts to get rid of sexual tension related to increased drives or unconscious searches for lost objects.

In this heightened sense of self, the adolescent feels alienation. Winnicott (1965) observes that before intimacy is possible, an adolescent must pass through a period of isolation. He sees the adolescent as an isolate and refers to groups of young as "aggregates of isolates." He describes them as struggling to start life again as though they have nothing to take over from anyone. There is a struggle to feel real by conflictual encounters with the environment.

The developmental failure in putting feelings and meaning together, the emotional and cognitive, is described as contributing to depression. To feel what another feels is a function of empathy and the lessons begin with mother. To understand what another (or oneself) feels is a more complicated task (Anthony, 1970). Beck (1972) described a developmental linkage between the cognitive and affective. A particular cognitive content such as an idea or fantasy produces the same affect as a real or actual depressive event. Affects are subjected to cognitive monitoring and interpretation so that any dysphoric affects can produce depression. Cognitive errors are seen by Feinstein (1975) as crucial to understanding depressive ideation. Affective-cognitive dysfuntion that contributes to depression is organized within the psychic structure and depression is virtually "ego syntonic." In addition, ego function may be aggravated by various traumas in preadolescent and adolescent phases. The ego somehow does not develop a capacity for finding humor, joy, or pleasure despite advanced intellectual (cognitive) achievement. The ego, rather, is characterized by humorlessness, masochism, self-hatred, prudishness, feelings of confinement, and isolated oppression. (Ego function without conflict results from lack of nurturance in the oral period, and lack of permission to explore and investigate in the anal and oedipal periods.)

Sidney Blatt (1974) has set out a useful way to categorize adolescent depression on the basis of development of object representation. Anaclitic, i.e., the loss of the need-fulfilling object or the self-object, is one type, introjective the other. Anaclitic depression takes place when there is real loss or environmental change. Guilt is not a factor, but ambivalence toward the object is great. There is intense clinging, pining, and longing to be soothed and comforted. There may be intellectual retardation; only the ready presence of the mothering object is relieving. Objects have not been sufficiently internalized and object removal is at a standstill. The need for nearness of primary love objects is great. There is inordinate reaction to needs not being met and it is difficult to make new attachments to objects other than in a need-fulfilling capacity.

Introjective depression is characterized by enormous guilt and moral masochism. There is difficulty in the expression of ambivalence toward important objects. There is identification with the aggressive parts of the object. Hence, there are continuous negative self-judgments, self-doubts, and a harsh superego. In anaclitic depression, fear of loss of the object is vital; in introjective depression, fear of losing the object's love is critical.

Precursors to introjective depression include impossible-to-meet aspirations in the form of demanding ego ideals. This state of affairs is often seen in student health centers. Depressed young patients reveal conflicts between their ambitions and their achievements. These conflicts mobilize guilt and anxiety connected to Oedipal types of rivalries with parents or rivalries with other primary love objects. Some conflicts revolve around ego ideal demands for achievement which are equated in fantasy with deposing love objects. College students away from home for the first time as well as culturally displaced students can suffer from both types of depression discussed above; these may be quite severe leading to ego disintegration and suicide.

Clinical Examples

Berlin, in this volume (see p. 103), has described a female inpatient with preadolescent features of clinging, demanding, and seductive behavior; she is seriously regressed and threatening suicide. The depression and wide mood swings that were characteristic of her mother contributed to confusing representations of the mother as a need-satisfying object. Object constancy could not be satisfactory. Perhaps sickness and asthmatic attacks brought more reliable and predictable responses from the mother. When the father, who was a more reliable authoritative person, was nearby, she was relieved of her need to control mother and his presence accounted for the child's diminished frequency of asthmatic attacks.

The patient had few friends and had poor social adaptation. Few friendships can tolerate the "demandingness" of the person functioning on a need-satisfying, dyadic basis. Her primitive anger and rage is what Margaret Mahler (1974) referred to as "affecto-motor storms." Oral rage was evident in her overdose of the medication given with the intention of helping her. She was in the hospital for a long time where her provocations were treated as part of her "negative identity." Ordinary needs were met and social life was provided as well. In this safe setting, development of self-representation improved and was reflected in better care of herself. She began to meet the challenges of social adaptation.

The firmness of the male occupational therapist is reminiscent of her father and was indispensible for reliability and predictability. The manipulative females were reminiscent of mother whose contradictory behavior caused rage. As a result of family therapy, Dr. Berlin's patient was helped to fuse the loving feelings she contained in reserve for her father, with her abundant hatred preserved for her mother.

The patient's responsiveness to the hospital staff, and especially to her teacher, indicated developmental advances of object relationships, as well as advances in ego-building cognitive development. This growth was connected to and facilitated by the appropriate developmental responsiveness of the staff. Thus, they reciprocally shared her newly acquired social skills and mutual satisfaction and gratification were experienced. Mahler (1974) refers to this in young children as the mirroring process whereby mother mirrors and shares in the growth process of her child. She sees this as crucial to healthy development.

A 14-year-old boy I considered to have borderline symptomatology was seen both with his parents and in individual psychotherapy. An eldest son, he was a heavy drug user and a chronic truant in frequent trouble with the law. The parents' marriage seemed stable. The father was a creative professional man and both parents were content with their individual achievements. They had enormous difficulty dealing with what they felt were sudden, unreasonable changes in the course of the family with the advent of their son's adolescent period. Pertinent to the boy's history was a 10-month period of being bedridden due to renal disease at age 11. This period, for the boy, was experienced in perspective as helpless, enforced passivity and associated with an enormous sense of shame because of compulsive masturbatory activity and sado-masochistic sexual fantasies. He felt severely arrested in personal achievement and sexual development. His parents were not aware of how the illness affected their son emotionally in terms of cognitive and social effectiveness but were preoccupied with his physical well-being, which was quite realistic since his condition was serious.

In evaluation sessions with the patient, he appeared sad, distant, and lonely. He was irritable, lacked capacity for mutual warmth, and was not responsive to cordial overtures. He acknowledged destructive and self-destructive urges including suicide, and he talked readily only about topics of violence. The patient was not able to describe his feelings and did not recognize himself as depressed. There was little capacity to speak about himself and his remarks about significant figures in his life were usually negative. He could not establish meaning to his feelings.

The most striking feature of this boy's mental life was that from every observation he viewed his parents as totally removed from him as comforting, empathizing figures whose love and approval were of no vital interest. This change in representation of his parents was linked by timing with the onset of provocative impulsivity that starkly contrasted the history of composure and self-regulation that before had kept him in harmony with the significant primary figures of his life. Now at age 14½ he frequently endangered himself with alcohol and drug intoxication. School and juvenile authorities were ready to identify him as irretrievably sociopathic.

While his behavior caused intense concern for his parents, he appeared triumphant and haughty. He was uninterested in their despair, and contemptuously dismissed their expressions of distress as "guilt trips" designed to rob him of freedom to master his own destiny. Family therapy was regarded as a trick to betray him and to lead him back to aggressively disavowed passivity.

I approached the boy's sullen and insular demeanor as manifesting a generally dysphoric state. He was uncomfortable with himself and his surroundings, particularly with adults. His greatest pride in himself was connected with the recounting of his participation in actions and events with family and school that led to his running away from both for several days at a time. Leaving seemed of great symbolic importance for his sense of mastery. My approach was to pay respect to his switching to an active mode of relating with adults. For him to be "bad" was the only way to be active and to be active was vital. Another vital factor was that to be real there must be immediate reactions and this was fused with badness and action. His ego capacities were under stress and in a state of reorganization to attempt a more active adaptational mode. This development was taking place in the face of the complexities of object removal and biological and social changes.

For this adolescent, such upheaval meant everyone concerned with him was coming in contact with and to terms with his negative identity (Erikson, 1968). This negative identity had never before been experienced by him in real interactions with the world outside himself. Negative identity was revealed projectively by omnipotently deprecating values upheld by important adults in his surroundings. He showed the contempt, envy, and aggressiveness he had heretofore been able to keep unconscious while parental attachment was of primary organizational importance to the ego. This was before the object removal of his adolescence. Internalized objects linked to parental values were undergoing a change in this young patient and there was suspension of their organizational capacities vis-a-vis the drives. The result was the regressive state of the ego function to primitive projective levels.

I accepted his view of family therapy as a genuine issue which threatened him with passivity. I told him this and acknowledged his need to remove himself and to be away from controls of any kind. I assured the patient I would not communicate with his parents except in his presence and with his approval. I understood his behavior as an important communication from him of how he wanted to live, to be viewed by others, and that he was interested in change. I emphasized the perspective of time by repeatedly telling the patient that at the moment his history with his parents seemed to stand in the way of getting along with them in the present, and his past now seemed to be the adversary of his future. Gradually his own feelings became more intelligible to him.

He indicated to me the persistent desire to reconcile with all facets of the adult world, and he wanted to be an adult too. However, he sensed that there was inherent danger for him in this urge to be with adults and this fear outweighed his efforts to reconcile.

In the early joint therapy sessions, he tormented his parents about various failures he perceived in their lives. He accused them of being inauthentic and insincere in dealings with himself and his younger siblings. This view of his parents proved ultimately to contain projected concerns about his own emotional achievements and capacity to care for and feel union with others.

Family therapy also demonstrated parental reverence for the past and their resistance to the progressive change in their son's life toward independence, which meant complicated changes for them. Each participant seemed to claim an exclusive hold on virtue as the tensions eventually brought about repetitive accusations of untrustworthiness.

The young patient's defensive make-up reflected a psychosexual conflict in pregenital ego organization. This was characterized by omnipotent denial of dependency and passive longings for support and comfort. Splitting predominated his mode of thinking and distorted his perceptions. This was reflected in vague and disconnected accusations and behavior which then led to his parents' obligatory controlling involvement in his life. He would be caught up fervently believing his own accusations and *at the same time* questioned them. He alternately accused his parents of shortcomings he later acknowledged in himself. The patient's self-representation fluctuated widely between the masterful, the victimized, and the helpless. Despite this, there was no overall loss of reality testing or generalized regression of all ego functions. The essential characteristic seemed to be various attitudes about reality coexisting at the same time.

I held to the view throughout his treatment that for this patient splitting represented as Shafer (1968) put it, "The enabling of change," i.e. that change (along with object removal) "opens the sluices of a dam" and was (in this case) "an essential mechanism" for a forward moving process in development. Splitting allows change but does not in itself provide psychic structuring required in object removal phases of growth, and trial by action becomes a prominent mode of testing and producing change.

One day the patient reported a series of dreams. This followed a day of carousing with sexually active peers who exchanged details of their heterosexual experiences. The dreams contained unmistakable fears about sexual potency. As his enormous fears of intimacy were disclosed to me, we formed a working alliance and a functioning observing ego was uncovered and began to develop. The observing ego development was viewed as a healthy split necessary for intensive collaborative psychotherapy. A more mature self-judgment with improved narcissistic balance followed from repetitive confirmation that his peers had similar fears. His improved cognition paved the way for a less alienated objective interest in looking at himself and the process he was undergoing. He enjoyed a creative experience as he discovered and pondered details of fears and fantasies of himself never before examined with another person. In time, self-reflection and the sharing of self-discoveries with others brought far more gratification than the less mature tension-relieving, pregenital devices of projective and splitting defenses that he had brought to therapy.

His fear over being unable to generate warmth in his peers was connected in therapy to heightened envy of his parents' love for each other and their capacity for love of his siblings. Fear and envy had in turn led to attacks on those relationships and was further aggravated by the separate ongoing process of object removal appropriate to adolescence. As interpretations surrounding the object loss were made in the context of the transference, fears of regressive fusion to the analyst-parent arose, but after elaboration and clarification, they greatly diminished.

These appropriate fears were understood and connected to new conceptualizations of himself and to his relationships with his parents from whom childhood bonds were loosening. As he dealt with his own relative incompetence as being realistic, he developed empathic appreciation and concern for the developments of life confronting his parents. He was relieved upon sharing his incompetence to the therapist. By age 17, the behavior which drew his parents into his life in a controlling fashion had greatly diminished. Group therapy was also quite useful to the patient. Through group work he was able to involve peers emotionally in his life in positive ways and in a "safe" setting.

DISCUSSION OF APPLIED THEORY

In a similar fashion, we find that through a therapeutic group experience, apathetic school dropouts can become enthusiastic and can experience achievement in learning about sexuality, reproduction, psychic development, and family relations. This enthusiasm is related to the discovery of having shared concerns and the establishment of bonds of camaraderie to replace those to primary objects.

In child-care learning experiments, adolescents have been observed to identify and relate empathically with the needs of the young. A similar phenomenon is the particular willingness of ex-convicts, ex-alcoholics, and ex-mental patients to be employed in roles connected with areas of difficulty in their own lives. These are often efforts to regain vicariously, through identification, lost and needed experiences with primary love objects, traumatically removed by the vicissitudes of previous interpersonal deprivations and the process of growing up.

SOCIAL IMPLICATIONS

Turning to external objects other than parents to facilitate psychic growth places peculiar responsibilities on institutions within society, and continues to be an area of unmet need. Erikson (1950), Pumpian-Mindlin (1958), and Derdyn and Waters (1977) emphasized that narcissistic injuries and similar issues are created by adolescent growth. These injuries continue in the adult phases of life and are contributing factors to failures by adults to deal in a helpful fashion with their adolescent children.

Jealousy and envy between generations is one explanation for the failure to provide for adolescents. This stems, in part, from unfulfilled wishes and needs experienced by adults; what was denied to adults earlier may not be provided to children later. There is a current trend to deprecate the importance of family integrity and its subsequent contribution of an environment favorable for growth and safety. The ordinary home with active interests and involvement of both parents shelters children from anxieties related to early and increasing open aggressiveness on playgrounds, in schools, streets, and in areas of entertainment. These institutions used to be extensions of safe homes. Now, too often, they are external counterparts of and stimulants to inwardly experienced aggressive drives threatening to get out of control. Drop-in clinics for adolescents, college rap groups, co-ops, and communes have attempted to become limited replacements for deprivations and losses related to real homes.

Creativity requires a facilitating environment in which curiosity and the desire to explore are safeguarded. Aggression contained in the adolescent's quest for autonomy may take on anxiety-provoking momentum in the presence of real environmental neglect and can lead to disabling defensive personality structuring.

There have recently been pioneering efforts to reverse this process, particularly in child placement. Advocates of children's rights such as Goldstein, Freud, and Solnit (1973) have raised serious questions regarding the legal decision-making processes for children. They view the law and social practice as having been uneven in responding to the process of development in childhood. Their concern is that children not continue to be viewed as chattels of the adult world. They suggest guidelines for the law in assuring for "each child a chance to become a member of a family where he feels wanted and where he will have the opportunity, on a continuing basis, not only to receive and return affection, but also to express anger and learn to manage his aggression." They point to the valuable body of applicable psychoanalytic theory and knowledge regarding child development that can be translated into guidelines "to facilitate making decisions that inevitably must be made" by the courts and society in general. These authors state "that to make the child's needs paramount is in society's best interest." Each time the cycle of grossly inadequate parent-child relationships is broken, society stands to gain a person capable of becoming an adequate parent for children of the future. What is needed is sound law combined with the hard-won knowledge of child and adolescent development contributed by psychoanalysis, ego psychology, and cognitive and social learning theories in the last two decades.

Friedenberg (1959) writes in his book, *The Vanishing Adolescent*, "There is obviously something in adolescence itself that troubles and titillates many adults. The teenager seems to let people vent hostile and aggressive feelings and declare themselves (parents) to be on the side of law and order."

Antagonism towards youngsters may represent filicidal impulses that we must consider as possibly existing in all of us. Norman Atkins (1970) writes that the theme of filicide has crucial meaning in the Sophoclean tragedy "Oedipus Rex." He sees filicide as a social issue. This is currently receiving attention in the medical press as "the battered child syndrome" as if it were something new. Atkins sees an intricate interaction between parent and child, assuming them to be mutually provocative and hostile. Rascovsky (1970) sees the parents as the initiator. Atkins and other writers think that the inevitability of generational succession leads to attempts to interrupt it; certainly, we tend to be blind to it. In view of the foregoing discussion, we can account for the many failures to provide for the health and safety for our children, in terms of adult hostilities towards adolescents who will succeed them.

In conclusion, object removal refers to the alteration in one's relationship to the objects from infancy and early childhood. This phenomenon in the phase of adolescence is associated with both psychosocial links to pubescence, and the underlying enormous energic shifts in libidinal and aggressive energies. In adolescence, there are heightened pressures in the direction of independence. A young boy or girl must adapt himself or herself to the external world. However, in adolescence with new mobility, physical strength, and new sense of self-awareness, the young person now tries to adapt the *external* world and *its* objects to himself. His adaptation may be more or less successful. "However, ... he takes his chances with the external world away from home. He leaves himself "vulnerable to the activity of outside objects—to its abandoning, rejecting, punishing, traumatizing, influences. . . . The adolescent cannot attempt to control his external objects with absolute confidence of success" (Shafer, 1968). Object removal creates a breech that may lead to depression of the anaclitic or introjective type. This dichotomous situation regularly engenders antagonism from the adult world and isolates the adolescent from his primary environment at a time when he continues to need its continued emotional presence to support his still immature psychic structure. Optimal responsiveness to the needs of the immature psychic structuring process is a developmental task for the parental world. A prerequisite for this task is adult capacity for the achievement of the life cycle phase referred to as "generativity" (Erikson, 1965). Mature adults in this phase of life have "as their primary concern, the guiding of the next generation," being absorbed in parental responsibilities, and a capacity for post-narcissistic love of the human ego.

References

Anthony, E. J. Two contrary types of adolescent depression and their treatment. *Journal of the American Psychoanalytic Association,* 1970, *18,* 841.

Atkins, N. B. The Oedipus myth: Adolescence and the succession of generations. *Journal of the American Psychoanalytical Association,* 1970, *18,* 860.

Beck, A. J. The phenomenon of depression. In D. Offer & D. X. Freedman (Eds.), *Modern psychiatry and clinical research.* New York: Basic Books, 1972, pp. 104–108.

Blatt, S. Levels of object representation in anaclitic and introjective depression. *Psychoanalytic study of the child,* 1974, *29,* 107.

Blos, P. The second individuation process of adolescence. *Psychoanalytic study of the child,* 1967, *22,* 162.

Derdyn, A., & Waters, D. Parents and adolescents: Empathy and vicissitudes of development. In *Annals of american society for adolescent psychiatry* (Vol. 5). Sherman Feinstein & Peter Giovachinni (Eds.) 1977. New York City, Jason Aronson, pp. 175–186.

Erikson, E. H. *Childhood and society.* New York: W. W. Norton, 1950.

Erikson, E. H. Identity and life cycle. In *Psychological Issues*, 1959, *1*, 1.

Erikson, E. *Identity, youth and crisis.* New York: W. W. Norton, 1968.

Feinstein, S. In E. J. Anthony & T. Benedek (Eds.): *Depression and human existence.* Boston: Little, Brown, 1975, pp. 313–335.

Freidenberg, E. L. *The vanishing adolescent* Boston Beacon Press, 1966.

Goldstein, J., Freud, A., & Solnit, A. *Beyond the best interests of the child.* New York: MacMillian, 1973.

Jacobson, E. *The self and the object world.* New York: International University Press, 1964.

Kohut, H. *The analysis of the self.* Monograph #4. New York: International Universities Press, 1971.

Levitt, M., & Rubenstein, B. O. Acting out in adolescence: A study in communication. *American Journal of Orthopsychiatry*, 1959, *29(3)*, 622.

Mahler, M. *On human symbiosis and the vicissitudes of individuation.* New York: International Universities Press, 1968.

Mahler, M. *Psychoanalytic Study of the Child.* 1974, *29*, 89.

Pumpian-Mindlin, E. Omnipotentiality, youth and commitment. *Journal of the American American Academy of Child Psychiatry*, 1958.

Rascovsky, A. Towards the understanding of the unconscious motivation of war. Read at scientific meeting of the Los Angeles Society of Psycholanalysis, November 1970.

Settlage, C. F. The superego in late adolescence. *Psychoanalytic study of the child,* 1972, *27*, 74.

Shafer, R. *Aspects of internalization.* New York: International Universities Press, 1968.

Trilling, L. *Sincerity and authenticity.* Charles Elliot, Norton Lecture Series. Cambridge, Ma.: Harvard University Press, 1972.

Winnicott, D. W. *The family and individual development.* London: Tavistock Publishers, 1965.

Winnicott, D. W. The location of the cultural experience. *Journal of Psychoanalysis,* 1967, 48:368.

Winnicott D. W. *Playing and reality,* 1971. Basic Books Inc., publishers.

Chapter 7

TREATMENT OF THE DEPRESSED CHILD

Harold Boverman
Alfred P. French

While theory building and research are essential, treatment is the core of clinical work. In this chapter, we explore the clinical use of the term *childhood depression,* seeking a balance between psychodynamic and biological positions as outlined by Akiskal and McKinney (1973). The central argument here is that psychiatric treatment in general requires both a balanced assessment of multiple current factors and awareness of the momentum of developmental processes; treatment of depression requires both generally supportive and specifically reparative responses to the perception that there is no point in trying to maintain one's balance or to experience ordinary well-being. Treatment of depression in children requires sensitivity to the child's developmental levels in multiple developmental lines (Freud, 1965), and sensitivity to the complex interplay of biological, psychological, family, and social problems. Treatment of a depressed child may be indicated on the basis of anticipated damage to development and to future function (Nagera, 1966) even though the child is not blatantly symptomatic at the time. The quietly withdrawn, modestly underfunctioning child may be in more urgent need of treatment than the aggressive child who is more likely to be referred for professional evaluation and care. Either child might be normal or depressed, either child might be in need of treatment.

The challenges encountered in evaluating and meeting a treatment plan for a withdrawn child are illustrated by our experiences with 8-year-old Bobby. His teacher, who referred him to the Mental Health Clinic, described a withdrawn, friendless child whose school performance was poor and who was alternately listless and "hyperactive." When she approached him, he responded with a broad but empty and unconvincing smile-like expression. The teacher was particularly concerned that Bobby might be "out of touch with reality," and she suspected that his parents "did not care" about him.

Bobby was small, clumsy and was temperamentally "slow to warm" (Thomas & Chess, 1977). His early development was complicated by severe parental discord, a divorce and a remarriage, leaving him the fifth of six children. The youngest in this new family, a delightful 5-year-old girl, identified closely with her biological mother and nicely fullfilled the "baby" role. By chance this new family contained three boys, all of whom were within 1-½ years of the same age. The oldest was always in favor with one of the other two, both of whom vigorously competed for the right to play with him.

A diagnostic session with the entire family moved slowly. The family circumstances seemed stable and the parents expressed a sincere interest in their large family. Family activities were family- and child-centered as much as their limited budget permitted. There were no major conflicts except for "the usual amount of fighting" among the children. The marriage was stable, and the family was suffering from no unusual stresses. Bobby appeared to be deteriorating in the midst of a relatively normal family. His past medical history included no major illnesses.

Toward the end of this initial session Bobby, grasping the back of his chair with both hands, leaned forward and stared intently at his knees. Speaking in a barely audible tone with his teeth clenched and his mouth held open in what appeared to be a grimace, he mumbled "Mommie didn't invite *Tony* to my birthday party." Asked to make this clear for everybody, Bobby first sat upright, then slouched in his chair, swung his feet, and withdrew. At the end of a long, expiratory sigh, his mother commented "Now that's just like him. When you try to talk to him he just clams up. You know, that's just *so* typical. Here I went and spent $30.00 for a skating party, rented a roller rink and all, and we had twelve kids from the neighborhood with presents and all." "And a cake," a sibling chimed in. "And ice cream," added another. Mother continued, "He just doesn't seem to appreciate all the things we do for him. I love Bobby very much but I must say that at times it's hard to like him." In a manner reminiscent of the dormouse at the Madd Hatter's tea party, Bobby raised his head and said in a quiet thin voice, "But Mommie didn't invite *Tony* to my birthday party." "Yes," his mother responded, "I told him that Tony lives 20 miles away, and I just couldn't drive 80 miles and do all the other things besides...."

Our understanding of Bobby began to deepen as we learned of this perceived loss. We inferred from his tone and from his mother's comments that Bobby's sense of loss was global, profound, and grievous. Further, it was clear that Bobby's behavior was such that perceived loss was virtually guaranteed. His mother's resources were limited, and when he criticized her inadequacy she found it difficult to recall the fun of the birthday party, recalling instead her enormous irritation at Bobby's criticism. Nothing was ever enough. The idea of childhood depression helped us to move to a formulation as Bobby's barely audible description of a perceived loss. This provided the first step to a clear understanding of his self-environment relationship.

A number of superficially minor changes had occurred in Bobby's life. A few months before, in the fall, he began the school year with a new teacher and a new set of classmates, none of whom he knew. A recent realignment among the boys in the family had left the older of the three in what appeared to be a permanent alliance with the other competing youngster, leaving Bobby out in the cold. In addition, the neighborhood youngsters had begun to play competitive sports. The mother reflected that as long as they had "played in the dirt with their cars" Bobby had had many playmates. Now, however, the emphasis on competitive games left him without a peer group since he was too small, clumsy, and shy to participate. Toward the end of the diagnostic session, she had a comment: "You know, he hasn't said much about it but maybe it's weighed on him. A few months ago his real father came by, unexpected, and sat down with him and said he could go live with him. And, do you know, he hasn't called since then. I don't even know where he is."

With depression in mind, we explored the structure of Bobby's life with respect to his capacity to gain a sense of well-being from his ordinary everyday experiences. We discovered the interplay of his temperament and small size with normal developmental events in his peer group and a power shift among the siblings in the family. No one of these attracted the family's attention nor would any one of them alone, in our opinion, have been likely to traumatize or disrupt Bobby's development. His biological father's recent visit with the promise of a special home for Bobby may well have been a special event in Bobby's life. The central question is, as Bobby moves through these various experiences does he gain an increasing sense of his capacity to master challenges and adapt to changes in a way that results in normal and healthy growth and development, or does he progressively perceive himself as incapable of establishing satisfying relationships? The importance of each of these events in Bobby's life is a problem to be researched with him. Each patient is a new research problem and treatment provides a series of unique research questions.

We do not propose yet another clinical entity, a new kind of depression. We believe that depressive symptoms have been overlooked by clinicians working with children and that many would not have seen Bobby as clinically depressed. We do believe that the pure culture, single-cause depression in childhood is rare, and we do not propose that Bobby was depressed simply in response to his father's visit and the broken promise of a new home. For the most part we must look to the metapsychological, (i.e., phenomena beyond those immediately observable) and multicausal models in order to gain insights viable in diagnosis and treatment. What, for example, is the importance to Bobby and for Bobby's development of his peer group's shift toward active sports? Does he rejoice that he has more time to spend playing with a special friend, who, like himself, is still interested in playing with toy cars in the dirt, or does he experience catastrophic loss?

There is broad agreement that a developmental approach must be the underlying unifying concept wherewith we seek a combination of developmental, maturational, and psychological viewpoints. In our evaluation, we see the generation of hypotheses to be subsequently tested in treatment. For example, we hypothesized Bobby will recreate in projective play many dramas that represent his perception of the conflicts with which he is struggling. For example, should he grieve the loss of his biological father and reinvest energy in the stepfather, thereby risking further loss should the biological father return and take him away? Can he be loyal to both? We further hypothesized that the specific reparative impact of treatment, which in this case would include Bobby's exploration of various alternative responses to his perceived environment (in the context of that process we expect that his perceived environment will change), will increase his degrees of freedom and reduce his sense of hopelessness and helplessness. Sensitive to his developmental level, specific interpretations might be made regarding links among his small size, clumsiness, ordinal position, and relationship with his biological father, to his tendency to withdraw and to criticize his mother's inadequacies. Above all, we seek to identify areas of development that are constricted, blocked, or distorted in a way that might significantly compromise Bobby's future development and function.

Development

The concept of development, one of the richest and most central in child psychiatry, is central to our understanding of depression and particularly of depression in children, since depression in children not only indicates that normal development is being blocked, but that further development may be compromised. Bobby's apathy and withdrawal may not only reflect his weariness in the wake of previous conflicts, but impinge destructively on his capacity to appreciate current resources.

But what, indeed, is "development"? A particularly rich discussion of this concept is found in Piaget's paper summarizing his own work (1970, p. 710), wherein he notes the broad similarity between developmental processes on biological and psychological levels: "the problem of stages in developmental psychology is analagous to that of stages in embryogenesis." The synthesizing concept of "epigenesis" refers to the construction, by the developing organism, of structures appropriate to its specific circumstances. In this process, the organism is facilitated and constrained by its basic biological nature on the one hand, and by interaction with the environment on the other. The process of development sometimes proceeds smoothly. Interruption of development demands decisions as to how development can proceed most efficiently. Piaget states that "if an external influence causes the developing organism to deviate from one of its creodes, i.e. expectable sequences of developmental events, there ensures a homeorhetical reaction which tends to channel it back to the normal sequence or, if this fails, switches it to a new developmental sequence as similar as possible to the original one." Piaget extends these comments to embryological and cognitive development and has recently extended them to affective development: "there exists a close relationship between the affective and cognitive organizations in the person ... I tried to show the analogies between the cognitive and affective unconscious" (Weiner, 1975). We, as clinicians, are concerned with the impact of the rerouting process. In Bobby's case, it appears that rerouting has been necessary in many areas of his life but has not, in many instances, proceeded well.

The notion of "areas of development" has been discussed by Anna Freud in her classic paper "The Concept of Developmental Lines" (Freud, 1965), in which she has summarized and articulated a scheme for the assessment of both the normal and the pathological in childhood in terms of forces interfering with normal movement along classic psychoanalytic, psychosexual lines of child development. In succinct form, she introduced her concept of developmental lines by first tracing the course of the formation of emotional self-reliance and adult-object relationship from the earliest precursers in dependent relationships of the human infant. She then proceeded to apply the concept to issues related to body independence: from sucking to rational eating, from wetting and soiling to bladder and bowel control, and from irresponsibility to responsibility in body managenemt. Other examples of developmental lines move from egocentricity to companionship, from the body to the toy, and from play to work.

In a further elaboration of this concept of developmental lines, Nagera's (1966) concept of developmental interferences and conflicts provides a conceptual base for our clinical search for multiple determined distortions of development. To paraphrase Anna Freud's introduction to Nagera's work, heretofore we have searched for clues to diagnosis and treatment of all behavioral and developmental conditions in one or another period of childhood, in one specific set of relationships, or in some specific cause external to the psychology of the individual. In his deceptively slim but powerful monograph, Nagera proposes a scheme to apportion the pathogenic impacts among external and internal interferences at any time and in any location in development, both internal and external. His view helps one to establish a hierarchy of disturbances in childhood in a way that guards against seductively clear but clinically and developmentally naive efforts at precise localization of pathology with a resultant simplistic view of treatment. Bobby, for example, is not likely to respond to any single intervention such as training in sports, advice to forget his biological father, tutoring, or individual psychotherapy in isolation from interventions from family and others. Treatment of this depression cannot be complete until Bobby has demonstrated to his own satisfaction a capacity to engage in and master problems of living, however small, and to gain a sense of satisfaction and well-being from his efforts.

In concert with the concepts of development, developmental line, and developmental interference, Kohut (1971) has proposed that an affirmative sense of self and affirmative narcissism develop as do other psychological structures. We see the affirmative sense of self as the mirror image, the opposite, of that sense of self which has depression as its appropriate affect and depression-withdrawal (Schmale & Engel, 1975) as its appropriate response. Our clinical hypothesis then becomes: Has Bobby been forced to retrack his development with sufficient frequency and insufficient success in enough developmental lines that the development of his affirmative sense of self has been significantly compromised? Does his mumbled and whispered statement of regret that Tony was not invited to his birthday party present a powerful metaphor facilitating our understanding of his perception that his caring environment cannot in fact care for him? In view of his age we are particularly concerned about the possibility that his egocentric and magical thinking will predispose him to conclude that, not only is his situation a bad one, but that he is personally to blame because he, himself, is bad.

Depression in childhood cannot be crisply localized and treated as can the inflamed appendix. On the other hand, it permits us to use available clinical material to explore the structure of Bobby's relationship with his average expectable environment. At the risk of oversimplification, we wish to integrate and summarize the work of the above and other authors including Joffe, Rawson, and Mulick (1973), French and Steward (1975), Watson (1977), Weck (1977), Seligman (1975), Schmale and Engel (1975), Murphy (1974), and many others: a healthy self-environment relationship can lead to the experience of a sense of ordinary well-being. Disturbance of any conceivable sort may lead the developing organism to perceive loss of a healthy self-environment relationship. This *perceived loss,* in turn, may lead to the loss or diminution of the sense of ordinary well-being. If the individual is able to regain a sense of well-being, he gains in addition a sense of mastery and the result is *increased* strength and adaptability. Certainly some stress and strain are required for optimal development. In the problem case, however, the perceived loss of a healthy self-environment relationship may lead to a loss of an ordinary sense of well-being with subsequent compromise of the sense of self and subsequent development of intrapsychic defenses against the pain of a compromise sense of self.

The tragedy deepens by way of the relationship between the pathological mental mechanisms, the distortions of development, and subsequent perceived losses as so dramatically illustrated in Bobby's case by the deterioration of Bobby's relationship with his mother. There is a point of compromised development beyond which there is a progressive spiral into hopelessness and helplessness as expectations of loss are progressively created and confirmed by experience, and the mental mechanisms involved in negative subjective experience and perception are strengthened further and further.

The above scheme is a general way of thinking about depression in children. Current clinical thinking regarding depression in children is well represented by Cytryn and McKnew (1972, 1974) and Malmquist (1971), while Anthony (1975), Akiskal and McKinney (1973), and Basch (1975) have presented a comprehensive review of the theoretical issues; current clinical and research findings are summarized elsewhere in this volume.

REFERENCES

Akiskal, H., & McKinney, W. Depressive disorders toward a unified hypothesis. *Science,* 1973, *182,* 20.

Anthony, E. Childhood depression. In E. J. Anthony & T. Benedek (Eds), *Depression and human existence.* Boston: Little, Brown, 1975, pp. 231–277.

Basch, Michael Franz. Toward a theory that encompasses depression: A revision of existing causal hypotheses in psychoanalysis. In E. J. Anthony & T. Benedek (Eds), *Depression and human existence*. Boston: Little, Brown, 1975, pp. 485–534.

Cytryn, L., & McKnew, D. Jr. Proposed classification of childhood depression. *American Journal of Psychiatry,* 1972, *129,* 149.

Cytryn, L., & McKnew, D. Jr. Factors influencing the changing clinical expression of the depressive process in children. *American Journal of Psychiatry,* 1974, *131,* 879.

French, A. P., & Steward, M. S. Adaptation and affects toward a synthesis of piagetian and psychoanalytic psychologies. *Perspectives in Biology and Medicine,* 1975, *18,* 464.

Freud, A. *Normality and pathology in childhood: Assessments of development.* New York: International Universities Press, 1965.

Joffe, R. M., Rawson, R. A., & Mulick, J. A. Control of their environment reduces emotionality in rats. *Science,* 1973, *180,* 1383.

Kohut, H. *The analysis of the self.* New York: International Universities Press, 1971.

Malmquist, C. P. Depressions in childhood and adolescence. *New England Journal of Medicine,* 1971, *284(16),* 887, 955.

Murphy, L. B. Coping, vulnerability, and resilience in childhood. In G. V. Coelho, D. A. Hamburg, & J. E. Adams (Eds.), *Coping and Adaptation.* New York: Basic Books, 1974, pp. 69–100.

Nagera, H. *Early childhood disturbances, the infantile neurosis and the adult disturbances.* New York: International Universities Press, 1966.

Piaget, J. Piaget's theory. In P. H. Mussen (Ed.), *Carmichael's manual of child psychology.* New York: Wiley, 1970, pp. 703–732.

Seligman, M. E. P. *Helplessness: On depression, development and death.* San Francisco: W. H. Freeman, 1975.

Schmale, A. H., & Engel, G. L. The role of conservation—withdrawal in depressive reactions. In E. J. Anthony & T. Benedek (Eds.), *Depression and human existence.* Boston: Little, Brown, 1975, pp. 183–198.

Thomas, A., & Chess, S. *Temperament and development.* New York: Brunner/Mazel, 1977.

Vaillant, G. E. Natural history and male psychological health II. Some antecedents of healthy adult adjustment. *Archives of General Psychiatry,* 1974, *31,* 15.

Watson, J. S. Depression and perception of control in early childhood. In J. G. Schulterbrandt & A. Raskin (Eds.), *Depression in childhood: Diagnosis treatment and conceptual models.* New York: Raven Press, 1977, pp. 123–134.

Weiner, M. *The cognitive unconscious: A piagetian approach to psychotherapy.* Davis, CA: International Psychological Press, 1975.

Chapter 8

A LONGITUDINAL STUDY OF TWO DEPRESSED, SELF-DESTRUCTIVE LATENCY-AGE BOYS: A SIX-YEAR AND FOUR-YEAR FOLLOW-UP

**Alfred P. French
Margaret Steward
Thomas Morrison**

INTRODUCTION

In 1975, two of the authors published a paper on a suicidal 7-year-old boy (French & Steward, 1975). One of us subsequently treated a depressed 5-year-old boy who, at the age of 3 years, 6 months, ingested 20 baby aspirins. In this chapter, we present the first case report, add the second, and present follow-up studies on both. Contrasting points in the two cases are discussed.

The literature on childhood suicide is sparse (Bakwin, 1957; Lukianowicz, 1968). Reports of suicide and suicidal gestures in children are rare although they have been collected for nearly 200 years. Available case reports dealing almost exclusively with the adolescent population focus largely on the circumstances immediately surrounding life-threatening behavior, include brief accounts of general situations preceding the event, or, more commonly, provide only basic demographic data. In the available literature, we find descriptions of the home and family in fewer than 70 cases of attempted suicide in children below the age of 13, and of these almost none exceeds a paragraph of description. With the uniform exception of age and sex of child, the most frequently cited statistic is the incidence of broken, disrupted, and disorganized homes (Bender & Schilder, 1937; Bergstrand & Otto, 1962; Lourie, 1967; Lukianowicz, 1968; Mattsson, Seese, & Hawkins, 1969; Toolan, 1962; Tuckman & Youngman, 1964). The impetus for the present paper arose from the opportunity to study in considerable detail the dynamics of a family who sought treatment for the first time when their 7-year-old boy made a serious suicidal attempt.

In searching the literature on childhood suicide, we have found that reference to depression in children has appeared only recently. The objective of this chapter is to link a review of the concept of childhood depression with clinical data that illustrates the utility of this concept in formulating a case of attempted suicide in a young child. Despert (1952), in an early study of suicide and depression in children, reported extreme disruption of social circumstances but specifically dissociated depression and suicide in children: "Depression in children is not uncommon . . . It is rarely associated with suicidal preoccupation. Suicide in children is predominantly of an impulsive nature." More recently, Lourie (1967) reported that, although suicide gestures were multiply determined, chronic depression was not a major determinant. Depression in childhood has been widely debated and has undergone considerably evolution since the studies of Bowlby (1953) and Spitz (1945). Rie (1966) reviewed the concept of depression and concluded: "An examination of the implications for child psychopathology of the dynamics of adult depression including the roles of aggression, orality and self-esteem, generate serious doubt about the wisdom of applying the concept of depression to children." King (1967), drawing from the classic Freudian discussion of object loss, noted that "in the child, depression generally takes the form of a pervasive personality characteristic, woven into many aspects of his life for many years," producing a clinical picture of depression in children and adolescents different from and more variable than that in adults, due to the continuing superego development.

In contrast to the position stated above, Davidson (1968) reported, in an unusual longitudinal study covering 15 years, the clinical history of childhood depression that was first observed at the age of 28 weeks. He defined depression as "an emotional state characterized by hopelessness, low spirits, fatigue and lethargy." The anlagen of the depression were attributed to specific characteristics of maternal handling from the outset, such that the infant could not be certain that her mother was sensitive to her signals of distress. The work of Chess, Thomas, and Birch (1967) has emphasized the variability of infants from the time they were born, and has provided the basis for interpreting children's depression by approaching mother-child interactions in terms of a homeostatic system, complimented by the interaction with other family members. Indeed, inadequate communication between infant and caretakers may lead to a posture of hopelessness on the part of both.

Malmquist (1971), in a comprehensive discussion of depression in children and adolescents, referred to the multiple uses of the term and proposed a classification. He emphasized the wide clinical variability of the depression syndrome in children, and delineated the means whereby depression becomes a significant coping mechanism at different ages. Intrafamilial dynamics are seen to provide a powerful mechanism for the transmission of subtle attitudes: "The concept of loss has subsequently been extended to include more subtle varieties of disruptions and distortions in parent-child relations. These have the possibility of being as devastating in their effects as gross maternal deprivation or separation . . ." (p. 888) and "Depressive proneness may develop in a child who does not have gross signs of disturbance" (p. 889). Rinsley (1965) has similarly emphasized that depression in children is best understood in terms of a disturbance, not necessarily a loss of object relationships. Engel (1968), on the basis of careful observation and physiological studies, arrived at an analogous conclusion by providing an important biological frame of reference for the concept of depression. The infant's only two alternative modes of relating to the world are to actively seek necessary stimuli and nurturance or, failing to find these, to withdraw in order to conserve energy in the face of a nonsupportive environment. Disruption of the caretaking process provides the basis for a helpless, hopeless, given-up, giving-up attitude that is the fundamental factor common to all depressions. In the event that this outlook predominates in infancy, depression-withdrawal becomes a basic ego mechanism, and depression is a readily available response strategy for meeting future stresses.

Therefore, we understand depression in children to be a manifestation of disturbed object relationships, leading to a posture of hopelessness and helplessness and resulting in withdrawal. A panpersonality disturbance inevitably results, as the child seeks to meet developmental tasks from this maladaptive frame of reference.

From a reading of the literature, one would expect a suicidal gesture to involve an older, male child from a home wherein severe disruption was immediately apparent. In contrast, the first case is that of a 7-year-old boy from a family that was, to all outward appearances, intact and healthy. Intensive work with the family over a period of time led to an understanding of the subtle intrafamilial stresses that resulted in depression, and finally a suicidal attempt.

Case Report: Tommy

Tommy, aged 7, was the fourth of five children; his siblings were males, aged 20, 10, 5, and a female, aged 15. His father, 41, and mother, 38, were high school graduates. The father was employed as a skilled tradesman and had held the same job for approximately 20 years. The parents had been married for 20 years, and had been living together for all but a few months early in their marriage.

All the children in the family were wanted by both parents. Tommy's gestation and delivery were normal, and the mother noted nothing unusual in her son until he developed a pattern of temper outbursts in early childhood.

Electroencephalograms of Tommy, his sister, mother, and maternal grandmother demonstrated abnormal temporal lobe activity. There was an extensive family history of violent temper outbursts in childhood. For several years prior to and during the course of therapy, Tommy was maintained on antiseizure medication by several physicians. Both parents expressed a sincere interest in the welfare of their children, and both were involved in the therapy from the outset, although the father initially seemed to consider himself primarily an observer of the process.

At the time the family brought Tommy to the hospital, he had a number of symptomatic behaviors as summarized in Table 1.

The acute episode preceding treatment was as follows: Tommy and his younger brother were playing together, and an altercation arose that was settled by the mother, who then left the room. The mother recalled nothing to distinguish this incident from innumerable similar ones. Several minutes after she left, she considered Tommy strangely quiet and returned to find him crimson-faced and struggling for air, having knotted a jumping rope around his neck and jerked it tight. She reported considerable diffi-

Table 1 Tommy's Symptoms

	Initial	At end of treatment
Interview behavior:	Sat on mother's lap, infantile speech, avoided therapist	Sat in chair alone, engaged therapist independently of mother
Play with siblings:	Fighting with younger brother; ignored by oldest brother	Less fighting with younger brother, befriended by oldest brother
Play in neighborhood:	"Vigilante Committee" protected smaller children from him	Had neighborhood friends
Accidental self-injury:	Frequent: (Missing upper front teeth)	None occured during last three months of therapy
Attitude toward discipline:	Violent resentment: "Uncontrollable"	Variable, sometimes accepted arbitration
Academic performance:	Mediocre, uneven	A's
Thought content:	Intermittent preoccupation with death	No preoccupations were apparent
Play-therapy activity:	Played alone, avoided competition with therapist	Sportingly competitive with therapist
IQ (WISC)		
Verbal:	100	125
Performance:	100	100

culty in loosening the rope and, having done so, sought professional help immediately.

For a period of 5 months, Tommy was seen weekly in play therapy; concurrently, his parents were seen jointly by the same therapists. Tommy was seen in a playroom equipped with a variety of toys, and the therapist was available for the boy to relate to as he chose. Initially, Tommy played alone and constructed mock battles in which there was an overwhelming victory and defeat. Gradually, Tommy moved to games that could include the therapist. At first, however, these were definitely "parallel play" and noncompetitive in nature, such as working on a puzzle. After a period of months, he began including the therapist in the play, which remained noncompetitive. At approximately 4 months, he initiated increasingly competitive play and during the final few sessions he demonstrated a very aggressive game of basketball.

The parents, at the outset, were considering the possibility of divorce, and at the end of therapy they no longer discussed this. It gradually became clear to both partners that no immediate dramatic change was going to occur in the other. The father's personality pattern was obsessive-compulsive; he stated with pride that his schedule in driving to and from work had not varied more than 10 seconds over nearly 2 decades. His behavior, as head of the household, was commensurate with this pattern, and he bitterly resented his family's failure to follow his specific and meticulous protocols for management of household matters. He perceived these failures as proof of their lack of concern for him, and he had progressively withdrawn from active interaction with the family. Conversely, other family members perceived him as gruff, critical, and unable to praise. The father expressed regret that, due to the generally disorganized nature of the family's life, he was unable to include himself in activities with them. His time at home was largely spent in reading the newspaper, sleeping, and working alone in the garage on his own projects. His Minnesota Multiphasic Personality Inventory (MMPI) profile was 634789-2.

The mother demonstrated features of the hysterical personality pattern. She came from a large and demonstrably warm family, but had lived in terror of her alcoholic father as a child. She expressed fear of her husband and a feeling of revulsion toward physical contact with him, as with men in general. She perceived the world as potentially damaging to her son Tommy and took a very protective role toward him. The parents' courtship had been uneventful over a period of approximately 18 months, but the mother stated that her husband "changed" the day of their wedding. She had had several surgical procedures, including a hysterectomy, and was prone to recurrent bouts of asthma that had required several emergency hospitalizations. Her MMPI profile was 1'''843''76'2–.

Tommy's perceptions of his parents, illustrated in his drawings were of distant and threatening figures. His father appeared as a faceless figure with a large extended hand and a massive phallus. The figure of the mother, drawn when the mother was present in the room, was initially "mommy." The final detail was the razor-sharp teeth, and as he drew them he commented, "This is a vampire."

However, during the course of therapy, the father became quite determined to reinstate his position as father and head of the household, although he felt that he had been actively sabotaged in this effort by his family, and began to recognize that his own feelings of anger entered into his efforts to discipline his son. He initially had perceived his son Tommy as a "bad boy," intrinsically and irrevocably different from the other children and in need of vigorous corrective measures. He gradually began to see that Tommy reacted, however unreasonably, to stresses within the family. The mother similarly came to the conclusion that her son was not simply suffering from a form of epilepsy, and stated that he was clearly reacting to "something very specific in the home." She recognized that her husband was not likely to change his pattern of behavior to any great degree, and with fear and determination she undertook long-term individual therapy directed toward her feelings about men.

On one occasion, Tommy was seen with both parents, and once the oldest son, aged 20, asked to be seen with the parents. He expressed fears that the marriage would not survive, and seemed intent on impressing upon the therapist the significance of the situation. A major shift occurred in the family following this visit in that the oldest son realized his younger brother's need for an older male companion. Subsequently, the mother reported his increased concern for and involvement with his younger brothers.

This patient's clinical picture was characterized not only by the unusual symptom of a suicidal gesture, but by the disturbance of all areas of functioning, as documented in Table 1. While Tommy did not initially fit our preconceived notion of the "classic" pattern of depression (derived, of course, from work with adults), it became clear that Tommy's symptomatology and response to therapy were readily understood in terms of the model of childhood depression outlined above. Caught between a distant, hostile, and threatening father on the one hand and a superficially warm and positive but destructively infantilizing mother on the other hand, Tommy perceived himself to be helpless in a hopeless situation. His response was that defined by Malmquist (1971) as a "depressive equivalent," in that there was no depressive affect; rather, the child sought to cope with the depression by hyperkinesis or impulsive acting out. It is altogether likely that many of the previously described cases of suicide in children would, on reexamination, fall into the same category. Akiskal and McKinney (1973), in an impressive formulation of the concept of depression, have pointed out the role of hyperarousal in the pathogenesis of depression. For Tommy, his suicidal gesture emerged from the context of a series of impulsive, potentially self-destructive behaviors. He was an accident-prone child. Schrut (1964) has pointed out that self-destructive behavior functions by lowering the child's anxiety as long as it elicits parental concern.

Glaser (1965) has noted that:

> almost any inner conflict in the child may reach proportions which make it seem impossible for the child to escape or solve his dilemma. The situation may be aggravated by a lack of supportive resources available to the child, especially if the parents are noncommunicative, detached, or absent, or if the child is afraid to communicate with the parents, as in the case when the conflictual situation involves forbidden behavior.
>
> The child's intelligence, maturity, past experience and tolerance for anxiety will influence his choice of coping mechanism. Here the direct purpose of the suicidal attempt may be to draw attention to the existence of a conflict. As in most neurotic behavior, the deeper aspects of the conflict-producing situation are concealed, rendering the defensive coping mechanism ineffectual.

Failure of what was previously a functional pattern (falling off the roof or running in front of cars) confirmed Tommy's helplessness. This experience in Tommy led to an escalation of self-destructive behavior resulting in a suicide attempt. The interpretation of a significant shift from mere accident-proneness to activation of suicidal strategies as a major means of coping is supported by the following incident, which happened early in therapy:

An argument between Tommy and his older brother escalated until they were preparing for battle in the backyard. As both parents arrived, Tommy was frantically trying to kick his older brother in the shins. Immediately the mother sided with Tommy, and the father, siding with the older brother, instructed him, "Go ahead, hit him in the teeth." However, the parents separated the boys and ordered them to go to the house. Tommy, finding his father standing between himself and the house, said, "I'll take off my belt and hit you," to which the father replied, "Go ahead." At this, Tommy abruptly sat down, dropped his head to his hands and mumbled, "I might just as well kill myself."

Tommy served as an ideal barometer to reflect the severe but hidden stresses that were present within the family. As an intelligent child, he picked up clues from his environment rapidly; as a hyperactive child, he reflected and exacerbated intrafamilial stresses. In this role of "identified patient," Tommy served several useful functions in the family. The mother had long used illness as a means to control a difficult environment, and was eager to use Tommy's special problems and weaknesses as a means to draw him closer to her as a special child. Simultaneously, her need to have a close relationship with a male was met by her Oedipal-age son more than by any other member of the family. The father seems to have used Tommy in two ways to vent anger in himself, since he seemed "primarily evil" and, therefore, a justified target for anger. Second, Tommy acted out his father's anger in a self-destructive manner and through aggressive acts in the neighborhood.

A close examination of the subtle intrafamilial stresses reveals that Tommy's suicidal gesture evolved from a series of increasingly dysfunctional coping maneuvers that failed to elicit the desired response. Therapeutic intervention resulted in several significant shifts. Tommy's cry for help was acknowledged by the therapist and interpreted to the family, decreasing his sense of hopelessness and depression. Concomitantly, play therapy behavior demonstrated increasing externalization of aggression. The family, particularly the father, decreased use of Tommy as a scapegoat, while simultaneously both the father and the oldest brother became more supportive. The mother felt less of a need to protect Tommy from the father's hostility and increasingly allowed Tommy independence.

Follow-up

The follow-up appointments with Tommy and his family were made approximately 6 years after they had terminated treatment, and getting together with him proved difficult. After initially agreeing in principal to a brief series of meetings, the mother refused several appointments, and accepted and canceled two different times because of illness in the family. After nearly a month of phone calls, she finally indicated that it would be impossible for us to see her son because she was preoccupied in caring for another family member. She was willing to allow us to provide transportation, however, and we were finally able to see Tommy again. The frustrating vignette permitted us to infer that the mother's use of illness as a controlling tool, and the struggle between holding on and letting go of her son, which had been important themes during treatment, continued to be powerful in the life of this family.

Tommy's parents had divorced and his mother had remarried within one year following our last contact. Tommy had grown, as expected, into a taller adolescent version of the child we had known. He was quiet, compliant, and worked with serious focus throughout the long session of psychological testing. His verbal responses were always brief, and at no time did he initiate spontaneous conversation. He seemed to have a sure sense of his own skills; he either tackled a request immediately or refused, saying he could not do it. He remained emotionally quite guarded, expressing little pleasure over obvious hard work that culminated in success and little frustration or dissatisfaction at failure.

Tommy was given the WISC-R, Berry Visual Motor Integration Test, Task of Emotional Development and was asked to draw his family.

On the WISC-R, Tommy received a verbal IQ of 114, a performance IQ of 101, and a resulting full scale IQ of 109. The verbal scale score falls in the bright normal range and the performance scale score falls well within the average range of intellectual functioning. The discrepancy between verbal and performance IQ's is important, especially in the light of the fluctuation in verbal scores previously seen and reported from the beginning to the end of treatment, when his verbal IQ shifted upward from 100 to 125 as important people in his world became more responsive to him and he was able to function in creative and positive ways in it.

The following test protocol thus did not demonstrate his superior potential and includes extensive subtest scatter from a high on Object Assembly (15) and Comprehension (14) to Coding (7) as the lowest scale score. This wide scatter suggests considerable cognitive interference and probable depression. Uneven responses and early intratest failure on Picture Arrangement and Similarities further support this impression. His success on Object Assembly may be a function of the fact that as a task it depends least on examiner-subject interaction of all the subtests. The sight of a scrambled puzzle carries the fairly explicit instruction to put it together, and the shape of the car or face when correctly assembled gives direct feedback. Under these conditions, Tommy worked quickly and alone to complete the task, and he succeeded well. His sensitivity to social and interpersonal demands, a result of inservice survival training in his troubled family, is reflected in his high score on Comprehension. Significant depressive features were seen in the low Coding score, especially in relation to high Vocabulary and Digit Span scores. Qualitative features of the record indicate continued concern with self and preoccupation with body. In response to the question about why criminals should be locked up, he responded, "So they won't harm you," and when asked about the need for meat inspectors, he again personalized the response by saying, "So you won't get germs or diseases or sick." Paperback books are handy "because you can put them in your pocket, but sometimes they bend and get spoiled." Anxiety is egocentrically focused through the perception of vulnerability.

The family constellation has changed dramatically in the intervening years and the family drawing done by Tommy reflected this change with simple clarity. Tommy drew his mother, stepfather, himself, and then his younger brother. It was significant that he omitted his father (whom he still sees weekly) and his three older siblings who no longer live at home. Rather than being the fourth of five children, Tommy is now the oldest child at home, and, at age 15, expects to play that role for two or three more years. He chose to draw himself next to his stepfather, positioning himself to share the family power with the current "man of the house." Tommy gave at least minimal indication of clothing to the rest of the family, but left himself essentially uncovered. He drew a hint of trousers, but gave himself no belt, likely to still be a highly charged piece of clothing since his suicide gesture was done with a rope and he was reportedly threatened with his father's belt as a younger child. Of the four family members drawn, Tommy's shoulders were broadest and the body most sturdy, as his characterization of "the baby," now a 13-year-old, was of a small, clown-faced figure placed at some distance from the rest of the family. Stepfather was tallest and distinguishable also by a moustache. Mother was identifiably feminine only by her longer hair, her body had no womanly shape, and was dramatically mutilated with the left hand missing and the right arm severed from the shoulder by repeated reworking of the pencil. All of the figures had fingers drawn with razor-sharp tips, not unlike the "vampire teeth" that Tommy had drawn on mother at the beginning of treatment six years before.

As is possible to infer from the descriptive material, the drawings were quite primitive. Applying the Harris-Goodenough scoring system to the best differentiated figure, the stepfather, Tommy received a total score of 15 points and a resulting age equivalency of 5 years. This is in sharp contrast to his age-adequate replication of the geometric designs from the Visual Motor Integration Test. These results documenting good perceptual motor coordination in combination with average skills demonstrated on the Performance Scale of the WISC-R lead to an understanding of the very disruptive influence that his family continues to have on his behavior. His own sense of vulnerability and anger toward the mother are portrayed in that simple rendering.

Signs of depression and vulnerability seen on the highly structured WISC-R were seen even more clearly in the responses that Tommy gave to the projective cards from the Tasks of Emotional Development, a series of 13 photographs that portray an adolescent boy in interaction with different family members, peers, or alone. Analysis of the responses included a judgment of the accuracy of the perception of the interaction pictured, affect, and problem solution. Tommy understood the action, surrounded it with negative affect, and had great difficulty providing a satisfactory resolution. He was able to identify the salient issues, reflecting his ability to quickly size up an interpersonal situation—an important strength. However, he made several unusual role assignments by misidentifying the boy in the picture as a father or husband, and thus diverting the pattern of responsibility from parent to child. In only one of the thirteen interactions did Tommy predict a positive outcome; this in response to the picture of a boy studying alone who later passed his test and was "happy." Academic achievement may provide the only safe corner for Tommy; but as we have seen above, even his cognitive skills are not conflict-free at this time. Woven among the developmentally appropriate stories of typical teenage/parent autonomy struggles was only one scenario created in which the others (parents) were seen as supportive or helpful. Every other story had painful, violent, angry interchanges inevitably with the central male figure (be he son, father, or husband) as target for attack; even an initially innocent experience of two boys who "ran into each other walking 'round the bushes" ended with a beating. His conversion of "mommy" into a "witch" in his drawing, which had occurred 7 years ago, appears to have been prophetic.

Sometimes the disaster or altercation started by others became the boy's fault. For example, in response to card seven, "the lady is washing dishes and the guy is fixin' up the cabinet . . . boy is standin' there . . . he'll drop the hammer and break the dishes . . . woman will be mad at him . . . the kid has to pick the stuff up." And the baby's father in card eight dropped the child when he was hit by the mother: "the baby has a broken arm . . . they fight . . . the lady kicks the guy out of the house." This latter vignette may reflect also Tommy's anxiety about his role as the special child responsible for his parents' divorce and his father's fate. We had initially hypothesized that, as a child, Tommy served as the "family barometer." As a bright boy he was sensitive and aware of the parental tension and as a hyperactive child he was able to express their pain overtly. As with many hyperactive children, physical maturity had lessened his heightened and relatively unfocused activity level. Tommy continues to incorporate the destructive impulses that still flow through the family; he continues to be the conduit, but is poorly defended and at considerable personal risk with the "quieter" transformation into depression.

Thematically important at this time for him is the confusion around his role: is he boy or man, son or husband? This issue, a residual from his parents' divorce and his mother's remarriage, is particularly salient now for there is the push of adolescence that demands clarification in his unique struggle for masculine identity. Tommy said he has not begun to date; given his perception of women as aggressive, powerful, and rejecting, one would predict as a corollary of this issue that heterosexual friendships will be difficult for him to establish and maintain. A second issue that seems to be crystallizing at this time revolves around the dimension of activity-passivity; is he responsible or just an innocent bystander? The broad shoulders in his self-portrait reflected one answer to this tension, to accept all the family pain himself. As the content of the tasks presented to him during the testing session became more personal, Tommy was less able to protect himself from essentially random attack, and he found it increasingly difficult to know how to "shoulder" what he perceived to be responsibility for another's destructive action. Thus, the feelings of hopelessness and helplessness which had resulted in his dramatic and life-threatening resolution 7 years ago continue to be evident in the follow-up material.

Case Report: Howard

Howard was seen at the university's Clinic for Hyperactive Children, on referral from school personnel, at age 5 years, 4 months, while in his second year of preschool. The presenting problems as stated by his parents were: 1) that the school had told them that Howard was probably hyperactive and 2) that Howard appeared "sad" much of the time. Howard's "sadness" was manifested at home by frequent (twice a day) crying spells with no evident cause, a reluctance to go to school, and numerous physical symptoms, such as vomiting, that tended to keep his mother at school with him. At other times at home he was reported to be hostile and violent towards his mother, often saying he hated her.

Howard's parents reported that he had begun to seem sad and that his behavior had become more erratic following the birth of his sister when he was three. At that time, he began to have intermittent nightmares, rapid changes of mood, and to engage in various "defiant" behaviors, such as getting up early in the morning and taking food from the refrigerator. The problems had gotten much worse in the prior few weeks. Howard's teacher reported that his maternal grandfather, to whom he had been quite close, had recently left the area without saying goodbye "since it would be so hard on the kids to say goodbye to us." However, school personnel had already decided that Howard would be unable to handle a regular first grade classroom and had retained him for a second year in the preschool program.

A school visit by the assessing psychiatrist revealed a pattern of behavior similar to that reported by the parents. Howard played with his peers in a remarkably controlling and demanding way. When his control was significantly threatened, his behavior changed dramatically—he seemed frightened, withdrawn, and about to burst into tears. His mother reported a similar phenomenon in his play in the neighborhood, saying that he occasionally ran inside to her, crying and saying,"I feel very sad."

The developmental history revealed life-long difficulty in the mother-child relationship that was intensified with the birth of his sister. Howard was wanted by both parents and was the product of his mother's third pregnancy. The pregnancy was very difficult as the mother was confined to bed for 6 months due to an amniotic fluid leak and was cared for by her own mother. Delivery was full term and uncomplicated after an "easy" 4 hours of labor. Birth weight was 7 pounds, 14 ounces and there were no neonatal distress indicators. Mother felt "fantastic" when she first held Howard and described the experience in almost religious terms.

During Howard's first months of life, his mother lived with her parents since his father was in military service in Vietnam. Early feeding experiences were a struggle, since grandmother wanted to bottle-feed the baby and contemptuously commented on the mother's unsuccessful attempts at breast feeding. She reported, "I got the blues real bad" during her son's first few months of life. Howard appears to have had a difficult temperamental type; in particular, irregularity of sleeping and other habits made his mother's life difficult.

The father returned when Howard was 4 months old, and the family moved into their own house. Developmental milestones were within normal limits, but Howard continued to be a difficult child throughout the toddler stage. He was "constantly into something" and did not respond to mother's attempts at discipline. Toilet training was a "two-year battle." Mother began confining Howard to his room, and later to the backyard.

Howard's general health and physical condition had been good, with one minor and one major exception: He was hospitalized at age 1 for three days for procedures to correct a congenital strabismus. At age 4 years, 11 months, he was hospitalized for a tonsillectomy that was enormously traumatic. Following the tonsillectomy, bleeding was excessive, requiring transfusions, and a "bleeding workup." According to his mother, he became wildly agitated, and "fought so hard that it took four people to hold him down" for the necessary intravenous lines and blood samples. He therewith developed a great hatred for doctors and hospitals which complicated the subsequent psychiatric evaluation.

At age 3 years, 5 months, and 6 months after the birth of his sister, Howard ingested approximately 20 children's aspirin. He was taken to the emergency room of the medical center, where he was examined and released. Unfortunately, the exact circumstances surrounding Howard's aspirin ingestion are not known. (One psychiatrist later recalled having been told that Howard had said to his sister that "if you take more than two, it hurts you real bad.")

In the final moments of the follow-up interview that was done 4 years after the conclusion of Howard's psychotherapy, we learned that when Howard's mother was in the 8th grade, she had ingested 30 aspirin tablets after being expelled from school for throwing a book at a teacher. She said she "cursed everybody as I counted them out." That night she awoke sick and was told by her mother to "take two aspirin, you'll feel better." She was subsequently hospitalized on the same ward where her son Howard was later evaluated for hyperactivity.

At the time of the initial interview the family included the father (30), mother (27), Howard (4 to 5), and younger sister (2 to 6). Father was happily employed as a salesman and mother described herself as a "traditional housewife," a role she said she disliked, but performed well.

Howard's parents had been married for 9 years, having known each other for 12. The marriage was planned as a result of an unwanted pregnancy. When the pregnancy resulted in a spontaneous miscarriage two weeks before the wedding date, the wedding plans apparently proceeded from their own inertia, with both parents stating they would have preferred not to marry. The parents have grown to appreciate each other over the years. They both reported that the major conflict between them was that the husband avoided conflict and did not give his wife much emotional support, especially during any period of crisis. Mother analyzed her problems with Howard by saying, "I don't yell at his father, so I take it out on him."

Howard's mother is the second of four children, with an older sister and two younger brothers. She stated that she was "supposed to be a boy." Her father was in the military. Both parents used alcohol heavily (when her father was hospitalized after an accident, her mother smuggled liquor to him) and became markedly overweight. The mother is remembered as "crying constantly at the least little thing" and having been very jealous of any attention that her husband gave to her daughters. The parents are remembered as being very distant and generally inattentive to their children. For her part, Howard's mother remembers having been quite independent by age 16 and stated, "I generally did whatever I could to aggravate the situation." Her suicide gesture in 8th grade has already been described.

Howard's father had one older sister. He flatly described his family as a good one with no problems. Others have described his older sister as very dominating towards him. There is no history of alcoholism or psychiatric problems in the family.

The clinical impression of the parents at intake was that both were quite depressed. Mother's depression was seen as more evident, but she was also seen as having more motivation to change. Father's depression was seen as being generally contained by his obsessional defenses with emphasis on work and his denial and avoidance of conflict.

The initial intake was extraordinarily prolonged by Howard's adamant, and even violent, refusal to leave the waiting room; apparently his pain from the bitter experience with doctors, in the context of his tonsillectomy and subsequent bleeding crisis, was bearing its predictable bitter fruit. Several stormy, unproductive waiting room encounters and a transfer to a new therapist occurred before Howard and his therapist sat in the office.

Howard looked intelligent and was highly articulate. He had fair skin, a small frame, fine features, and somewhat inhibited movements that combined to make him look "intellectual." The appearance was heightened by thick glasses. The psychiatrist experienced this first interview with Howard as intense. Howard sat silently for 20 minutes, visually exploring the therapist's facial features. He then fell asleep. He did agree to take a walk toward the end of the session, but spoke very little.

Howard was seen for 18 weekly individual play therapy sessions. In the initial sessions, he actively refused to participate in activities with the therapist. During one session, the therapist took Howard for a walk to the store where he bought him an orange. Howard participated more readily in sessions following this event, and his mother reported that he began to anticipate coming to sessions with some eagerness. Trips to the store for food subsequently shared in the office became central; Howard later tolerated being weaned away from this gratification and, for the first time in therapy, began to use toys and relate to his therapist in a normal manner. His father brought him unfailingly to every session.

By the 15th session, the therapist's note indicated that Howard "looks like an entirely normal youngster during the session." Therapy terminated shortly thereafter, with the therapist noting, "affect variable, good laughter, competitive in age-appropriate way, less controlling... Now age-appropriate; depressive-proneness and obsessional defenses remain."

Howard's mother was referred for therapy and remained in weekly therapy for one and a half years. She described the experience as "very useful," saying, "I learned to like myself; now I like me better."

Follow-up

As part of the follow-up study, Howard was seen for a psychological assessment at the age of 9 years, 11 months, 4 years and 2 months after the conclusion of his therapy.

Assessment instruments used were the Wechsler Intelligence Scale for Children—Revised (WISC-R), Wide Range Achievement Test (WRAT), Berry-Buktenica Test of Visual Motor Integration (VMI), Benton Visual Retention Test (BVR), Tasks for Emotional Development (TED), Kinetic Family Drawing, Human Figure Drawing, and Walker Problem Behavior Identification Checklist (completed by mother).

Howard was a good-looking boy with short, straight blond hair who was dressed in short pants and a T-shirt that seemed to be "color coordinated." He related in a friendly but passive way to the examiner and carried himself somewhat stiffly. His physical appearance closely matched the description written by his therapist when he was 5: His fair skin, fine features and thick glasses combined to make him appear "intellectual." In reply to questions, he reported that he got "twelve A's" on his year-end report card, and he acknowledged that he felt "happy" about that.

In general, the assessment material suggested that Howard was functioning well within normal limits for a 9-year-old, with some tendency to depression and denial of conflict. His Verbal (111) and Full Scale (111) IQ scores were in the Bright Normal range and his Performance IQ (109) was in the high end of the Average range of intellectual functioning. There was little interest scatter of his scaled scores on the WISC-R subtests, except for a relatively lowered score on the Picture Completion subtest (8) and a slightly elevated score on the Object Assembly subtest (14). This indicates relatively consistent functioning over a wide range of cognitive skills. His scores on the Reading and Spelling subtests of the WRAT were at the 8th grade level. Since his standardized scores on these subtests (133 and 131) were equivalent to IQ scores in the Very Superior range, Howard could reasonably be called an "over-achiever," with the achievement higher than predicted by intellectual capacity as measured by IQ.

The Visual Motor Integration and Visual Retention tests, both measures of visual-motor functioning, were administered because Howard had some tendency to rotate designs on the Block Design subtest of the WISC-R. The results were equivocal, indicating the possibility of mild difficulty in integrating visual percepts with motor output.

The stories told by Howard to the 12 stimulus pictures of the Tasks of Emotional Development test are remarkable primarily for their consistent "normality." An overall title for the 12 stories might be "Things will be better tomorrow," or "It'll go away." In each story, Howard readily identified the appropriate emotion for the child protagonist (ranging from scared, happy, mad, sad to jealous—mentioned three times), and ended each story by indicating that any "bad" feeling would be gone by the next day, when the characters would be relating more happily. For example, Howard's story on card 7 of the T.E.D. was: "One day a boy was feeling jealous because his mother and father were fixing up the kitchen and he couldn't help. So the next day the whole family went on a camping trip and they fished for a while and when they came home they went to bed." Examiner: "What is he thinking about?" Howard: "When he'll be able to do that kind of stuff." The theme of happy normality was continued in the Kinetic Family Drawing wherein Howard drew a schematic and relatively undifferentiated picture of his family playing baseball (which he said was a frequent event) with him at the plate. Examiner: "What's going to happen?" Howard: "I'm going to hit a home run."

There are several indications that the image of normality presented by Howard on the projective materials is not without some psychological cost. Howard's low score on the Picture Completion subtest of the WISC-R, which requires identifying what is missing in a picture, indicates that he may have trouble allowing himself to see things being "wrong." In addition, Howard literally did not see the rather clear suggestions of mother-child conflict in two

Table 2 Comparison of Howard and Tommy

	Howard	Tommy
Presenting problem	School demanded evaluation for "hyperactivity"	Parents sought help in response to attempted self-strangulation
History of the problem	Life-long difficulties in mother-child relationship	Long history of accident-proneness
Initial clinical observation	Initially refused to enter office, vigorously and actively negativistic	Withdrawn, infantile, and passive but eagerly used playroom, quietly avoiding therapist
Developmental history	By parental report, temperament very difficult in infancy; especially low rhythmicity, traumatic hospitalization	By parental report, temperament very difficult in infancy, gradual emergence of violent outbursts, "uncontrollable"
Family history	Depression (continual weeping) in maternal grandmother, alcoholism, both maternal grandparents, depression and poor self-esteem in mother	Seizure disorders in several relatives, chronic serious undiagnosed illness in maternal grandmother was source of much of mother's energy drain

Initial diagnosis	Depression (self-report, "sad")	Seizure disorder (treated); adjustment reaction of childhood; multiple developmental lags and deviations
Treatment course	Responded well to critical feeding; tolerated weaning from feeding without recurrence of symptoms; enjoyed active play, no unusual content (mother in treatment quite successfully for 1½ years)	Progressed from solitary to parallel to interactive play, midway in treatment he repeatedly presented themes of overwhelming force destroying the weak and helpless, parents involved in treatment intermittently
Follow-up	Pleasant, cheerful, cooperative boy doing well but occasionally "stubborn"	(Parents divorced tumultuously after termination). Shy, quiet, cooperative, pleasant teenager, doing well
Formulation of depression	Emerges from family and developmental histories, depressive mood is obvious to family clinical observers, relationship of aspirin ingestion to depression not clear	After months of play therapy, the perception of hopelessness and helplessness in the face of an overwhelming environment was inferred: self-destructive wish and behavior were clearly direct responses to this perception

WISC-R Picture Arrangement items. This again suggests the important role played by denial of conflict in maintaining his psychological equilibrium.

Howard's human figure drawing seemed to provide an important clue to the psychological state underlying his socially appropriate, conforming responses to the T.E.D. Howard described the boy in his picture as "just standing there smiling." To the examiner, the boy appeared to be on his knees with eyes wide open and arms outstretched, a position of begging or pleading. This posture, combined with other data such as misplaced pockets on the female human figure drawing, the frequent mention of jealousy, and the sense of being left out in the T.E.D. stories, suggest that many of Howard's unmet needs to be cared for and nurtured are out of his awareness and are currently channelled into the search for recognition through conformity, compliance, and high achievement. Since he has considerable skills in these areas, he seems at present to be receiving enough substitute gratifications to keep his needs in check.

Discussion

There are a series of points that need to be brought into sharp relief against the background of these case studies. In any statistical tabulation of "unsuccessful suicide attempts" made by children under 10 years of age, these two boys by definition would be grouped together, grouped with the implicit assumption that they were children too young to know what they were doing. Indeed there is some support in the research literature for such a position. It has been found that children less than 10 years of age do not understand death as either inevitable or irreversible. Thus, it would be fair to assume that neither child conceptualized the severity of his act, nor the potential finality were it successful. It would also be fair to posit that at the time each child made a self-destructive attempt, neither wanted to live at that moment. Young children do indeed feel strongly. Freud (1953) made that point very clearly. Rage, terror, passion, depression can be as overwhelmingly debilitating or facilitating to the behavioral repertoire of the child as for the adult.

As clinicians, however, we know how dangerous it is to overgeneralize. Though the children shared strong feelings and potentially self-destructive behavior, what they did, the context within which the behavior arose, and the meaning of that behavior for each child must have been quite different. Contrasting points are summarized in Table 2. To categorize the two children as being under 10 years of age is not sufficiently explanatory to understand their behavior. Howard was only 3 years old at the time of the incident and was functioning with what Piaget (1952, 1967) terms the "intuitive stage" of cognitive abilities. This stage is conceptualized by prelogical or preoperational thinking where the child's behavior is predominantly imitative, and things appearing together in time or space are perceived necessarily to be causally linked. The preoperational child lives in a binary world of good and bad, fat and thin, hot and cold, mine and yours. He does not remember well, nor does he predict the future. Indeed, experiences are sharp, clear, and existential. In contrast, Tommy, at the time of suicidal gesture, was functioning in the concrete-operational stage that is characterized, at least in part, by considerable experimentation with the world of things and people around him. Trial and error strategies predominate, if X does not work then try Y, and if that does not work, then try Z. The child in the concrete stage can understand more than one cause and can expect more than one effect. Selma Frailberg (1959) has noted that the alligator under the bed of the 3 year old is a considerably different critter than the alligator under the bed of the 6 year old.

It is this developmental point that we wish to make here. The suicide attempt of Howard was an attempt to solve an immediate problem, the feeling of overwhelming sadness, with the strategy he copied from mother. Tommy, on the other hand, with more cognitive flexibility acted to "stop the world and try to get off" after having exhausted a repertoire of possibilities, none of which worked. Again, from the Piagetian developmental perspectives, the first child's behavior could be seen as primarily accommodative, the second as assimilative. The first child was more responsive to the solutions, pressures, and possibilities modeled for him in the world; the second child was more sensitive to the meaning which he attributed to external people and events. This framing from Piagetian theory becomes powerful as we focus again on the findings from the follow-up studies. Howard continues to be particularly sensitive to the demands of those in his world. He is identified as "an overachiever" who takes his important cues from the demands of the external world. Tommy, in contrast, is much more explicitly reflective with the assimilative functions predominating. He continues to perceive the world as a disappointing and hurtful place, and he continues to perceive himself as vulnerable and his repertoire of possible responses as being insufficient for his needs.

As social scientists we are boggled, but as clinicians not surprised, to find that the family context within which these children were raised differed considerably. Tommy was raised within a deteriorating marriage; Howard was an infant whose parents built from a rocky start a solid and comfortable relationship. There has been improvement in the home environment in the homes of both children since they were first seen. That is undoubtedly important and contributes to the essentially clean bill of health each child received in the follow-up studies. Though there are striking dissimilarities between the two marriages, there may be an important commonality in the mother's experiences as children in the homes of the boy's grandparents. Both grandfathers were alcoholics and each woman suffered the rage, terror, and abuse common to children in alcoholic families. There is strong suggestion within the social science literature that in the process of socialization of children within a family that children model not only on the role available (in this case the son modeling on his father) but that the mother too provides important clues and cues to her male child about appropriate masculine behavior; and that she uses her own father as her primary model. Thus, the child is socialized directly by his father and indirectly by his mother's portrayal of the grandfather. It is impossible now to reconstruct the damage that an alcoholic father did to his girl child and which, in turn, she passed on in her relationships with her son. But it is possible to speculate that it has been significant and continues to be an important component in the personality structure and the behavior of these two boys.

Since we first saw Tommy, the concept of "childhood depression" has achieved widespread recognition, and the literature is shifting to discussion of the assessment and developmental implications of depression in childhood. The two cases permit a longitudinal view of two boys' development as influenced by the self-awareness of sadness (Howard) and the self-awareness of helplessness in a hopeless situation (Tommy). These cases illustrate clearly the critical distinction between depressive affect in the first child and impulsive self-destructive behavior in response to helplessness and hopelessness manifest by the second child. These boys are coping with very different life situations with different mechanisms: Howard seems to have imbibed sadness with his mothers' milk and subsequently learned to cope with life more optimistically. In fact, his optimism may have a somewhat forced quality. Tommy, in contrast, learned through bitter experience that life is hard and that one may periodically encounter threatening situations where one is hopeless and helpless. He is learning to live in this world with integrity, dignity, and caution.

Fortunately, both families are amenable to further follow-up. We anticipate a review, 5 years hence, of the rapidly evolving interface between two boys' developmental processes and our concept of depression.

REFERENCES

Akiskal, H. S., & McKinney, W. T. Depressive disorders: Toward a unified hypothesis. *Science,* 1973, *182,* 20.

Bakwin, H. Suicide in children and adolescents. *Journal of Pediatrics,* 1957, *50,* 749.

Bender, L., & Schilder, P. Suicidal preoccupation and attempts in children. *American Journal of Orthopsychiatry,* 1937, *7,* 225.

Bergstrand, C. G., & Otto, U. Suicidal attempts in adolescence and childhood. *Acta Pediatrica,* 1962, *51,* 17.

Bowlby, J. Psychopathological processes set in train by early mother-child separations. *Journal of Mental Sciences,* 1953, *99,* 265.

Chess, S., Thomas, A., & Birch, H. Behavior problems revisited: Findings on an anterospective study. *Journal of the American Academy of Child Psychiatry,* 1967, *6,* 321.

Davidson, J. Infantile depression in a "normal" child. *Journal of the American Academy of Child Psychiatry,* 1968, *7,* 522.

Despert, J. L. Suicide and depression in children. *Nervous Child,* 1952, *9,* 378.

Engel, G. L. A life setting conducive to illness: The giving-up given-up complex. *Annals of Internal Medicine,* 1968, *69,* 293.

Frailberg, S. *The magic years.* New York: Charles Scribner, 1959.

French, A. P., & Steward, M. S. Family dynamics, childhood, and attempted suicide in a seven-year-old boy: A case study. *Suicide,* 1975, *5,* 29.

Freud, S. Three essays on the theory of sexuality. *The standard edition of the complete psychological works of Sigmund Freud,* (Vol. VII). New York: Hogarth Press, 1953.

Glaser, K. Attempted suicide in children and adolescents: Psychodynamic observations. *American Journal of Psychotherapy,* 1965, *19,* 220.

King, J. W. Depression and suicide in children and adolescents. *GP,* 1967, *34,* 95.

Lourie, R. S. Suicide and attempted suicide in children and adolescents. *Texas Medicine*, 1967, *63*, 58.
Lukianowicz, N. Attempted suicide in children. *Acta Psychiatrica Scandinavica*, 1968, *44*, 415.
Malmquist, C. P. Depressions in childhood and adolescence. *New England Journal of Medicine*, 1971, *28*, 887.
Mattsson, A., Seese, L. R., & Hawkins, J. W. Suicidal behavior as a child psychiatric emergency. *Archives of General Psychiatry*, 1969, *20*, 100.
Piaget, J. *The origins of intelligence.* New York: International Universities Press, 1952.
Piaget, J. *Six psychological studies.* New York: Random House, 1967.
Rie, H. E. Depression in childhood—A survey of some pertinent contributions. *Journal of American Academy of Child Psychiatry*, 1966, *5*, 653.
Rinsley, D. B. Intensive psychiatric hospital treatment of adolescents. *Psychiatric Quarterly*, 1965, *39*, 1.
Schrut, A. Suicidal adolescents and children. *Journal of the American Medical Association*, 1964, *188*, 1102.
Spitz, R. Hospitalism—An inquiry into the genesis of psychiatric conditions in early childhood. *Psychoanalytic Study of the Child*, 1945, *1*, 53.
Toolan, J. M. Suicide and suicidal attempts in children and adolescents. *American Journal of Psychiatry*, 1962, *118*, 719.
Tuckman, J., & Youngman, W. F. Attempted suicide and family disorganization. *Journal of Genetic Psychology*, 1964, *105*, 187.

Chapter 9

PSYCHOLOGICAL IMPLICATIONS OF TOTAL MOTOR PARALYSIS IN A FIVE-YEAR-OLD BOY

J. Allen Miller

INTRODUCTION

Child psychiatrists are sometimes asked to see children by their pediatrician colleagues. Referrals range from requests to evaluate purely psychiatric problems to evaluation of the stress of illness. Several authors have described general aspects of the psychological impact of physical illness in children (Freud, 1952; Mattsson, 1972). These reviews have pointed to the stress imposed by issues such as the origin of the illness, subjection to nursing care, and changes in the emotional climate of the family. In each instance the child's reaction to stress may lead to regressive behavior, isolation, and the withdrawal characteristic of depression. The child's reaction may also lead to hiding both the overwhelming fear of loss of nurturant support and abandonment and the great anger or rage to which he is so vulnerable when so helpless to alter the conditions of illness, hospital care, or family reaction.

The case presented in this chapter offers an opportunity to look at some of the psychological stresses of total motor paralysis in a preschool child. Therapeutic efforts directed at reducing the impact of those stresses are also discussed. Medical aspects of the illness in question, the Guillain-Barré syndrome, are outside the scope of this chapter. Readers interested in the specific illness are referred to a review by Markland and Riley (1967).

Case Description

Chad, aged 4 year, 10 month, Caucasian boy, had an upper respiratory tract infection from which he recovered in a few days. A week later he complained of weakness in both legs. Within hours he could no longer stand and was brought to the pediatric clinic where he was noted to have a progressive motor paralysis and was admitted to the hospital. By the next afternoon the paralysis had affected both upper and lower extremities and the respiratory musculature making it necessary to perform a tracheostomy and place Chad on a respirator in the pediatric intensive care unit. Within a 48-hour-period, the disease had reduced Chad from an alert, active boy to a frightened, paralyzed patient with no functional speech.

The progression of paralysis stopped and a diagnostic work-up revealed findings consistent with Guillain-Barré syndrome. The parents and Chad were informed of the favorable prognosis. Chad would probably recover completely in a matter of months but would need to be hospitalized for supportive physical care.

During the next 30-day period, Chad remained mentally alert but his only means of expression was eye movement. Recovery was slow, and he remained in the pediatric intensive care unit. Efforts were made to protect him from the knowledge of other children dying. Because he was without speech but seemed to hear, a sign was placed above his bed which read, "speak to me, not about me." By the end of this period he was able to roll his head and speak a few words through his tracheostomy tube. His first communications were negativistic and uncooperative, i.e., he said "no" and rolled his head to avoid cooperation with procedures. The parents and staff were happy to see the paralysis rolling back but were unprepared for Chad's attitude. At this point, the pediatric intern requested evaluation and suggestions from child psychiatry.

The parents were pleased to have a psychiatrist involved and reported the following history. Chad was born out-of-wedlock and has never known his biological father. Within months of his birth, mother married Chad's stepfather who feels he has developed a close relationship with Chad similar to that of many fathers with adopted sons. A sister was born a year later. Father, a union roofer, was unemployed when Chad became ill and the family was on welfare. Chad was always an attractive child and got on well with adults and other children. He showed great interest in physical activities and always seemed "on the go" but equally enjoyed swapping stories or having stories read to him. He was successfully enrolled in a preschool program. Past illnesses had always been acute and mild, usually upper respiratory. He had never been hospitalized before.

The parents described the first 24 to 48 hour period as progressively frightening as they watched their son become paralyzed. They felt helpless and feared for his life. As they were bringing Chad into the hospital, he begged not to come because "that is where people die." After the paralysis stopped progressing they remained helpless and began wondering if they had somehow caused his illness. Once they heard the diagnosis and prognosis they were relieved but the recovery was so much slower than they had expected that they were once again anxious. They visited Chad daily for 4 to 8 hours depending on the demands of the intensive care unit. They refused to allow themselves to look at the other patients, many with terminal illnesses. When Chad began to respond to others, they were dismayed that he should be so negative and uncooperative. Mother's inclination was to give in to Chad's demands because he had been so ill for so long. Father, on the other hand, felt the relationship should be as consistent with the pre-illness relationship as it could. Although in mild disagreement, mother followed father's lead.

Initial Psychiatric Interviews

My first interview with Chad was difficult since he still could only roll his head and say a few words through his tracheostomy. I introduced myself as a doctor who specializes in worries and told him other children in his situation often had worries to talk about. He looked dismayed. I told him I knew it was difficult for him to talk and maybe I could bring some play materials to help. He suggested playing cards or marbles, representing his wish to have motor function returned. I suggested bringing puppets who could do the talking for both of us. He brightened and said, "yes."

For the next session I took four puppets, an adult male and female and a child male and female. Chad identified both males as doctors and both females as nurses. He suggested the story line with one or two words such as "Doctor. Mad. Nurse." After clarifying that he meant the doctor was mad at the nurse, I enacted a scene wherein the doctor puppet yelled at the nurse puppet.

Because he was easily fatigued, these early sessions were limited to 15 to 30 minutes and Chad was seen 3 or 4 times a week. His theme remained consistent, the doctors and nurses were angry with each other. Slowly he admitted he was angry with the nurses also. As his speech improved he began giving the puppets direct commands to hit each other and say go away, come back, shut up, and so on. His delight was demonstrated by his laughter.

Many children in similar situations would have withdrawn, become inert, and not experienced the continuous support from the presence of parents and interested nursing staff, nor have available a psychotherapist. Severe depression in this case was avoided, in part, by the open negativism and, later, the open playing out of hostility.

Involvement in Play Therapy

By the end of the second month in the intensive care unit, and one month of play therapy, Chad was able to say in words and choppy sentences whatever he wanted. He was also able to move his shoulders and raise his arms. He had endeared himself to the intensive care nursing staff who enjoyed spending time with him. He remained abusive to the puppets but also used them as objects to chase, thus exercising his arms.

When it was time to wean Chad from the respirator, he objected violently and refused to even try to breathe. He called the respirator his "friend" and insisted he would take it with him when he left the hospital. He asked the puppets what they thought. The puppets looked the machine over closely and decided it was too big to take home. Chad argued briefly, then knocked the respirator off with his chin and began breathing rapidly to show the puppets that he could. The respirator alarm sounded but Chad was in no distress. Four days later he was completely weaned from the respirator.

Following this, Chad was free to go on short wheelchair rides. He enjoyed these rides and the nurses began talking to him about moving onto the regular ward. This frightened both Chad and his parents because it meant cessation of 24-hour intensive care. Chad began refusing to eat. Because the intensive care unit routine would not allow prolonged battles over feeding, Chad was force fed by putting the food into his mouth and holding his nose. Although advised against this practice, the nurses continued it because ordinary feeding took up to two hours. Chad's puppet play began to involve feeding the puppets food that turned into "blood" once swallowed. In addition, he fed them garbage, animal food, and rocks with great delight. If the puppets refused to eat they were spanked.

Working Through During the Recovery Period

The anxiety of loss of support from the respirator, the depressive feeling of vulnerability, and the inability to function on one's own was minimal and was dealt with quickly. Similarly, the fear of leaving intensive care and doing more on his own had marked depressive elements. Once helpless and dependent, even with his parents' help, he felt that he could not become self-sufficient without the risk of being destroyed.

One week short of his third month in the intensive care unit Chad was transferred to the pediatric ward where he made steady progress and was quite a hit with the nursing staff and hospital volunteer foster grandparents. Puppet play during this time varied a great deal but the characters remained doctors and nurses. Some of the play themes follow. Chad delighted in giving the puppets a "Hawaiian punch" to knock them out; then to tie them up. Once tied up, Chad stripped the puppets of their clothes and belongings, throwing them in the dump. When the puppets protested, Chad told them they were "dead" and could not talk until he untied them. In another sequence, Chad chopped a hole in a doctor's neck and put in a tracheostomy, going through the process of suctioning ("This will be hard," he told them) and cleaning. The feeding theme mentioned above continued with the addition of putting a tube down the puppets' noses for gavage feeding.

Finally, a decision was made to remove Chad's tracheostomy and send him home. Similar to his reaction to weaning from the respirator, Chad refused to breathe with the tracheostomy hole covered even though he did well if the hole was covered while he slept or was preoccupied. He had two pulmonary arrests during one week when the hole was covered. These were thought to be psychophysiologic but of major concern. Again, the anxiety about being independent of a life-giving support carries the threat of not being taken care of at all. Revenge for desired autonomy may make the regressive state more secure which is characteristic of the more pervasive struggle in depression. It is safer to be helpless and in need of care than effective and assertive with the fight that it may bring about.

During this sequence of events, he smothered the puppets under the covers and held their noses. Gradually he let them practice breathing and then practiced with them. He also paid close attention to my breathing and observed my nostrils flaring slightly. He then wanted to try nose breathing to see if his nostrils could flare. The next time the tracheostomy was removed, Chad requested that the puppets and I be present. He was frightened but the procedure went smoothly. Understanding of the fear and support at a fearful moment permits the shared experience of fear without a sense of being overwhelmed. Tomograms of the trachea revealed a stricture at the site of the tracheostomy tube and the otolaryngologist replaced the tube until the stricture could be treated. Chad was disappointed that they had not left it out altogether but proudly announced, "I don't need it anymore!"

Chad was discharged home the next week with plans to return to the hospital in two weeks for removal of the tracheostomy tube. His paralysis had resolved enough to allow some fine motor movement of the fingers. Gross motor movement of the lower extremities had returned enough to crawl. Total time in the hospital was 4½ months.

Once out of the hospital, Chad's struggles over eating ceased. He also became very active, crawling and exploring his home with vigor. His parents were happy to note that he was not "spoiled" by his hospital experience and discipline was not a problem. They observed a significant increase in Chad's ability to observe events and discuss his feelings about them.

I saw Chad next on the day of his readmission to the hospital. The pediatric staff, nurses, and foster grandparents made a great fuss over his return. Chad was sullen, wished the staff would leave him alone, and did not want his parents to leave. He asked how the puppets had been since he last saw them. When the puppets said they had missed him, Chad cut out their tongues and pulled off their eyes. I commented "you do not like people to say they missed you nor to see that you are back in the hospital." He agreed. The fear of abandonment, regression, repetition of the helplessness and dependence that occurred in the first hospitalization were healthy signs that nothing had been repressed. His ability to express murderous anger in play rather than to retreat and withdraw into a depressive stance demonstrated his healthy ego functions and effective resolution of previous developmental conflicts.

I saw Chad again the following day after the otolaryngologist had done a bronchoscopy to determine the status of the stricture. The decision was to leave the tracheostomy tube in place and reduce the stricture by serial dilatations over a 6-week period as an outpatient. Chad told me he wished they could take it out now but was happy he did not have to stay in the hospital for the dilatations. He quickly focused away from the tracheostomy to show me the gains he had made in muscular strength and coordination. For the first time he spoke confidently of entering kindergarten next year when all of this would be behind him. He did not wish to play with the puppets except to say goodbye since he would be leaving the hospital the next morning.

Several days after discharge from the hospital, Chad's father was offered a job in another state and the family transferred there. Chad promised to telephone me whenever he came back to visit his grandparents.

Discussion

What is the psychological impact of a month of total motor paralysis in a 5-year-old child previously very active and effective? Chad's first communications showed a change from a pleasant boy to a negative, uncooperative patient. Since the frequent reaction to overwhelming stress in a 5-year-old is withdrawal and depression, why was Chad's reaction different? Chad's interaction with the hospital staff and use of puppets dramatized his conflicts and gave at least a partial answer to this question.

The preschool child often misunderstands the cause of illness. In the case presented here, Chad told his parents not to take him to the hospital because that is where people die. After admission to the hospital he did get worse and was put in the intensive care unit where children did die. There was an accusation, "you did this to me," in Chad's dealings with his parents once he got his speech back. The parents felt guilty even though they "knew" they had not caused his illness. The parents needed help in separating themselves from their child's misunderstanding enough to help their son with the facts.

Dealings with the severity of illness can be complicated by the child's inability to comprehend certain concepts such as death. Easson's (1968) discussion of the concept of personal death stresses the preschooler's notion of the reversibility of death. As evidenced by Chad's puppet play, he saw his paralysis as "I am dead, but I will be alive again when I get untied." Only once did Chad ask his father where children go when they die. Father told him they go to heaven and Chad appeared satisfied.

Loss of bodily control and dependence on nurses for total care can be difficult for a preschooler who has become quite independent and competent. From his play it seemed that Chad saw his paralysis as leaving him at the mercy of the nurses who could "strip" him of his clothes and possessions at their whim. His first communications were rebellion against nursing care, refusing to cooperate as much as possible, rather than indifferent, passive, depressive acceptance of care. These communications indicated the healthy anger of an effective, loved child who previously felt secure enough in adult relationships not to fear expressing anger at adults for their treatment of him. There reawakened the infant's struggle of "I need you, I would like to do without you, but I'm afraid I'll be deserted or disliked." Equally important is the concept "I get angry when I can't do it myself and, when you insist on doing it for me, I fear losing my independence." The intensity of this struggle for Chad was demonstrated in his refusal to deal with subsequent forced feedings, a struggle that ended as soon as he left the hospital. The struggle for independence is the antithesis of the dependence and helplessness of the child who is depressed in the hospital and fearful that adults will desert him if he does not behave as they want him to. The ambivalence of the situation is illustrated by Chad's "addiction" to his "friend" the respirator while rejecting the human nurses. The respirator being life saving and inanimate does not require assertion of independence from persons who were not seen as life-saving agents. The task of the therapist in this instance was to help Chad deal with current stresses while working toward integration into nonhospital life once the illness subsided.

David Levy (1939) was influential in introducing the idea of structured play situations to conserve time in dealing with stress. Hospital-based child therapists have found his concepts helpful in dealing with children's reactions to illness. The child under stress will structure play material to deal with the most pressing stress. In this case, Chad identified the nondescript puppets according to his need, i.e., they were doctors and nurses. Early in his therapy, Chad could not engage in direct dialogue nor physical activity with the puppets but was able to "direct" the activity using the doctors to punish the nurses through a third party, the therapist. Chad thus illustrated two tenets of play therapy possible even to severely limited children. These are the opportunities to change from suffering party to aggressor and to change the outcome of events (Waelder, 1933). With return of motor function and verbal ability, Chad took a more direct role in the interaction. This behavior again indicated the lack of depressive adaptation and a more healthy independence of his caretakers whom he could punish and make suffer as he had suffered.

Chad also used the puppets to master the various procedures that had been done to him. He drew blood, inserted a tracheostomy tube, gave gavage feedings, and resuscitated the puppets when they were smothered. He chose to tell the puppets things he kept from the hospital staff, his parents, and his therapist. The puppets served as the objects of his aggression, his teachers, his friends, and the sharers of his confidences. Finally, Chad was able to say goodbye to the puppets to signify the separation he felt from the entire hospital experience. This child's healthy rather than depressed adaption to very severe stress of paralysis, his freedom to be negativistic and defiant, and to use the puppets in play therapy to express his anger and revenge for what was done to him indicates that he was an emotionally secure child without major developmental conflicts on admission.

REFERENCES

Easson, W. M. Care of the young patient who is dying. *Journal of the American Medical Association,* 1968, *205,* 63.
Freud, A. The role of bodily illness in the mental life of children. *Psychoanalytic Study of the Child,* 1952, *9,* 69.
Levy, D. M. Trends in therapy: Release therapy. *American Journal of Orthopsychiatry,* 1939, *9,* 713.
Markland, L. D., & Riley, H. D., Jr. The Guillain-Barré Syndrome in Childhood. *Clinical Pediatrics,* 1967, *6,* 162.
Mattsson, A. Long-term physical illness in childhood: A challenge to psycho-social adaptation. *Pediatrics,* 1972, *9,* 801.
Waelder, R. The psychoanalytic theory of play. *Psychoanalytic Quarterly,* 1933, *2,* 208.

Chapter 10

DEPRESSION IN THE CHILD ABUSE SYNDROME

Charlotte Bible
Alfred P. French

Abused young children frequently appear subdued, isolated, and are unable to function in social situations appropriately. In general, they appear depressed, as do the parents. Their hopeless and helpless feelings have often been described as precursors to abusing the child. The child who is at risk is one who will not respond to the parents' needs or to their instructions to be quiet and not to bother them. Rather, they demand attention from their parents who are in a psychologically and emotionally depleted state. The frequent parental history of very minimal parental nurturance and of frequent physical abuse is repeated with the abused child, who may be singled out as the unwanted child for a variety of reasons.

Thus, the abused and neglected children we see usually present as very depressed. The effects of a nurturing and stimulating environment that does not permit the child to get into old circular conflicts with the adults often results in a marked reduction of the depressed affect and beginning sense of hopefulness and pleasure in many activities.

Other abused children present a facade of cheerfulness with very manipulative and hostile-destructive behavior that appear to mask the underlying depression. Thematically in treatment, the hopeless aspects of their feelings may be manifest in the incapacity to trust anyone in the recurring destructive or murderous themes that do not abate for some years. The impulsive aggressive behavior towards others also may be viewed as masked depression as well as a recapitulation of the treatment they have received from parent figures. This case presented here very nicely depicts the clinical picture of one variety of masked depression.

Since the pioneering work of Kempe et al. (1962), child abuse has become recognized as a major medical and social problem. The many aspects of child abuse have been discussed elsewhere. In this chapter, we will present a review and discussion of the definition, epidemiology, and causes of abuse, and a detailed case report of a latency-age girl who is a typical abused child. Depression is a common presenting symptom in abused children. We therefore present this chapter as a clinical example of one type of severe childhood depression and its treatment. We hope that our clinical opinions and approaches can be extrapolated to other abused children, and that the practicing clinician may find our considerations and interventions useful in his or her work with similarly abused children.

DEFINITION

There is little consensus on what comprises abuse. It can be considered a range of behavior, varying from "simple disciplinary measures through uncontrollable angry outbursts, often under the influence of alcohol, to premeditated murderous attacks" (Gil, 1969). Generally, filicide is considered distinct from abuse (Resnick, 1969), though death may result from abuse. It is the opinions of Steele and Pollock (1968) that "direct murder of children is an entirely different phenomenon and is instigated during a single, impulsive act by people who are clearly psychotic." Sexual molestation is also generally excluded from the definition of child abuse. There are indistinct boundaries between righteous disciplinary measures gone awry, deliberate punishment of older children in response to provocative behavior (Gladston, 1965), and purposeful vindictive abuse. For Young (1964), however, there is a clear albeit not frequently clinically noted distinction between abuse and punishment:

> It is the perverse fascination with punishment as an entity in itself, divorced from discipline and even from the fury of revenge. It is the cold calculation of destruction which in itself requires neither provocation nor rationale.

Broader definitions are discussed later. In most studies abuse fits Morse's (1970) definition: "Any willful or grossly careless act on the part of the parent(s) or designated caretaker which resulted in overt physical injury to the child in question."

A third category is accidental physical injury, as described by Malone (1966). These children, the offspring of disorganized families, grow up in an environment of danger and deprivation and have a "heedlessness and general disregard for body care" so that they "trip and fall or stumble into things frequently."

Epidemiology

Epidemiological studies are in fair agreement as to the age and sex of abused children: They are young; the peak age of incidence occurs between 3 months and 3 years (Gelles, 1973). Nineteen of twenty children studied by Elmer and

Gregg were less than 40 months (1967); 20 months was the median age in the Lauer, Broeck, and Grossman report (1974). In another study, 75 percent were 3 years or younger and 50 percent were less than 1 year (Cohen, Raphling, & Green, 1966). Gil's (1969) large study of nearly 6,000 abused children, however, shows 25 percent were 2 years or less, 25 percent were between 2 and 6 years, 25 percent were between 6 and 10 years, and 25 percent were older than 10 years. These data may be misleading, as Gelles (1973) points out. Younger children are more vulnerable to physical damage because they are less durable and more defenseless than older children. The sexes are abused almost equally (Cohen et al., 1966; Elmer & Gregg, 1967; Kempe el al., 1962). In Gil's report slightly more than half were boys.

Incidence reports vary; Gil states that in 1967 a total of 5,993 physically abused children was reported nationwide. In a more recent paper by Solomon (1973), the estimate is 200,000 to 250,000 children based on extrapolated data from California and Colorado. Later, Gil (1975) estimated the upper limits between 2.5 and 4.1 million. Of note is that in New York City the incidence of reporting increased 549 percent once a central registry was established; this suggests the same may be true across the county, i.e., as it becomes more readily recognized and more acceptably reportable, the reports of abuse may rise sharply. This does not necessarily indicate an increased incidence, but may more accurately count a truly high incidence.

Causes

Abuse has a multiplicity of causes. Therefore, it is difficult to tease out its separate causative strands. When left as a whole cloth, discernable patterns emerge as to which children are abused, which parents abuse, and which environments promote or allow abuse to occur.

The Role of the Child

First, there is the fascinating role the child plays in his own abuse. Retrospectively, it has been noted that "retarded and problem children" are frequent victims of abuse and neglect (Morse et al., 1970). By virtue of medical-physical problems (Gil, 1969) and personality-temperament, certain children may be more at risk than others for abuse. Friedrich and Bariskin (1976) provide a good review of this subject. The high-risk child may be conceived premaritally, unwanted, and unplanned (Cohen et al., 1966; Steele & Pollock, 1968), or premature (Elmer & Gregg, 1967.) Case histories are described where the children had medical problems including poor feeding (Cohen et al., 1966), pyloric stenosis (Martin, 1972), mental retardation (Morse et al., 1970), brain damage secondary to herpes encephalitis (Elmer & Gregg, 1967), and schizophrenia (Green, 1968).

These conditions require more than the usual amount of attention and care, may place a financial strain on the family (Gelles, 1973), and may result in a child who is less responsive and rewarding than hoped for (Steele & Pollock, 1968). Mothers of such children may feel inadequate, confused, and out of control (Morse et al., 1970). Simply because he is an infant or toddler and therefore lacks the motor and verbal skills needed for meaningful social interaction that deprived lonely parents require, he may therefore frustrate the parents to the point of physical abuse (Gelles, 1973). And once he has frustrated the parent, he is more vulnerable because he cannot evade the angry parent as could an older child (Lauer et al., 1974).

Often the abused child is singled out as being different from other children. He may be linked in the parent's mind

—consciously or unconsciously—with individuals who are associated with ambivalence and/or rejection; e.g., he may symbolize a despised former lover. Besides being described by parents as "sickly," these children are also said to be "bad," "selfish," "spoiled rotten," and "defiant" (Morse et al., 1970), as well as "evil," "born wicked," and "unlike other children" (Young, 1964). Though the parents may misperceive the child, other less subjective observers find them difficult to manage. The children Milowe and Lourie (1964) describe are those who "were frequently in the cubicle farthest from the nurses' station" and had a "particularly irritable cry." Some nurses think them not only difficult to manage but unappealing (Gladston, 1965). A corroborative item used to support the theory that many abused children are intrinsically different and provocative of abuse, is that some abused children, placed out of their homes, will be abused by foster parents (Milowe & Lourie, 1964).

Of course, there is always the dilemma of whether the cart follows the horse or vice versa. Milowe and Lourie (1964) state the problem succinctly:

> What the added effect of neglect, lack of parental stimulation, and varying amounts of physical pain may have upon the child's irritability is difficult to ascertain. Since these children characteristically also have a developmental lag, we are involved in the difficult area of trying to ascertain whether they were atypical from birth, or if the lack of necessary emotional stimulation, coupled with physical abuse, has made them so unresponsive.

Martin (1972) cites the study of Gregg and Elmer, in which there were "no differences in mood or activity level" between 30 abused children and 83 accidentally injured children. Further, he points out and gives examples that parents' perception of the child may have little correlation with reality. But no child can be used as an adequate excuse or cause for abuse.

The Role of the Parent

Here, too, a recognizable pattern is woven from the threads of the parents' personal and social identities, family history, and mental set.

Generally, the abusing parent is young (Cohen et al., 1966; Gladston, 1965; Lauer et al., 1974; Steele & Pollock, 1968). Moreover, he or she is immature and is overwhelmed by and unable to take up adult responsibilities (Morse et al., 1970). The educational level is low (Gladston, 1965; Gil, 1969). Often the abusing parent is isolated and estranged from the community (Cohen et al., 1966; Green et al., 1974; Steele & Pollock, 1968; Young, 1964). There may be a reversal in the husband-wife role, with the wife leaving the home as the breadwinner and the husband remaining at home as the babysitter (Gladston).

Families in which abuse tends to occur are deviant and disruptive, frequently mobile (Lauer et al., 1974; Martin, 1972) not intact (Morse et al., 1970), headed by females (Gil, 1969), and characterized by alcoholism (Young, 1964). Or, the marriage may be stable by partners who cling to each other out of fear of loneliness (Steele & Pollock, 1968). Young (1964) found that the parents may be set into a well-established aggressor-victim conflict between themselves. The aggressive partner dominates the passive partner by evoking fear. The victim defends the aggressor, denies the abuse—even when it befalls a child— and clings to the aggressor.

Often the abusive parents were themselves abused (Cohen et al., 1966; Gil, 1969; Spinetta & Rigler, 1972; Steele & Pollock, 1968; Young, 1964). The current history parallels the parents' past history. A developmental deviation occurs and repeats itself from generation to generation. Morris and Gould (1963) summarize the process: "Relationship learning appears fixed at brutal experiences with their own parents, without modification from later relationships or observations of relationships." The original parents did not satisfy and could not be satisfied; the abusive parents do not satisfy and cannot be satisfied (Steele & Pollock, 1968). In fact, the abusive parents have unrealistic expectations of their offspring, expectations that cannot be satisfied. They look upon the infant or child as an adult who will provide meaning to their lives, gratify their needs and wishes, love them totally, and perform perfectly. This is the role reversal in which the parent wishes to be the dependent child and wishes the child to be the caretaking adult (Morris & Gould, 1963). Conjointly, since the child is viewed as an adult, he is seen as having the adult attributes of purposeful deliberate behavior and judgment (Gladston, 1965). So, the child is at risk for abuse if he does not gratify the parent, "deliberately" displeases and antagonizes the parent, or evokes the parent's envy and retaliation. Or, the child may be seen as a threat to the parent, displacing the parent from the comfortable, sought-after dependent position (Cohen et al., 1966).

Several authors have described a sense of righteousness that the parents have about "disciplining" their offspring (Steele & Pollock, 1968). Morris and Gould (1963) talk of the abusing parents' view that brutality from their own parents was "good" (retrospectively) and that it is now their "own natural prerogative in dealing with the dependency of their infants."

Abuse may be culturally permitted. Childrearing practices and the use of physical punishment or force vary among different ethnic, national, and social groups. Further, there being no "clear-cut legal prohibition and sanctions against this particular form of interpersonal violence" (Gil, 1969) may encourage its prevalence.

Finally, the abusing parents may be naive about the social and moral injunctions against child abuse; "they seemed unaware that there was anything wrong with their behavior or that others might find it reprehensible" (Young, 1964).

The question must be asked: What is the mental set of the abusive parent? It has been described as composed of emotional disturbances, mental retardation (Morse et al., 1970; Young, 1964), severe personality disorders (Gil, 1969), psychosis (Young, 1964), and developmental deviations (as noted above). Since the early 1960s a change of thinking has occurred in considering this question. Initially, the tendency was to regard all abusive parents as psychotic. As Gelles (1973) states, the predominant model has been that "the parent who abused suffers from a psychological pathology or sickness that accounts for abusing or battering a child." Now the trend is to see the majority of them as having personality defects that result in the release of aggressive impulses. To bring order out of confusion, Green, Gaines, and Sandgrund (1974) list six personality characteristics: reliance of the parent on the child to gratify parental dependency needs, impaired impulse control, poor self-concept, shifting identities dominated by hostile introjects, defensive use of projections and externalization, and misperception of the child.

The major proponents of the psychodynamic theory of abuse have been Helfer (1973) and Steele and Pollock (1968). Because of their monumental contributions to the understanding of child abuse, these authors and their theories will be reviewed separately.

Steele and Pollock in their classic paper state clearly that the demographic, social, and economic factors are somewhat irrelevant to the act of abuse. "Probably the crux of the problem of distinguishing the non-abusing from the abusing parent lies in the fact that in the latter when there is significant environmental and intrapsychic stress, with a contest between ego ideal and superego, the punitive superego wins out." Though the parents in their study came from all socioeconomic strata and had a heterogenous psychopathology, all of them "without exception" were raised in the same style that they were now raising their own children. They lacked basic mothering, in the sense of showing and being shown tenderness, gentleness, empathy. The original parents were excessively critical and demanding, expecting the child to perform tasks he could neither comprehend nor accomplish. When the child failed, as he inevitably did, he learned to feel unloved, disregarded, and unsure of himself, without basic trust. He came to identify with the insufficient and punitive mother. Because as a child his aggressive drives were frequently directed toward his insufficient mother and because, through identification, he had the rudiments of a strict superego, he felt guilt over these aggressive impulses and turned them inward against the self. Hence, he is as an adult depressed and has low self-esteem.

These identifications persist into his adulthood. The abused parent looks to *his* child as the last source of care and comfort, the abused parent "misidentifies the infant as the embodiment of his own bad self" and turns abusive, directing the aggression of his punitive superego against his own child. The process repeats itself from generation to generation.

For Helfer (1973), three components are necessary for abuse to occur: the potential for abuse; a very special kind of child; a crisis or series of crises. Subsumed under the first are several considerations: How was the parent himself raised? (Almost invariably he experienced poor early parenting.) What is the parent's ability to seek outside help when he's "uptight" with his children? What is the marital relationship? (Can the spouse come to the aid of the distressed parent?) How does the parent view the child? (Does he expect too much, too soon from the offspring?)

Gladston (1965) sees the abuse syndrome as a "transference psychosis" in which the parents, who otherwise show no other major psychotic symptoms, have a "circumscribed distortion in the perception of a particular child at a particular stage in its development." Along the same line is Milowe and Lourie's (1964) observation that some parents and children seem to have excellent relationships "until particular times in the life of the child, when the dynamics of the child's stage of development corresponded with problem areas in the parents' own lives. This seems often to determine at what age a particular child gets battered."

But the argument to the whole psychodynamic theory of abuse is that *no specific abuse personality exists*. In fact, and this is made abundantly clear by the above researchers themselves, the causes of abuse are multifactorial. There is more to abuse than either the child or the parent.

THE ROLE OF THE ENVIRONMENT

The third major etiological factor is the environment, specifically the socioeconomic class and individual or collective crises. Abuse reportedly occurs predominantly in low socioeconomic families (Elmer & Gregg, 1967; Gelles, 1973; Morris & Gould, 1963). However, this reported high incidence may be falsely elevated. More abuse than is reported may occur in middle- and upper-class families. Private physicians who tend to see these latter families are less likely to report suspected abuse than are doctors working in public clinics, and hospitals likewise have greater hesitation in taking action against middle-class families (Young, 1964).

Gil (1969) places the ultimate responsibility and cause of abuse within society itself. He looked upon abuse as an aspect of the poverty life-style and thought poverty simultaneously generates extra stresses and diminishes coping mechanism. Later (1975), he broadly expands his definition of abuse. Abuse occurs and is measured by the deficit between where the child actually is and where, with optimal development, he ought to be. It is the gap between actualization and potential. It is "conceived of as inflicted deficits on a child's right to develop freely and fully and occurs on three levels—in the home, in institutions, and in society." In an all-encompassing view, Gil believes abuse is caused by an interplay of factors:

> social philosophy and value premises of a society, its social, economic, and political institutions, and the quality of human relations to which these institutions, philosophy and values give rise.

The argument to the social theory of abuse is that "the great majority of deprived families do not abuse their children" (Spinetta & Rigler, 1972). And some well-to-do parents engage in child abuse. In short, abuse crosses class lines.

Many authors have noted that environmental stress seems to precipitate abuse (Cohen et al., 1966; Gladston, 1965; Gil, 1969; Milowe & Lourie, 1964; Morse et al., 1970; Steele & Pollock, 1968). The immediate precipitating event might be a difficult feeding, irritability on the child's part, a toilet-training mishap, the breakdown of the family washing machine, loss of job, the breakdown of family arrangements. According to Steele and Pollock (1968), the attack may occur when the one parent feels rejected or deserted by the other. They believe the parent wants to do right by his child, but may attack him when something either increases his low self-esteem and feeling of being unloved or prevents his successful care-taking attempts. The child becomes the easy target on which the parent vents his hostilities, anxieties, and frustrations. Justice and Duncan

(1976), using Holmes' and Rahe's Social Readjustment Rating Scale, have found that abusive parents, as compared to nonabusive parents, undergo too much change too fast, that they have a decreased ability to cope with a series of life stresses, and are therefore at greater risk of losing control.

Gelles (1973) attempts to explain the causes of abuse by his sociopsychological model. For him, abuse is an adaptation to stress. The abusive parent often was himself abused as a child. Hence, he has learned to use force and violence as a means of problem solving. "It is the way he knows of responding to stress and bringing up his child."

Case Illustration

Jennifer is, we believe, the eldest of her mother Marie's four children. She was born in March 1970 when her mother was 17 years old. (When Marie was 16 she reportedly was pregnant by her own father through rape, but we do not know how that pregnancy ended, whether in abortion or childbirth.) Children born after Jennifer are two brothers, Sam in 1972 and James in 1973, and one sister, Brandy in 1975. Each had a different father.

The family has been known over several generations to several social agencies in the medium-sized city where they lived. Complaints of general neglect involved Protective Services in 1971, when Jennifer was a year old. Twice the police found Jennifer, then a toddler, wandering the streets, and returned her home. Finally, in the early summer of 1973, she and her brother, Sam, were removed from the home, after Marie had called her welfare worker, saying that Jennifer was sick and asking him to take her to the doctor. He arrived at the house to find that Marie apparently had changed her mind and did not wish his help; she was cool and detached. The worker found Jennifer bruised and harnessed to a chair. Marie at first excused the bruising as accidental and then claimed that Jennifer's stepfather had beaten her with a two-inch-wide leather strap to correct her misbehavior. Authorities removed the two children that day, and Jennifer was taken to the hospital.

There she was found to have multiple (some 20) ecchymoses on her extremities, back, abdomen, and face. Her two upper incisors were missing, and she had a subconjunctival hemorrhage and deep scratches on her face. Her weight plotted between 25 and 50 percentile for her age and her height 50 percentile. In general she was described as well developed. Neurologically she was intact, and radiographs of her skull, ribs, long bones, pelvis, and shoulder girdle showed no fractures. Scant nursing notes state "very quiet—will not talk," "cheerful," "up and about ward," and "had a good appetite." No psychological evaluations or further behavioral observations were made at the time of that brief hospitalization.

Upon leaving the hospital, Jennifer—and Sam—spent several months at a receiving home. Then Sam was returned to the care of Marie, but Jennifer was relinquished by her mother who had been charged with failure to prevent abuse to minors; it seems that she viewed her daughter as a troublemaker and was glad to be rid of her. It was as though by giving up this one child she might appease the authorities who periodically and persistently intervened in the management of her household. In a court-ordered report to a psychologist, she complained that Jennifer was "hyperactive" and that she had to restrain her to keep her from running into the street or playing with the gas stove jets. She wanted treatment for Jennifer so that she'd "improve in her activity level and be taught to mind." Sam, on the other hand, was viewed as a good and placid child. It was the psychologist's impression that Marie was overwhelmed by responsibility.

A senario of neglect, if not of abuse, has continued. Twice more Marie has been cited for neglect of her children and recently the remaining three were removed temporarily from the home. Sam was seen by a psychologist who assessed him as having "infantile depression"; his speech is unclear and delayed; and he stares off into space. According to welfare records, this is "at least the third generation in which physical beatings were the principal means of behavior shaping." Marie's mother was known to the Court as an abuser.

Jennifer was tested by a psychologist at 3 years, 3 months, and scored 2 years, 6 months on the Stanford-Benet. Her IQ overall was 76, but the tester noted that the score might be underestimated by 10 points. On the Vinline Social Maturity Scale she was 2 years, 10 months, and had a social quotient of 85. At the testing session she cried and appeared withdrawn and frightened. She was not judged hyperactive, attended well to the tasks, was not unduly distracted, and was easily entertained. Her vocabulary was limited; she associated words together at the 2-to-3-year-old level; she had some echolalia and perseveration.

Jennifer lived in a foster home for over a year. Descriptions of her behavior at that time come from several sources. Her foster mother placed her general behavior at the 2- or 2½-year level. Her speech at first was practically unintelligible; she was withdrawn. At night while asleep she covered her face with a clenched fist, as though to ward off blows. She abused her dolls, hitting them and tearing off their heads and limbs while wearing a tense smile. When reprimanded, she would flinch and punish herself by slapping her face or head, and picking at her arms 'til they bled. She demanded the constant attention of anyone around her. When a new baby came into the foster home, she became enuretic. She used eating in a manipulative way to gain attention, eating either too much or too little. She would wander off at any time, including the night if left alone. If she did something that displeased herself, she would hit her head or whirl repeatedly. One of her case workers, reflecting on these times, says, "Jennifer drove me up a wall because she wanted me to be with her all the time. She was extremely angry if I wanted to talk to her parents, and when I did, she'd become sticky affectionate, maudlin ... She talked about hostile angry parents who beat up on kids and asked people—anyone—to take her home to live. She would say, 'I want to go to an empty house.' "

Jennifer was sad and eager to please. But her life remained in flux. In her 4th year she was placed in the home of a childless couple, the Dales, who were themselves eager to love and adopt a child. The mother made a list of problem behaviors that Jennifer exhibited in various degrees of intensity from the time she began living with them through the time she began treatment: enuresis day and night, running away from home when angry, poor speech, self-injury, especially hitting her face. She destroyed all her dolls except one. She had little self-control and was constantly running, rocking, and interrupting conversations to the point that relatives and friends asked her parents not to visit or come by because she could not be controlled. She appeared indifferent to animals and did not even acknowledge the death of the family dog. She seemed to have an intense interest in fires and would stare at the fireplace flames and spoke about a real fire at her former foster home as though she had been there, when she had not. She was harshly overbearing with other children; her preschool teacher noted that when she touched her classmates, they thought she was shoving and were frightened and shied away from her. By the time the Dales sought help they were "grasping at straws," totally exhausted from the 24-hours-a-day job of caring for Jennifer.

Jennifer presented an unusual first impression to the man who was to become her long-term therapist. She was then a 6-year-old slender blond girl with large blue eyes, pink cheeks, and a clear complexion. She was pretty and stylishly dressed, but had odd mannerisms. At their first meeting she goose-stepped rapidly into the center of the office, spun around, and slapped herself vigorously on top of her head. She fixed the therapist with an intent stare and stated clearly, "Doctor, I just can't say it."

The issue that lay before the clinician, her prospective parents, and the adoption agency was: Had the severity and intensity of the abuse and neglect brought about potentially irreversible damage to this child? If Jennifer was reparable, the Dales were eager to adopt her. If not, they would give her up. Each of them, as well as the adoption agency, had tremendous investment in making the treatment successful and the adoption workable.

Jennifer's potentially adoptive parents were in their late 30s, middle-class, hard-working, and Christian in attitude. Their marriage was childless. Mr. Dale had previously been married to a reportedly schizophrenic woman who had threatened suicide repeatedly and who had literally kidnapped their daughter (who, ironically, was also named Jennifer). As a result Mr. Dale had lost his wife and daughter and was estranged from his family of origin. For her own self-esteem, Mrs. Dale badly needed to mother a child successfully. The couple had earlier adopted an infant boy from the same agency who was now handling Jennifer. After having him three months, he was found to be mentally retarded and was returned. The agency assured the Dales that Jennifer was traumatized but basically normal. In turn, the Dales emphatically stated they were not prepared to cope with an "emotionally disturbed child."

The child's twirling, self-injury, odd interpersonal manner of thought processes suggested a borderline psychotic state. Thorazine, 75 mg at bedtime was prescribed, with immediate and dramatic improvement. Her gait became normal, her twirling ceased, and her interpersonal function improved somewhat. The Dales were delighted; their spirits lifted. They hoped this was the kind of improvement that would occur as a consequence of therapy and looked forward to having a normal child in their family.

Most of her play in play therapy was mundane. She simply reenacted ordinary household scenes in a bland fashion, with occasional interruption to check the room for "monsters." Her drawings, play, and verbalizations, while not indicating gross psychotic content or process, were collage-like and had no clear organizing theme. During therapy she was pleasant, cooperative, and well-mannered. She manipulatively delayed terminating the hour.

At home, Jennifer became increasingly demanding and difficult. She learned to play the parents against each other. During the day she was tyrannical with her mother; in the evening she was cooperative with her father. On one occasion she became so provocative that her patient, long-suffering Christian mother slapped her across the face, and was instantly remorseful, remembering the source of Jennifer's difficulty in the first place—abuse. Finally Mrs. Dale, in a fine idea born of frustration, suggested that a woman therapist was also needed, that Jennifer was "all right when a man is around, since her troubles were with her mother and all her misbehavior is with me." At this point, following 6 months of individual sessions with her male therapist, a female therapist joined the therapy.

Jennifer's play regressed to the infancy stage. She baby-talked, drank water from a bottle, and sat stiffly in the female doctor's lap. Occasionally she would arrange disasters for her dolls: auto accidents, sickness, and death would befall them. She always brought in an ambulance and administered aid, but the outcome was usually fatal. One session a handful of marbles accidentally rolled underneath the playroom door into the hall beyond. Jennifer grinned at the sight and proceeded to scatter the rest of the marbles across the floor and under the door. It seemed symbolically to fit her scattered state well. It was at this time that Mrs. Dale reported two instances in which Jennifer had asked her if she'd seen the "bad girl." This bad girl was making Jennifer misbehave, she said, in a description that set it apart from the usual fantasized childhood companion. She remained on the Thorazine.

The child's behavior deteriorated, the Dales became more weary and ambivalent. A conflict emerged and grew between them. Mr. Dale did not see Jennifer's tyrannical behavior toward his wife. She, in turn, felt unsupported, misunderstood, and wrongfully blamed for failure to continue to accept Jennifer's insincere, manipulative, and demanding behavior. A videotape was made to illustrate this to the father, and conflicting parental views led to conjoint family sessions. Whereas initially Mrs. Dale had tried to reach Jennifer through warm physical intimacy (hugging, holding), she now tried to appeal to Jennifer in a pleading rational way. She looked exhausted. Indeed, she never left Jennifer except for one 1-hour-a-week art lecture. Valium was prescribed for Mrs. Dale. Mr. Dale was isolated and participated minimally in the sessions. A blank unchanging joyless grin seemed to be covering increasing pain as he faced the possibility of yet another loss. Jennifer jockeyed for a more secure position with each parent by appealing to them in an animated but mechanical way.

Therapy was interrupted when the three went to visit Mr. Dale's family in a distant state. A successful visit was crucial because it would test Jennifer's ability to gratify the Dales' need and wishes in front of Mr. Dale's family. Jennifer did present herself to some of the relatives as a delightful, endearing child, but continued her tyrannical attacks on Mrs. Dale in private. On their return from the vacation, Jennifer became obstinate, ran off a short distance from their campsite to sit by herself on a tree stump in the pouring rain, and went on a three-day hunger strike.

Caught between a wish to care for her adequately on the one hand and anger at being manipulated on the other, the prospective parents were increasingly morose, depressed, ambivalent, and immobile. The therapy metaphor became that of two parents sitting on a narrow ledge above a precipice, wondering how much longer they could endure. The adoption paper lay openly in the house, unsigned, a visible reminder of their ambivalence and of Jennifer's insecure position and future in their home.

Finally, a veritable ton of bricks broke the camel's back. One afternoon Jennifer began raiding the refrigerator. Disgusted with her voracious, insatiable eating, Mrs. Dale came to the end of her Job-like patience and left the house. Mr. Dale stood by, in disbelieving attendance, as Jennifer ate all the food in the refrigerator, regurgitated it, ate the vomitus, and regurgitated again. He later claimed he was simply powerless to stop this behavior. It was as though he needed as dramatic a demonstration as this to convince him of Jennifer's abnormality.

Hope for normality was gone for both the Dales. Shortly after this incident, the Dales, together at last in their perception of Jennifer, requested that she be removed from their home. However, so great was their continued attachment to her that in the midst of planning her departure, they moved her into the biggest, sunniest bedroom.

Placement was arranged at a residential treatment center, where the consulting psychiatrist described her as "far and away the sickest kid in the place."

With this resolution of her living situation, Jennifer's play therapy changed dramatically. She became organized and presented two themes that replaced the earlier mundane repetition of daily events that had occupied her play. The new themes were a vain search conducted by the therapists for a missing cat, a part skillfully played by Jennifer, and a flood of monsters who besieged all three. At first these imagined monsters were so frightening that Jennifer allowed them to come no closer than the outside office window. Over a period of months she perceived them as more manageable and allowed them to approach. In one memorable session the three cowered in a corner of the playroom, hidden behind a wall of chairs, as the monsters came closer and closer. Then Jennifer announced that one of them had gained entry into the enclosure! She named him "Fedder" and took him on as a household pet. A part of the beast had been tamed.

A third theme came into play, in which the female therapist played a mean witch. Jennifer, alternating between "good" and "bad" roles, would "melt" the witch, then bring her back to life. Once, in the midst of this play, she picked up a small heavy metal object from the floor and hurled it directly toward (and past) the female therapist's face. Immediately Jennifer froze. The play stopped and the clinician said to her in a firm tone, "You must not do that." Jennifer turned away, her body rigid. Through clenched teeth she stated with great intensity, "When I do that I could kill myself." The therapist gently touched her shoulder and asked if she wanted to talk about it. She did not respond. A short time later Jennifer resumed the play, but maintained a controlled and detached manner for the remainder of the session.

During this period, after about one year of therapy, she became increasingly uncontrollable in the waiting room. She had always used her striking good looks and lively manner to charm the secretarial staff. Now she turned her charm toward the waiting adult patients, and hustled free drinks at the vending machine. Then she discovered an open jar of Tang in the staff lounge. She loudly and angrily resisted her therapists' initial attempts to keep her from barging into the lounge and helping herself to cups of the powder, which she would convert with modest adding of water into a thick sludge. Management of this sticky food became a central theme of the play. For several sessions the therapists sought to grab her cup of Tang, which Jennifer held just out of reach, gleeful at the therapists' howls of frustration. At the outset of the fifth of these sessions, she turned to a large waiting room audience, loudly announced that she'd brought a second cup for the doctor, and proudly handed him a cup of the sludge.

Toward the end of these sessions she began to devote brief periods to play with a playhouse and dolls. Themes of child abuse, child neglect, child abandonment, men who came in the night to sleep with the mother, and brutalization of all family members (except the midnight male callers) were enacted. Jennifer alternately identified with identical twin female dolls, one who was "good" and one who was "bad."

Two changes occurred at the end of 15 months of therapy. The male therapist moved to a new office across town, while the female therapist moved to a nearby town and stopped seeing Jennifer on a regular basis. Jennifer spent the first sessions at the new office exploring it and vigorously expressing her resentment over limits set on her explorations.

As of this writing, Jennifer has settled on three themes in her play: child abuse and abandonment, hiding from monsters, and careful observation of the therapist to see if he is ready to "go home forever."

Discussion

In the 18 months of therapy, Jennifer has almost always maintained an air of fixed cheerfulness. But her poignant comment, "I want to go to an empty house," reveals her inner state.

We find it useful to differentiate two processes at work in Jennifer. First, she had suffered physical trauma and internal and external losses since early development. Understandably, she manages interpersonal relationships with a manipulative, superficial, and seductive behavior that allows contact with others but minimizes the chances for intimacy. Second, she occasionally strives for or is enticed into brief contacts of genuine intimacy. She responds to this intimacy with fear and rage, and it is this fear and rage that temporarily sends her spiraling into a recognition of self-hate, hopelessness, and helplessness. As she said, having hurled the object at the therapist during the witch play, "When I do that, I could kill myself."

Steele and Pollock (1968), based on their extensive clinical experience, report that battering parents frequently have a deep underlying depression. Here we come full circle. In these parents, as with Jennifer, the classic theory seemed to be upheld: Violence-outward has its violence-inward counterpart in the form of depression. Child abuse occurs from generation to generation. The burning question is, will Jennifer grown up to be a battering mother? For motherhood *is* an intimate encounter. On recent walks in the office's neighborhood, Jennifer has chanced upon a domestic cat. She has tried to pet this cat, who is a stranger and not too pleased with Jennifer's attention. When the cat attempts to leave Jennifer, she squeezes the animal hard, with force, to keep him by her side. It is obvious to the observer that at that point Jennifer cannot decide whether to pet or abuse the cat.

Perhaps "depression" is less useful here than that persistent, but often maligned, term, *depressive equivalent.* If this illusive concept could be defined with sufficient rigor, it may have considerable clinical value. We propose the following criteria for a depressive equivalent:

1. Is not accompanied by depressive affect, either observed or reported, and which
2. The perception that the self-environment relationship is hopeless and that the individual is helpless to change matters.

Jennifer's aggressiveness may therefore be conceptualized as a depressive equivalent since she is hopeless in the face of a horde of angry monsters who have wrecked havoc in her life and she is helpless to tame them. She is at risk to enact her hopeless-helpless perception with violence. Tragically, self-recrimination and the development of the classically described "punitive super-ego" seem to follow. As Anthony (1975, pp. 257-259) stated, "this ego psychology has a number of advantages that seem especially pertinent to the childhood situation . . . hopelessness is the bread and butter of childhood and a constant existential experience coupled with humiliation, and any theory that concentrates on it is speaking very much to the condition of childhood . . . all the metapsychological difficulties associated with the operation of classic theory—oral fixation and incorporation, aggression against the self—are here given merely a peripheral or complicating role. *The child's depression can assimilate them later when he becomes an adult.*" (Italics added.)

Her development of a close friendship, the disappearance of severe symptomatology (hallucinations, destroying dolls, abnormal gait, and self-mutilation), her progressive willingness to name and tame her monsters in play, and the clear emergence of nurturing characteristics in play and interpersonal relationships demonstrate impressive progress. Yet, the reversability of Jennifer's depression is greatly in question. In contrast to youngsters discussed elsewhere in this book, Jennifer suffers pain that is less accessible. Her depression is not only less reversible, but its release is potentially harmful. She has diminished capacity to meet the enormous tasks of facing, owning, and reintegrating her fear and rage.

The dilemma of treatment is to achieve intimacy without triggering the sequence of destructive responses: anger directed outward followed by anger directed inward.

Jennifer's fixed smile, manipulative style, and bright-eyed good looks present the antithesis of "depression" as commonly defined. The therapist must be prepared to respond whenever and wherever to her basic conceptualization of her self-environment relationship. In this task, "depression" may not be a perceptible affect but is an indispensible clinical tool.

REFERENCES

Anthony, E. J. Childhood Depression. Anthony, E. J. & Benedek, T. (Eds.), *Depression and Human Existence.* Boston: Little, Brown, 1975.

Cohen, M. I., Raphling, D. L., & Green, P. E. Psychological aspects of the maltreatment syndrome in childhood. *Journal of Pediatrics,* 1966, *69,* 279.

Elmer, E., & Gregg, G. Developmental characteristics of abused children. *Pediatrics,* 1967, *40,* 596.

Friedrich, W. N., & Boriskin, J. S. The role of the child in abuse: A review of the literature. *American Journal of Orthopsychiatry,* 1976, *46,* 580.

Gladston, R. Observations on children who have been physically abused and their parents. *American Journal of Psychiatry,* 1965, *122,* 440.

Gelles, R. J. Child abuse as psychopathology: A sociological critique and reformulation. *American Journal of Orthopsychiatry,* 1973, *43,* 611.

Gil, D. G. Physical abuse of children: Findings and implications of a nationwide survey. *Pediatrics,* 1969, *44,* 857.

Gil, D. G. Unraveling child abuse. *American Journal of Orthopsychiatry,* 1975, *45,* 346.

Green, A. H. Self-destructive behavior in physically abused schizophrenic children. *Archives of General Psychiatry,* 1968, *19,* 171.

Green, A. H., Gaines, R. W., & Sandgrund, A. Child abuse: Pathological syndrome of family interaction. *American Journal of Psychiatry,* 1974, *131,* 882.

Helfer, R. N. The etiology of child abuse. *Pediatrics,* 1973, *51,* 777.

Justice, B., & Duncan, D. F. Life Crisis as a Precursor to Child Abuse. *Public Health Report,* 1976, *91,* 110.

Kempe, C. H., Silverman, P. N., Steele, B. F., Droegemeuller, W., & Silver, H. K. The battered child syndrome. *Journal of the American Medical Association,* 1962, *181,* 17.

Lauer, B., Broeck, E. J., & Grossman, M. Battered child syndrome: Review of 130 patients with controls. *Pediatrics,* 1974, *54,* 67.

Malone, C. A. Safety first: Comments on the influence of external danger in the lives of children of disorganized families. *American Journal of Orthopsychiatry,* 1966, *36,* 3.

Martin, H. The child and his development. In C. H. Kempe & R. E. Helfer (Eds.), *Helping the battered child and his family.* Philadelphia: J. B. Lippincott, 1972, pp. 93–114.

Milowe, I. D., & Lourie, R. S. The child's role in the battered child syndrome. *Journal of Pediatrics,* 1964, *65,* 1079.

Morris, M. G., & Gould, R. W. Neglected children. Role reversal: A necessary concept in dealing with the "battered child syndrome." *American Journal of Orthopsychiatry,* 1963, *33,* 298.

Morse, C. W., Sahler, O. J., & Friedman, S. W. A three year follow-up study of abused and neglected children. *American Journal of Diseases of Children,* 1970, *120,* 439.

Resnick, P. J. Child murder by parents: A psychiatric review of filicide. *American Journal of Psychiatry,* 1969, 126, 325.

Solomon, T. History and demography of child abuse. *Pediatrics,* 1973, *51,* 773.

Spinetta, J. J., & Rigler, D. The child-abusing parent: A psychological review. *Psychological Bulletin,* 1972, *77,* 296.

Steele, B. F., & Pollock, C. B. A psychiatric study of parents who abuse infants and small children. In R. E. Helfer, & C. H. Kempe (Eds.), *The battered child.* Chicago: University of Chicago Press, 1968, pp. 103–147.

Young, L. R. *Wednesday's children: A study of child neglect and abuse.* New York: McGraw-Hill, 1964.

Chapter 11

THERAPY VIGNETTES

Harold Boverman
Alfred P. French

The following case vignettes are examples of various constellations of depressions. They are illustrative of the many different clinical pictures all subsumed under the diagnostic label of "depression."

A clinician rarely sees a "pure culture" of any disease entity, and illustrative case examples are rarely of crystalline clarity. Perhaps a sorrowful latency-age boy is too convenient a case. Each case is a new research project, as well as an opportunity for treatment; the term *depression* has no value unless it is a flexible clinical tool, useful in a wide variety of situations. In this section, the total field of depressed children will be divided into four major categories, by means of two general concepts, around which examples of treatment can cluster: First, there is the *intensity-severity* dimension. Here the *degree* of disturbance of the specific lines of psychological development and of intra- and interpersonal resources are considered; we can also consider the development of the sense of hopelessness-helplessness in order to plan treatment. The second dimension is the *degree of reversibility* of the developmental disturbance. These two dimensions, reversibility and severity, require that we present four types of cases: severe and not readily treated, mild and not readily treated, severe and readily treated, and mild and readily treated. These considerations arise from our convictions that understanding and treating the depressions of childhood can only come from a *multidimensional* approach. In addition, treatment must be *multileveled;* the dimensions of intensity and reversibility may be applied to phenomena on the biological, psychological, familial, or social level.

Severe and not Readily Treated

A 14-year-old girl, Judy, had been living in a well-managed residential treatment center for several months when the counselors requested psychiatric consultation. They reported wide mood swings; at the high extreme Judy slept seldom and briefly, shouted, sang and disturbed the staff and other residents at all hours, and charged about the quarters day and night with seemingly inexhaustible energy. She reported feeling "absolutely great" during these times. The low extreme presented the staff with a heap of blankets beneath which, curled up, could be found a withdrawn and hopeless Judy who expressed self-deprecatory comments and suicidal ideation. The staff responded to these extremes as flexibly as possible, condoning in the name of sympathy the broken furniture, which followed Judy's wake during her high phase and spending great amounts of time supporting, reassuring, and consoling her during her low phase.

Keenly aware of the use of lithium in the management of manic-depressive disorder, the staff informed Judy that staying at the center would be contingent upon her agreeing to accept a therapeutic trial of lithium. As her serum levels of lithium rose, the mood swings disappeared; but the cure was limited to the biological level. Judy dramatically and triumphantly presented innumerable side effects, complained of "being poisoned by a crazy shrink," and howled with pain during the necessary venipunctures. She angrily protested, "I'm losing all my power." In this case, we have a severe, but readily reversible, biological, manic-depressive disorder, which was obviously the least of our management problems. Clearly, this manic-depressive process had been built into a life-style. It appeared that loss of the coping maneuvers that were built around the manic-depressive disorder led to a reactive depression and we speculated about a deeper, underlying process (probably including a depressive component) that led Judy to use manic-depressive disorder as a primary coping tool. This latter depression seemed to be severe and minimally reversible. We noted in retrospect that the treatment of manic-depressive disorder had been *done to,* rather than *carried out with* Judy.

Mary was an unwanted infant, raised by her mother under deprived conditions. In infancy she cried pitiously and inconsolably when wet, tired, or hungry. She refused to play and became a hyperactive toddler. By the time she was 3, she had been treated repeatedly for unexplained bruises before physical abuse by her mother was recognized. At 9, she began individual psychiatric treatment, which proceeded slowly because of her distractability, staring episodes, and unwillingness (or inability?) to follow through the thoughts or action. In addition, treatment was periodically distracted by an endless battle for her custody. Almost every line of psychological development had been traumatized and distorted at every important stage of her short life span, from the earliest beginning of the development of the sense of trust to the subsequent development of a sense of self and a sense of mastery. Important people in her life were, at best, disinterested; at worst, hostile and negative. Even her special relationship with her therapist was traumatized by disorganization in her caretaking environment and by her own difficult behavior.

At 9, Mary could hardly express her wants and deal effectively with her world; she could not begin to find pride in her own competence. She was still learning about herself in her own elementary ways. Preoccupation with issues of separation prevented development of cooperative play, the capacity to delay gratification, and the ability to work through conflicts to mutual resolution. She seemed so overwhelmed that she could hardly play alone; she could not be included in simple table games, follow rules, or participate in group play. These developmental problems made it impossible for her to use play as an outlet for healthy drive expression. She could neither impose appropriate limits on her own impulses nor gracefully accept limits imposed by others. She apparently did not recognize that she might develop useful self-control and other helpful regulatory mechanisms. Her use of language was aggressive, hostile, and loaded with street jargon, reflecting her perception that control of her impulses originates from a punitive environment.

In this case, the complex of psychological forces leading to the development of an affirmative sense of self have been consistently sabotaged, diverted, and distorted. Even if she had been optimally prepared for a healthy development on the biological level, the trauma to her development would have been overwhelming.

MILD AND NOT READILY TREATED

Elsewhere in this book, the case of Bobby, who was quite disappointed and angry that his mother did not invite Tony to his birthday party, was presented. Bobby's depression was not blatantly obvious, and his life situation was stable. From his developmental history, we inferred that his development of an affirmative sense of self had been traumatized by his small size and clumsiness as well as by repeated losses of important relationships. At the time of intake, Bobby's depression was not incapacitating; yet his reluctance to actively engage his current environment (reflected, for example, in the great tentativeness with which he shared with us the crucial information that "Mommy didn't invite Tony to my birthday party") presented an urgent need for treatment. At that point, it appeared that the developmental traumas had resulted in such sufficient distortion of his development that individual therapy was indicated, while keeping a "weather eye" out for any indication that the family would be uncomfortable with resulting changes.

Severe and Readily Treated

A normal, happy 4-year-old girl in a normal family developed typhoid fever and was hospitalized; her illness required isolation, to which she responded with the usual sequence of protest, despair, and withdrawal. The situation was complicated by discovery that her dog was the primary carrier, which was followed by the necessary destruction of the animal. The psychiatrist was asked how the transition to a new dog should be handled. The parents were advised to visit the child as often as possible during the hospitalization, to respect the rate at which their daughter would emerge from her reactive depression, to wait for her to raise questions about the missing animal, to answer these questions in a direct, straightforward manner without elaboration, and to await the child's anticipated interest in a new animal. The parents later reported a normal child who had formed a strong attachment to a new pet.

A 9-year-old boy, John, was adopted at two weeks of age. When he was 2 years old, a "natural" brother was born. John was diagnosed as "hyperactive" and stimulant medication was prescribed at the age of 6 because of his temper tantrums, clowning, aimless destruction, poor school performance, and continuous squealing and wiggling. Almost overnight there was a dramatic shift in his ability to acquire and retain school related skills and knowledge. Nevertheless, his social behavior remained unacceptable and his school work was never good enough. By the time he was 8 years old, he was at home more than he was at school; his most notable misbehavior was urinating on another boy.

Individual psychotherapy focused on development of a therapeutic alliance and observing ego through a dialogue facilitated by play and board games. The medication was gradually withdrawn. The parents were encouraged to be carefully consistent in their actions with John, and to be candid and forthright in their responses to his misbehavior. Teachers were incensed when they learned that the medication was being discontinued and the parents were supported in their struggles with the school.

Initially, John was listless and preoccupied with complaints about his brother and other children, complaining that he was picked on by his parents and teachers. Feeling sad and sorry for himself, he found comfort in food and fantasy. His original play themes concerned the control of monsters; eventually it was possible to discuss the "monster" in him which the therapist conceptualized as the intolerable pain of uncontrollable incompleteness. This depressive affect was worked through again and again for more than a year, while John's gradually increasing mastery accompanied an ever-growing sense of well-being and accomplishment. Most important, John developed an ability to think and to concentrate. Even in termination, however, there remained a wish for an "energy" pill even though there was no need for it.

Here, the basic developmental lines had not been severely interfered with although one might have made a case for the specialness imposed upon both child and parents by John's adoption. As is often the case with adopted children, John had often longed for knowledge of his "real" mother, and particularly so when in conflict with his adoptive mother. Finally, the prompt favorable response to medication permits the inference of a biological predisposition to irritability and fragmentation of thinking.

Mild and Readily Treated

Edna was 14, the youngest daughter in an educated, middle-class family with an older "perfect" sister and a competent older brother. The family included loving, but overinvolved grandparents. Intellectual and financial resources were more than adequate, and the family lived accordingly. Since infancy, Edna had been quiet and pleasant. In the past few years, however, she had become increasingly and annoyingly more quiet; at the time of referral she was sullen and uncommunicative. Her disheveled room and grooming suggested inner disorganization and turmoil. Her schoolwork was most often incomplete and inarticulate. The results of projected psychological tests suggested a depressive affect, but were inconclusive because of the paucity of material. She was quite clear and articulate, however, as she expressed opinion about her family and their interpersonal conflicts.

She was baffled by her inability to deal with her family members and, after establishing a trusting relationship with her therapist, expressed regret that she had had to resort to silence and withdrawal. Her confusion and despair were genuine, as were her warm and affectionate regard for her parents, siblings, and grandparents. She continued to explore these issues with the psychiatrist for several visits. Coincidentally her parents discussed the behavior that led to referral. She soon took an antagonistic attitude toward treatment even though she was candid and vocal with her therapist. At home, she became increasingly aggressive about a variety of family issues. Eventually, under the umbrella of "dealing" with her parents, she attended to her room, her grooming, and her schoolwork if only they would excuse her from "that psychiatrist."

Here we find an intact and psychologically healthy family; there is an interested, invested, and competent extended family. Psychological deficits are in the realm of overinvestment in the value of appearances and action. Edna has a long history of smooth development. She had prided herself and could express this pride in her competence and achievements. Family members and peers were accustomed to working through interpersonal conflicts to personal mutual resolutions. She had long been familiar with drama, good use of fantasy, and organized sports. Finally, albeit with a struggle, she was able to recognize that she had some capacity to recognize her feelings as her own and to integrate them appropriately into her life. She developed a further ability to delay gratification and to accept external controls when her own were inadequate or threatened. She recognized some impulses as arising from within herself. Most importantly, she was able to use language to express impulses and related feelings. Each of these functions has its own history of development in her life, and each contributes to her optimism and sense of well-being.

Summary

Drawing on the work of many authors, we have discussed "depression" as a multilevel response to the perception of an unfavorable self-environment relationship. The intensity and reversibility of these responses are widely variable. Opportunities to reexamine the appropriateness and value of this perception occur with widely varying frequency and therapeutic power. In this process, we find "depression" an indispensable clinical tool, in work with patients of any age.

Chapter 12

ANNOTATED BIBLIOGRAPHY
Alfred P. French

The following annotated bibliography contains abstracts of bibliographic references to date relevant to childhood depression that the editors felt would be useful to all child mental health workers.

It has been the intention to include here all references available in English directly related to childhood depression (I have made an exception of Bowlby's extensive work, bibliographies of which are readily available elsewhere). Apologies are extended to those whose papers in the field were missed or those whose related works have been excluded.

Papers marked with an asterisk are those of central importance. Those with a dagger (†) are taken from a bibliography on depression in children prepared by the National Institutes of Mental Health.* Otherwise, the discussions are my own.

*I am indebted to Dr. Charles Schaffer for bringing this bibliography to my attention.

Depression In Children

Abraham, K. The infantile prototype of melancholic depression. In *Selected Papers of Karl Abraham*. New York: Basic Books, 1927, pp. 464–469.

Abrahams, M. J., & Whitlock, F. A. Childhood experience and depression. *British Journal of Psychiatry*, 1969, *115*, 883.

> This clinical study examines "the relationship of childhood bereavement and adverse childhood experiences to adult affective illness ... in 152 depressed patients and 152 controls matched for age, sex, civil and social status." The authors found that "more of the depressed patients had experienced unhappy childhoods than the controls ... physical loss of a parent does not necessarily contribute to the later development of that affective disorder but ... unsatisfactory child-parent relationships may be important determinants of personality and neurotic symptom formation ... " Thus, we see the emergence of the central concept that chronic stress over a period of time, rather than a single childhood trauma, has pathogenic potential.

Ackerly, W. C. Latency-age children who threaten or attempt to kill themselves. *Journal of American Academy of Child Psychiatry*, 1967, *6(2)*, 242.

> This study discusses 31 children, twelve years of age and under, who threatened or l41empted to kill themselves. Ackerly argues strongly that children who threaten to kill themselves and children who make a suicidal attempt are clinically distinct groups who should not be confused. He presents vignettes representative of these types. He proposes that "in general, latency-age children who threaten or attempt to kill themselves are expressing at least three basic wishes. This triad constitutes a core conflict of oral aggression, which is a consistent feature in these children. The wishes are to kill, to be killed and to die." Ackerly proposes that the first task of treatment is that of "modifying the projection-introjection systems so that the child can introject a good object; when he then projects onto the world, there will be better and more hopeful image and ego ideals." The therapist may then perceive to help the child toward a more optimistic view of the world.

Adam, K. S. Childhood parental loss, suicidal ideation and suicidal behavior. *The Child in His Family*. New York: Wiley, 1973, pp. 275–297.

Agras, S. The relationship of school phobia to childhood depression. *American Journal of Psychiatry,* 1959, *116,* 533.

In this brief, clearly-written, and delightful paper, Agras presents an interesting formulation of school phobia. On the basis of his own clinical observations of seven cases, supplemented by the appropriate review of the literature, Agras proposes the following mechanism that he refers to as the "depressive constellation in the family: The child's mother suffers from depression, as does the child: The mother-child system therefore tends to move toward infantilization of the child, one component of which is the refusal of the child to attend school. Agras (commendably) extends his formulation to include the father. Inadequate supportive function by the father exacerbates the mother-child depression and the tendency of the mother-child pair to cling to each other. He emphasizes that a primary underlying characteristic in these patients is their denial of any depressive affect," ... "in one instance, for example, the mother came to each interview with tear-filled eyes and a depressive facies, but maintained that 'she felt just fine.'"

Unfortunately, Agras does not discuss the treatment of the families but does outline a number of hypotheses which arise from his formulation. Agras' interesting formulation of the family dynamics and school phobia may well be quite general and applicable to a number of syndromes. One might easily infer on the family level; however, he does not use this term.

*Akiskal, H. S., & McKinney, W. T. Depressive disorders: Toward a unified hypothesis. *Science,* 1973, *182,* 20.

Akiskal, H. S., & McKinney, W. T. Overview of recent research in depression, integration of ten conceptual models into a comprehensive clinical frame. *Archives of General Psychiatry,* 1975, *32,* 285.

In these two papers, the authors integrate previous work on depression on the biological, psychodynamic, and environmental levels.

Amir, M. Suicide among minors in Israel. *Israel Annals of Psychiatry and Related Disciplines,* 1973, *11(3),* 219.

Anonymous. Depressive illness in children. *British Medical Journal,* 1971, *2(756),* 237.

*Annell, A. *Depressive states in childhood and adolescence.* Stockholm, Almqvist and Wiksell, 1972, p. 541.

This book presents the proceedings of a symposium held in Uppsala, Sweden in 1972 concerning depressive states in childhood and adolescence. The 73 papers by authors from all over the world are divided into twelve sections: Basic concepts, etiology and background factors, depressions in childhood, brain damage and depression, depression in school performances, depression and adolescence, depression and schizophrenia or obsessional neurosis, psychotherapy, psychopharmacotherapy, and symptomatology course and prognosis of depressions of childhood. This symposium clearly suffered from its obvious and inevitable Achilles' heel: There is no uniformity regarding the diagnosis of depression in children. The paper, therefore, discussed every kind of childhood psychopathology from a wide variety of points of view. The symposium was of major historical importance in stimulating thinking on an international level concerning depression in children. I will leave to the individual reader the task of ferreting out specific papers relevant to particular areas of interest.

Anthony, E. J., & Scott, P. Manic-depressive psychosis in childhood. *Journal of Child Psychology and Psychiatry, 1860, 1,* 53.

Anthony, E. J. Two contrasting types of adolescent depression and their treatment. *Journal of American Psychoanalytical Association,* 1970, *18(4),* 841.

*Anthony, E. J. Childhood depression. In Anthony, E. J. & Benedek, T. (Eds.), *Depression and Human Existence.* Boston: Little, Brown, 1975, pp. 69–100; 231–278.

This fine paper is discussed in the introductory chapter to this volume.

Archibald, H. C., Bell, D., Miller, C., & Tuddenham, R. D. Bereavement in childhood and adult psychiatric disturbance. *Psychosomatic Medicine,* 1962, *24(4),* 343.

These authors examined "the instance of childhood bereavement . . . for a serial sample of 1000 patients in a V.A. Mental Hygiene Outpatient Clinic." These were compared with data obtained from a life insurance company. The authors found "an appreciably greater frequency of bereavement in childhood generally than (in) the general population." They present the particularly interesting finding that, in their study group, the incidence of parental death decreased with the age of the child, in clear contrast to the control group, wherein as one would expect, the incidence of parental death increased with the age of the child. In other words, the psychiatric group was characterized by parental loss earlier in life. Although the authors present their "impression that men who have lost their fathers in childhood have difficulties in masculine identification, whereas those who have lost mothers have oral problems and express in their marital relationships unusual dependency and hostility . . . " the authors conclude that "the loss of a parent in early life constitutes a *non-specific* trauma whose effects depend upon complex interactions among (a wide number of) variables . . . " (see also Birtchnek, J.).

Arthur, B., & Komme, M. L. Bereavement in childhood. *Journal of Child Psychology and Psychiatry and Allied Disciplines*, 1964, *5*, 37.

Bakwin, H. Loneliness in infants. *American Journal of Disturbed Children*, 1942, *63*, 30.

Bakwin, H. Suicide in children and adolescents. *Journal of Pediatrics*, 1957, *50*, 749.

Bakwin, H. Depression—a mood disorder in children and adolescents. *Maryland State Medical Journal*, 1972, *21(6)*, 55.

Bakwin, R. M. Suicide in children and adolescents. *Journal of the American Medical Womens Association*, 1973, *28(12)*, 643.

This paper, which is primarily concerned with suicide in adolescents and young adults, notes that suicide is rare under 10 years of age, and that "young people seem more matter-of-fact about death. Most children express death wishes for themselves or others at some time, usually without any real intention or understanding." On the basis of a comparison of statistics from seven different countries, she notes that "the suicide rate for teenagers resembles that for adults in each country."

Balser, B. H., & Masterson, J. F. Suicide in adolescents. *American Journal of Psychiatry*, 1959, *115*, 400.

Barrett, A. M. Manic-depressive psychosis in childhood. *International Clinics*, 1931, *3*, 205.

†Bauersfeld, K. H. Diagnosis and treatment of depressive conditions at a school psychiatric center. In A. Annell (Ed.), *Depressive states in childhood and adolescence*. Stockholm: Almquist and Wiksell, 1972, pp. 281–285.

At the Fourth Congress of the Union of European Pedopsychiatrists in Stockholm, August 30–September 3, 1971, diagnosis and treatment of depression in children suffering from various learning and behavioral disorders were described, based on observations over a 10-year period at a school psychiatric center. Of 2,238 children studied, 307 presented with depressive mood or other symptoms of depression. Most were between 8 and 13 years of age and were more intelligent than their nondepressed counterparts. Clinically, many of the boys were the outgoing type, whereas most girls had passive personalities. Physical symptoms were frequent with many subjects reporting a wide variety of subjective somatic complaints. Other symptoms included disorders affecting articulation, school work, social adaptation, and antisocial and neurotic reactions (lying, truancy, stealing, enuresis, and encopresis). In most cases, development of chronic depression passed unnoticed by parents and teachers. Drug therapy was carried out with most patients and both child and parents required detailed advice before treatment began. In some cases, psychotherapy was used in combination with the drug treatments. Response was good in about one third of the patients as their mood, school work, and social adaptability improved (Author abstract modified).

Bayer, M. Suicide: Some children really mean it. *RN*, 1975, *38(9)*, 23.

Beck, A. T., Sethi, B. B., & Tuthill, R. W. Childhood bereavement and adult depression. *Archives of General Psychiatry*, 1963, *9*, 295.

These authors studied 297 patients selected from routine admissions to outpatient and inpatient facilities. Their objective was to "present further findings regarding the relationship of the development of depression in late adolescence and adulthood to the death of a parent in childhood." Depression was assessed with a Depression Inventory. The authors found "significantly greater incidence of loss of a parent during childhood in the high-depressed as compared with the non-depressed patients ..." The authors conclude that "the death of a parent in childhood may be a factor in the later development of a severe depression in the significant proportion of psychiatric patients. The precise nature of this relationship cannot be determined without further research."

Beichi, L. On accumulation of suicides in a family. *Wien Klin Wochenschr*, 1965, *77(41)*, 727.

Bender, & Schilder, P. Suicidal preoccupation and attempts in children. *American Journal of Orthopsychiatry*, 1937, *7*, 225.

This classic and widely-quoted paper presents case vignettes of hospitalized children with suicidal preoccupations. They present vignettes of 24 cases, ranging in age from 6 years to 15 years and conclude that "in the majority of our cases we have found obvious conscious motives for the suicidal preoccupations in the situation of the child. The child wants to escape a situation which seems to be unbearable." The authors emphasize that escape from the current situation, however, is not the only motivation: "the suicidal threat asserts the independence of the child and punishes those that have interfered with the child. There is hardly any suicidal case in which the motive of spite does not play an important part." The authors formulate that the deprivation of love, or the assumption thereof, is at the core of the unbearable situation and that deprivation of love increases the aggressiveness of children.

Bergmann, T. Personality development of two chronically ill children. *Bulletin of the Philadelphia Association of Psychoanalysis,* 1967, *17(3),* 158.

Bergstrand, C. G., & Otto, U. Suicidal attempts in adolescence and childhood. *Acta Paediatrica,* 1962, *51,* 17.

This study examines the frequency of suicide and suicidal attempts in Swedish children and adolescents. The authors examine a sample of 1,727 patients collected over a period of four years and all patients under 21 years of age. The majority of their patients were poor and the authors noted a high incidence of disruption of the families in virtually all of their cases.

†Berrini, M. E., & Tommazzolli, C. M. Depressive aspects of mental inhibition and pseudoretardation. In A. Annell (Ed.), *Depressive states in childhood and adolescence.* Stockholm: Almqvist and Wiksell, 1972, pp. 273–280.

At the Fourth Congress of the Union of European Pedopsychiatrists in Stockholm, August 30–September 3, 1971, learning disabilities and mental inhibition of a group of children aged 6 to 11 years suffering from depression were studied. Clinical examinations, analyses, and psychological testing enabled identification of the psychodynamic elements of mental inhibition and retardation based on emotional factors (pseudoretardation). These factors include envy of the mother, failure to satisfy basic curiosity and transforming it into action, and lack of encouragement by adults. The presence of depressive anxiety, revealed by anamnestic data in these children suggests that their learning process was interrupted at the point at which they felt it to be a destructive attack on the mother in the exact moment of the depressive position. The serious delay in speech development in four of the eight children also suggests difficulties in overcoming anxiety connected to depression. Excessive dependence was also noted, particularly in the case of the pseudoretarded subjects. Mental inhibition and pseudoretardation can be considered as two stages in a continuum, a process of inhibition of the wish for knowledge that appears in all children in a very early stage of development. Such inhibition is connected with anxieties characteristic of depression at a time when the wish of approaching and knowing the mother is excessively filled with aggressive feelings (18 references).

*Bibring, E. The mechanism of depression. In P. Greenacre (Ed.), *Affective disorders.* New York: International Universities Press, 1961, pp. 13–48.

This is certainly one of the classic papers in the literature on depression and, like papers by Bonime, is important to those of us concerned with depression in children because it is a critical part of evolution of the ego-psychology point of view. Bibring first presents a brief review of the theories of Freud, Abraham, Fenichel, Weiss, Federn, and Jacobson. He summarizes the psychoanalytic literature on depression as falling into "two major trends in explaining the structure and genesis of depression." The first major school of thought divides depression into at least two types of the uncomplicated grief reaction and the melancholic, due to narcissistic injuries; the second major type proposes that "a loss of self-esteem is common to all types of depression." Bibring's core statement is that "depression is an ego-psychological phenomenon, a 'state of the ego,' an affective state. This refers to all 'normal' and 'neurotic depressions' and also probably what is called 'psychotic' depression." Bibring thus defines depression "as the emotional expression (indication) of a state of helplessness and powerlessness of the ego, irrespective of what may have caused the breakdown of the mechanisms which established his self-esteem." (See also the paper by Engle and Schmale.)

Bierman, J. S., Silverstein, A. B., & Finesinger, J. E. A depression in a six-year-old boy with acute poliomyelitis. *Psychoanalytic Study of the Child,* 1958, *13,* 430.

This paper may be the first detailed case report in literature regarding a depressed latency-aged child. The authors described a 6-year-old boy whose deep depression of two months' duration followed his hospitalization for acute paralytic poliomyelitis affecting his legs. The authors formulate the depression in terms of a loss of the ambivalently loved object and compare the boy's depression to that occurring in adults in that lowered self-esteem occurred in their patient as is classically observed and described in adults with depression.

Birtchnell, J. Some psychiatric sequelae of childhood bereavement. *British Journal of Psychiatry,* 1970, *116*(532):346–347, March, 1970.

In this letter to the editor, Birchnell criticizes a paper by Monroe and Griffith concerning bereavement and mental illness and concisely summarizes the literature and methodological problems in the area of the psychiatric sequelae of childhood bereavement.

Blatt, S. J. Levels of object representation in anaclitic and introjective depression. *Psychoanalytic Study of the Child,* 1974, *29,* 107.

Blinder, B. J. Sibling death in childhood. *Child Psychiatry and Human Development,* 1972, *2(4),* 169.

In response to previous studies demonstrating that loss or death of a sibling during childhood affect timing and appearance of depression in adulthood, Blinder has reported in detail three case reports of children who experienced sibling loss. Blinder emphasizes that, although the literature in the development of psychopathology emphasizes the importance of trauma in early life, severe trauma in later childhood may also have a significant pathogenic potential.

Blotcky, M. J., & Kimsey, L. R. Childhood depression. *Texas Medicine,* 1970, *66(4),* 64.

†Bodtker, S. Psychotherapy of anaclitic depression with severe autistic withdrawal (report from a long-term psychotherapy). In A. Annell (Ed.), *Depressive states in childhood and adolescence.* Stockholm: Almqvist and Wiksell, 1972, pp. 405–411.

At the Fourth Congress of the Union of European Pedopsychiatrists in Stockholm, August 30–September 3, 1971, the techniques of long-term psychotherapy of anaclitic depression complicated by severe autistic withdrawal were described. In such situations, the therapist must be able to carefully regulate his emotional contact with the patient both physically and psychically. This is only possible by being thoroughly acquainted with psychotic experiences, preferably also with self experiences gained in training and other analytic situations. The control of sadistic and aggressive drives is of great importance and is achieved partly through selection of therapeutic material and partly through the therapist in offering his own superego without reluctance. Many patients cannot be successfully treated due to the time-consuming nature of such treatment. Prevention seems possible only through a gradual widening of understanding of children's emotional needs by professionals and society (Author abstract modified, 6 references).

Bollea, G., & Giannoti, A. Repression and episode obsessive-compulsive reactions: In A. Annell (Ed.), *Depressive states in childhood and adolescence.* Stockholm: Almqvist and Wiksell, 1972, pp. 389–394.

At the Fourth Congress of the Union of European Pedopsychiatrists in Stockholm, August 30–September 3, 1971, two case histories were examined to demonstrate the possibility of the presence of a depressive personality when obsessive-compulsive phenomena appear in the transition from one developmental stage to another in children. The possible psychopathological significance of such phenomena is considered, as well as the reasons for their appearance at the most critical periods of personality development when the demands for adaptation to the family and to society evoke aggressive tendencies. These aggressive feelings further depress the ego, which feels threatened by destructive demands from without. The obsessive-compulsive symptoms thereby acquire the special significance of a defense mechanism (Author abstract modified).

Bonime, W. Dynamics and psychotherapy of depression. *Current psychiatric therapies.* New York: Grune and Stratton, 1962.

Bonime, W. The psychodynamics of neurotic depression. In S. Arieti (Ed.), *American handbook of psychiatry.* New York: Basic Books, 1966.

In this classic paper, Bonime, a leading proponent of the "ego psychology" school of psychoanalysis, discusses neurotic depression from the ego psychology point of view. The importance of this work for those concerned with depression in children is made clear by Anthony's discussion (see Anthony, E. J., this bibliography) written some 10 years later wherein Anthony states, "This ego psychology theory has a number of advantages that seem especially pertinent to the childhood situation ... there is nothing in the theory that would preclude the consideration of clinical depression on the grounds of immaturity."

After reviewing the previous work in the field, Bonime presents his point of view which is to "regard interpersonal experience as the dominant force in the development and dynamics of personality (to regard) constitutional factors as co-determinants (to) see environment and personality related in constant structure-determining and function-determining reciprocal interaction.

Bonime outlines his basic concept as follows: "the depressive is an extremely manipulative individual who, by helplessness, sadness, seductiveness, and other means, maneuvers people toward the fulfillment of demands for various forms of emotionally comforting response." The crucial categories of depressive pathology are manipulativeness, aversion to influence, unwillingness to give gratification, hostility and anxiety. Bonime hypothesizes that "the depressive character develops in an environment in which the normal needs of a child for solicitous parents are unfulfilled ... "

Boulanger, J. G. Depression in childhood. *Canadian Psychiatric Association Journal*, 1966, *11* (suppl.), 309.

Bowlby, J. Grief and mourning in infancy and early childhood. *The Psychoanalytic Study of the Child*, 1960, *15*, 9. (with subsequent discussions by Anna Freud, Max Schur and Rene Spitz.)

This paper and the three following discussions are discussed briefly in the first chapter in this volume. I have not included an extensive bibliography of Bowlby's voluminous work, which is well-known and readily available.

Brandes, N. S. A discussion of depression in children and adolescents. Clinical Pediatrics, 1971, *10(8)*, 470.

Branzei, P., Pirozynski, T., Scripcaru, G., Avramovici, J. A., & Pirozynski, M. Considerations upon the attempts of suicide during infant-juvenile growth period. *Revista Medico-Chirurgicala a Societatii di Medici si Naturalisti din Iasi*, 1973, *77(1)*, 25.

Brown, F., & Epps, P. Childhood bereavement and subsequent crime. *British Journal of Psychiatry*, 1966, *112*, 1043.

In this study the authors interviewed 546 female prisoners and 168 male prisoners. They concluded that "18.2% of the (female) prisoners' fathers died before fifteen, and 8.6% of the mothers. This is also significant." The authors emphasize that "both paternal and maternal orphanhood are significant factors in both male and female criminality, but more marked in female criminality. It is probably not the bereavement itself so much as the train of events which is likely to follow that provides the damaging situation."

Brown, F. Childhood bereavement and subsequent psychiatric disorder. *British Journal of Psychiatry,* 1966, *112(491),* 1035.

Brown, F. Bereavement and lack of parent in childhood. In E. Miller (Ed.), *Foundations of child psychiatry.* Oxford: Pergamon Press, 1968, pp. 435–455.

In this study which was carried out over a period of 5 years in the Hamstead General Hospital in London, the author was concerned with the hypothesis "that a depressive illness in later years is often a reaction to a present loss or bereavement which is associated with a more serious loss or bereavement in childhood. The depressive illness is thus regarded as a kind of anaphylactic reaction which occurs in later life where there has been an early sensitization." In order to examine this hypothesis, the author studied cases of depression over a period of 5 years, rejecting those cases where there was inadequate information concerning childhood development. He found that "forty-one percent of people suffering from depressive illness now lost a parent in the first fifteen years of their life, compared with sixteen percent of the general population (and therefore) it would seem that something could be done to prevent the present illness by increased care of these orphans." Brown, therefore, concludes that the general hypothesis, stated above, is upheld by his study.

Brumback, R. A., Dietz-Schmidt, S. G., & Weinberg, W. A. Depression in children referred to an educational diagnostic center: Diagnosis and treatment and analysis of criteria and literature review. *Disease of the Nervous System,* 1977, *38,* 529.

This paper is, no doubt, typical of the kind of work that will now be done in the field of childhood depression. It is a well-done piece of work and a fine contribution to the literature. The authors, in their study, use the following criteria for diagnosis of childhood depression: Both dysphoric mood (melancholia) and self-deprecatory ideation, and two or more of the remaining eight: aggressive behavior (agitation), sleep disturbance, changes in school performance, diminished socialization, change in attitude toward school, somatic complaints, loss of usual energy, or unusual change in appetite and/or weight. Using these criteria, the authors found that 58 percent of their sample (72 consecutive new patients referred to an educational diagnostic center for evaluation of learning and/or behavior problems noted in school) meet their criteria. Interestingly, the authors note "a positive family history of affective disorder was present in 89% of the depressed children" and that "treatment with antidepressants (Imipramine or Amitriptiline) resulted in clinical improvement in 95% of the depressed children."

This study is of interest for several reasons: First, the authors have, admirably, crisply delineated their criteria for the diagnosis of depression. Their list of criteria is nicely compatible with discussions of depression in children found elsewhere in the literature. This list would lend itself well to the obvious next step in research, i.e., study of the development of reliable and valid scales. Second, the report is of interest because of high proportion of children (58 percent) who were found to be depressed—in remarkable contrast to prior literature.

Special note must be made of these authors' enthusiastic comments regarding the use of tricyclic antidepressant medication in their patients. The ages of the children are reported as "9.5 + 1.4 years" for males and "9.8 + 1.7 years" for females. Medications were used in "dosages ranging from 25 mg to 125 mg per day (varying with age and body size) in nineteen of the thirty-four children who were available for follow-up after eleven to thirty weeks." It must be vigorously emphasized that the use of tricyclic antidepressant medication in children is quite controversial; at least one unpublished case of which this writer is aware demonstrates that these medications may be lethal in children. Certainly, there may be a hazard that the authors' highly enthusiastic comment that "while 95% of the treated depressed children showed improvement, only 40% of the nontreated depressed children showed any improvement" may encourage others to try tricyclic antidepressant medication without adequate caution.

Burks, H. L., & Harrison, S. I. Aggressive behavior as a means of avoiding depression. *American Journal of Orthopsychiatry,* 1962, *32,* 416.

This well-written clinical paper discusses the evolution of sadness into aggression. The authors describe their experience with a group of children who were severely deprived in early childhood and in later life were unable to have any real fun: "the laughter heard consisted of bitter, sardonic chuckles when someone was hurt or when adult authority had been successfully circumvented. An exception was the occasional incident when a child was able to enjoy a very infantile sort of gratification from a staff person who was for the moment trusted." The authors discussed the relevance of depression defined in Bibring's terms: "An ego-psychological phenomenon, an affective state referring to the helplessness of the ego."

The authors conclude that *some* aggressive behavior is enhanced when it is viewed as a means of avoiding feelings of depression. This seemed particularly true in those children whose early years were characterized by some degree of true rejection and deprivation. In particular, the authors noted the children's sensitivity to situations which threatened adequacy, threatened to force the child to recognize his own cravings for affection, and situations recalling memories from the past which highlighted feelings of worthlessness. The authors make an interesting distinction between aggressive behavior as a way to avoid feelings of depression, as opposed to "impulsive acts designed to placate feelings of guilt."

Burks, H. L. and Hoekstra, M. Psychiatric emergencies in childhood. *American Journal of Orthopsychiatry*, 1964, *34*, 134.

Campbell, J. Manic-depressive psychosis in children: Report of 18 cases. *Quarterly Journal of Child Behavior*, 1952, *4*, 389.

Caplan, M. G., & Douglas, V. I. Incidence of parental loss in children with depressed mood. *Journal of Child Psychology and Psychiatry and Allied Disciplines*, 1969, *10*, 225.

†Caplan, M. G., & Douglas, V. I. Childhood depression: Separation and aggression. *British Journal of Projective Psychology* (London), 1972, *7(1)*, 5.

The reactions of a group of 20 depressive boys were examined in two conflict areas: Reactions to the threat of separation and modes of dealing with aggression. Test instruments were two story completion tests and a collection of the children's earliest childhood memories. Control groups were 40 normal boys and 20 boys who, though emotionally disturbed, did not show symptoms of depression. Subjects were matched for age (8–13 years old), IQ, and socioeconomic status. In comparison with normal subjects, both clinic groups showed evidence of insecurity over separation and abandonment. Depressive children were differentiated from both control groups on a number of responses which suggested attitudes of passive withdrawal and an inhibition of active goal-directed behavior. The findings suggest that the depressive reaction in childhood is characterized by feelings of hopelessness and an inability to assert oneself positively (20 references, Author abstract).

†Cebiroglu, R., Sumer, E., & Polvan, O. Etiology and pathogenesis of depression in Turkish children. In A. Annell (Ed.), *Depressive states in childhood and adolescence.* Stockholm: Almqvist and Wiksell, 1972, pp. 133–136.

At the Fourth Congress of the Union of European Pedopsychiatrists in Stockholm, August 30–September 3, 1971, the incidence, etiology, and pathogenesis of depression in Turkish children investigated in a group referred to a university clinic were discussed. Among 10,661 Subjects examined over the last 10 years, 85 were depressed. Only two manic-depressive psychoses were observed. A cyclothymic personality, psychosis in the family, and intermittant attacks of manic-depressive psychosis were seen in these two cases, with subjects in the age range of 12 to 16 years. All other cases were depressive equivalences. Depressive syndromes were thus 0.8 percent of the total. A total of 82 percent of the subjects had neurotic (reactive) depression; 8 percent were endogenous; 3 percent had anaclitic depression. Family conflicts caused 30 percent of the cases; loss of a love object, 20 percent; depression parents, 27 percent; and 25 percent of the causes were unknown. In children prone to suicide, the symptoms, such as psychomotor retardation or sad expression, are not as evident as in adults. Usually, depression in children is hidden behind depressive equivalent symptoms, such as psychosomatic complaints, anxiety and hyperactivity (16 references, author abstract modified).

Cearny, L. Suicides in children and adolescents in Czechoslovakia. *Acta Paedopsychiatra* (Basel), 1968, *35(2),* 380.

This paper is in French, with a summary in English. The author presents statistics concerning suicides in children and adolescents in Czechoslovakia from 1948 to 1966 and suicide attempts from 1963 to 1965 "from a viewpoint of motivation, of employment and social structure." The paper also presents a remarkable summary of statistics concerning suicides in youngsters aged 10–14 and 15–19 in 31 counties (although the variations in diagnoses and reporting might well be expected to be so great from one country to the next that one might question the accuracy of such figures).

Chrzanowski, G. (moderator). The management of depression in children and adults; a panel discussion. *Contemporary Psychoanalysis,* 1965, *2(1),* 26.

Contents: Communication with depressive patients by Rose Spiegel; Depression in infancy and childhood by E. Kleinberger; Depression in adolescents by M. R. Freen; A psychotherapeutic approach to depression by Walter Bonime.

Connell, H. M. Attempted suicide in school children. *Medical Journal of Australia,* 1972, *1(14),* 686.

This paper discusses 15 cases of attempted suicide in children ranging in age from 11 to 14 years. Brief case vignettes describe chaotic and destructive home circumstances. Connell found that "the picture which emerged was remarkably uniform; children lacking normal support of adult relationships appeared to have personality structures inadequate to cope with a combination of environmental stress and an aggressive drive ... the importance of retroflexed aggression—that is aggressive feelings meant for disappointing love objects redirected toward self—as an etiological factors in depression and suicide is clearly demonstrated. These children were continually frustrated in their expectations of love and support from parent figures. Aggressive behavior was commonplace in these homes in the level of physical violence unusually high."

†Connell, H. M. Depression in childhood. *Child psychiatry and human development,* 1973, *4(2),* 71.

The symptoms of 20 children regarded as suffering from depression were compared with those described as indicative of depression in standard texts. It was found that the children fit the clinical picture well and that there was some indication that the rudiments of the two types of depressive illness seen in adults may be recognizable in childhood. 10 references (Journal abstract modified).

Connell, P. H. Suicidal attempts in childhood and adolescence. In J. G. Howells (Ed.), *Modern perspectives in child psychiatry.* New York: Brunner/Mazel, 1971, pp. 403–427.

†Cuk, S., Haasz, A., & Haasz, I. Die rolle des vaters bei der entstehung depressiver zustande im kindes—und jugendalter. (The role of the father in the development of depressive states in childhood and adolescence). In A. Annell (Ed.), *Depressive states in childhood and adolescence.* Stockholm: Almqvist and Wiksell, 1972, p. 91–94.

At the Fourth Congress of the Union of European Pedopsychiatrists in Stockholm, August 30–September 3, 1971, the role of the father in the development of depressive states in childhood and adolescence was studied in 25 cases of infantile juvenile depression. It was found that the fathers had failed to fulfill their parental role, being passive, weak and remote in their relationship with their children; whereas, in a control group with delinquent behavior, the most striking characteristic was a general and serious disturbance of the family environment. Despite the great significance of a disturbed father image in the formation of depression in childhood and adolescence, the entire family must be included in any investigation. 7 references. (Author abstract modified)

*Cytryn, L., & McKnew, D. H. Proposed classification of childhood depression. *American Journal of Psychiatry,* 1972, *129(2)*, 149.

These authors propose that "neurotic depressive reactions of midchildhood may be classified into three distinct categories: Masked depression, often characterized by 'acting-out behavior'; acute depression in which there is '. . . a history of a relatively normal adjustment prior to a traumatic event that is followed by the onset of a depression'; and a chronic depression characterized by marginal premorbid social adjustment, depression and repeated separation from important adults . . ."

*Cytryn, L., & McKnew, D. H. Factors influencing the changing clinical expression of the depressive process in children. *American Journal of Psychiatry,* 1974, *131(8)*, 879.

This brief and interesting paper is certainly one of the gems to appear in the burgeoning literature concerning depression in children. Starting with a clinical observation that " masked depression is by far the most common form of depression in children, while overt depression is more common in adults" the authors proceed to present a formulation of the development of the clinical expression of depressive process. The authors propose that "the depressive process manifests itself in three different ways" which are fantasy, verbal expression, and mood and behavior. Similarly, the authors propose three levels of defenses: level of fantasy, wherein the defenses are denial, projection/introjection, acting out, avoidance and splitting; the second level of depressive talk, wherein dissociation of affect and reaction formation of the predominant defenses; and the third level wherein the defenses against depression fail and mood and behavior are affected. The authors discuss the "uneven distribution of overt depressive symptomology through the life cycle" on the basis of this scheme.

Davidson, J. Infantile depression in a "normal" child. *Journal of the American Academy of Child Psychiatry*, 1968, *7(3)*, 522.

In her summary, Davidson states that "This paper is an attempt to document the theoretical assumption of the etiology of depression by examining the occurrence of depression in a 'normal' 20 week old infant who lived in an intact family." This child, who showed "signs of misery, unhappiness and depression at the ages of 5, 12 and 15" experienced disruption of the mother-infant relationship. Davidson summarizes that "her problems were rooted in her response to her mother's handling of her. The mother was . . . fighting to stave off her own depressed moods by extreme activity." This paper emphasizes that depression may arise within the context of the stresses and strain occurring within a relatively normal and intact family, and from the matrix of an overstressed mother-infant relationship. This is in contrast to other literature on depression in children written at that time, which reported only massive and profound disruption of the normal intrafamilial processes.

Dennehy, C. M. Childhood bereavement and psychiatric illness. *British Journal of Psychiatry*, 1966, *112*, 1049.

This paper includes a rather extensive discussion of the methodological aspects of research in the field of relationship between loss in childhood and subsequent psychiatric disorder. The objective of the study "was to determine the incidence of bereavement, that is the loss of a parent by death in a psychiatric population." The author studies 1,020 psychiatric patients presenting the consecutive admissions to three hospitals. All patients were below the age of 60 years. The authors conclude that, in this population, there was "an excess of both male and female schizophrenics who lost their mother before the age of five . . . alcoholic male drug addicts showed an excess of father loss and female drug addicts an excess of mother loss."

Despert, J. L. Suicide and depression in children. *Nervous Child*, 1952, *9*, 378.

Despert reviews the literature concerning depression and suicide in children, noting the lack of uninamity regarding the association between the two. Reviewing the statistical data regarding suicides and deaths in children, Despert notes that there is a high frequency of accidental deaths for the age groups under consideration. Despert then presents a study of the records of 400 consecutive cases of children who were seen for behavioral, neurotic, and psychotic problems. In this series, they found 26 children (18 boys and 8 girls) with depressive moods and/or evidence to preoccupation with suicide or else expressed realistic suicidal threats. The youngest, a girl 4 years and 8 months old, was depressed and not suicidal; the oldest, a girl 16 years of age, was suicidal. Of these 26, five manifested intense suicidal preoccupations and had made suicidal attempts. Despert concludes that "depression and suicide are relatively rare in children and depression and suicide do not have the close association assumed to exist in adults." Case vignettes of the five suicidal children point out the extensive disruption of development in these children. In three boys, she found a profile consisting of a "massive character of these boys associated with intense hostility toward the mother figure with inability to express aggression other than in sudden violent outbursts and the tendency for the aggression to be turned toward oneself. It is also striking that in the three cases a satisfactory male identification had not been achieved, this owing to factors in the parental figure which varied in the individual cases."

DeYoung, H. Homicide, children's division. *Human Behavior,* 1976, 5(2), 16.

†DiCagno, L., & Ravetto, F. Depression et carences maternelles partielles: aspects cliniques et psychopathologiques. (Depression and partial maternal deprivation: Clinical and psychopathological aspects.) In A. Annell (Ed.), *Depressive states in childhood and adolescence.* Stockholm: Almqvist and Wiksell, 1972, pp. 84–90.

At the Fourth Congress of the Union of European Pedopsychiatrists in Stockholm, August 30–September 3, 1971, the relationship between partial maternal deprivation and depression in a group of children between the ages of 4 and 13 years was studied, with a focus on the clinical and psychopathological aspects of the condition. In 40 patients with depressive reactions related to a situation of partial maternal deprivation, as compared with a control group in which this factor was absent, the data confirm the importance of such deprivation in the genesis of depressive manifestations. Factors of particular significance are: 1) the importance of inadequate maternal care and of a distortion of the mother-child relationship for formation of depressive reactions, apart from the loss of, or a true separation from, the mother; 2) the role played by discontinuity in the mother-child relationship in formation of the personality and the specific clinical aspects of depression; 3) the reappearance of depressive manifestations in new situations of loss or separation; and 4) the variability of clinical manifestations associated with depression according to the manifestations associated with depression according to the chronological age and to the level of ego maturation. 15 references.

Dizmang, L. G. Loss, bereavement and depression in childhood. *International Psychiatric Clinics,* 1969, *6(2),* 175.

*Dorpat, L. L. Depressive affect. *Psychoanalytic Study of the Child,* 1977, *33,* 3.

This is a magnificent review of the field; with this paper "childhood depression" truly comes of age. Dorpat clearly presents the argument, arising from the seminal work of Bibring, Engel, Sandler and Jolle, and others, that depressive affect, like anxiety, "is a basic psychobiological affective reaction which becomes abnormal when it occurs in inappropriate circumstances or persists too long." The clear distinction between depressive *affect* and depressive *illness* does much to clarify our thinking and greatly simplifies our approach to "depression in children." Of particular interest are Dorpat's discussions of the developmental line of depressive affect, the *reciprocal* relationship between superego development and the development of depressive affect, and his discussion of the depressive equivalent.

Drotar, D. Letter: Concern over the categorization of depression in children. *Journal of Pediatrics,* 1974, *85(2),* 290.

Duch, E. Attempted suicides of the child and the adolescent. *Acta Paedopsychiatra* (Basel), 1968, *35(11),* 345.

Easson, W. M. The management of depression in children and adolescent. *Ohio State Medical Journal,* 1968, *64(9),* 1024.

Editorial: Suicide in children. *British Medical Journal,* 1975, *1(5958),* 592.

Emde, R. N., Polak, P. R., & Spitz, R. A. Anaclitic depression in an infant raised in an institution. *Journal of the American Academy of Child Psychiatry,* 1965, *4(4),* 545.

*Engel, G. L. Anxiety and depression-withdrawal: The primary effects of unpleasure. *International Journal of Psychoanalysis,* 1962, *43,* 89.

*Engel, G. L. A life setting conducive to illness. The giving-up given-up complex. *Annals of Internal Medicine,* 1968, *69(2),* 293.
*Engel, G. L., & Reichsman, F. Spontaneous and experimentally induced depressions in an infant with a gastric fistula. A contribution to the problem of depression. *Journal of the American Psychoanalytic Association,* 1956, *4(3),* 428.

This is certainly one of the very classic papers in literature of depression and essential reading for any student of depression in children. From this initial study have come many papers; in particular, the reader is referred to Schmale, A. H. and Engel, G. L.: The role of conservation—withdrawal and depressive reactions. In Anthony, E. J. & Benedek, T. (Eds.), *Depression and human existence.* Boston: Little, Brown, 1975, pp. 183-198. In this 1956 paper, Engel and Reichsman present the case report of an infant studied over a nine-month period with congenital atresia of the esophagus and surgically produced gastric and esophageal fistulaes. Due to the resulting severe disruption of the mother-infant bond, the child withdrew to a state which was characterized by "muscular inactivity, hypotonia and sad facial expression, decreased gastric secretions and eventually a sleep state. It vanished as soon as the baby was reunited with a familiar person." The authors state that "Darwin's classic description of grief, dejection, and despair coincide to a remarkable degree with Monica's appearance." On the basis of their observations, the authors concluded that "Monica's condition on admission is properly classified as a *depression of infancy.*"

The authors complement their clinical observations with a discussion of papers by Freud, Abraham. Jacobson, Rado, Bibring, Benedek, and Selye. In conclusion, the authors propose that "in depression there is not only the active, oral, introjective anlage emphasized in classic theory, but also an inactive, pre-oral, pre-object anlage." They propose that "Monica's reaction of depression-withdrawal, including the gastric hyposecretion, (is) representative of the inactive pre-oral phase ..."

Evans, J. Depression in adolescents. *Proceedings of the Royal Society of Medicine,* 1975, *68(9),* 566.
Faigel, H. C. Suicide among young persons. A review for its incidence and causes, and methods of its prevention. *Clinical Pediatrics,* 1966, *5(3),* 187.

This essay concerns suicide in both adults and children and presents a brief discussion of suicide and review of the literature.

Fast, I. Some relationships of infantile self-boundary development to depression. *International Journal of Psychoanalysis,* 1967, *48,* 259.

Faux, E. J., & Rowley, C. M. Detecting depressions in childhood. *Hospital and Community Psychiatry,* 1967, *18(2),* 51.

Feinstein, S. C., & Wolpert, E. A. Juvenile manic-depressive illness: Clinical and therapeutic considerations. *Journal of the American Academy of Child Psychiatry,* 1973, *12,* 123.

This interesting paper presents the case history of a girl first seen at the age of 3½ "because of hyperactivity, low frustration tolerance, impulsive and destructive behavior and an inability to concentrate" in whom the authors made the diagnosis of manic depressive illness. The authors propose that "manic depressive illness appears in early childhood, manifesting itself as erratic, rapidly shifting mood behavior with a basic intactness of intellect." They emphasize that this use of separation-individuation are essential and that psychotherapy in addition to pharmacotherapy are indicated.

†Forster, E. Kinder endogen-depressiver eltern—Verhaltensstorungen una personlichkeitsstruktur? (Is there such a thing as a depressed or an elated mood state which can be regarded as characteristic of a personality structure?) In A. Annell (Ed.), *Depressive states in childhood and adolescence.* Stockholm: Almqvist and Wiksell, 1972, pp. 77–83.

At the Fourth Congress of the Union of European Pedopsychiatrists in Stockholm, August 20–September 3, 1971, data on the nature and frequency of behavioral disorders, personality and intelligence level, social level, adaptation, and family integration of children of depressed parents were presented. A total of 106 children from 61 families, where either the father or mother suffered from endogenous depression, were investigated. All such parents had undergone several episodes of illness. A symptom questionnaire for psychosomatic and neurotic disorder, the Minnesota Multiphasic Personality Inventory, and the WIP test were used, as well as a procedure for objectively analyzing interfamily relationships and identification behavior. 4 references. (Author abstract modified).

French, A. P., & Steward, M. S. Family dynamics, childhood depression and attempted suicide in a 7-year-old boy: A case study. *Suicide,* 1975 *5(1),* 29.

In this paper the case of an attempted suicide in a 7-year-old boy was described and the case was formulated in terms of his depression, which was in turn linked to the dynamics of the family. (For a follow-up on this same case, see French, Steward, & Morrisson in this volume.)

*French, A. P., & Steward, M. S. Adaptation and affect—toward a synthesis of Piagetian psychoanalytic psychologies. *Perspectives in Biology and Medicine,,* 1975 *18(4)*, 464.

This paper grew out of the need to define "depression" of sufficiently general terms that the term could be applied to children. It grew out of interest in publishing a case report (see French and Steward, 1975) concerning a suicidal and depressed 7-year-old boy. As the clinical paper was rejected by one journal after another, we realized that we must write a second theoretical paper justifying our underlying assumption that depression was possible in children. The result was this theoretical paper in which we have tried to pull together basic concepts from cybernetics, general systems theory, Piagetian theory, and psychodynamic theory. The core of the theoretical model is the proposal that basic functions of the feedback loop may be related directly to the processes of assimilation and accommodation described by Piaget. The result is a formal definition of various states or an organism, and a discussion of the subjective (affective) signals appropriate to these states. In one of these states the organism perceives that there is failure of homeostasis *and* there is no reference readily available with respect to which the organism could maintain homeostasis. The corresponding affective state may be depression.

Freud, S. *Mourning and melancholia* (1917). London, Hogarth Press, Standard Edition, Vol. 14, 1957, p. 237.

†Friedman, J., & Doyal, T. Depression in children: Some observations for the school psychologist. *Psychology in the Schools,* 1974, *11(1)*, 19.

Depression in children is discussed, and case material is provided to illustrate the phenomenon. Depressive symptoms, especially sad affect, are relatively common in children. Three forms of depression are reported: acute, chronic, and masked. Symptomatology and etiology are considered. Object loss in children frequently leads to feelings of helplessness and loneliness. Self-abnegation often results from real or imagined assaults on self-esteem. Family and sociocultural influences on the etiology of childhood depression are considered as are various methods of treatment. 9 references.

Frommer, E. A. Treatment of childhood depression with antidepressant drugs. *British Medical Journal,* 1967, *1(5542),* 729.

In this paper, one of the very few concerning the treatment of childhood depression with antidepressant drugs, Frommer reports "a comparison of the effects of Phenobarbitone against a combination of Phenelzine (Nardil) and Chlordiazepoxide (Librium) was made in a group of children whose symptoms were thought to be depressive in origin." Frommer emphasizes the diverse nature of depressive symptoms in children, proposing that depression should be "suspected in children who complain of non-specific recurrent abdominal pain, headache, sleep difficulties and irrational fears, or mood disturbances such as irritability, unaccountable tearfulness, and associated outbursts of temper." The author studied a total of 32 children, ranging in age from 9 to 15 years of whom "the majority were still prepubertal and physically immature."

They divided their group into "phobic" group and "mood disorder" group. The authors conclude that "despite the limitations and inaccuracies . . . antidepressant drugs are much more useful for treatment of depressed children, whether with 'functional' somatic symptoms or 'behavior disorder', than is the Phenobarbital that is so often used." Frommer emphasizes that precautions must be taken when prescribing monoamine oxidase inhibitors for children.

Furman, R. A. A child's capacity for mourning. In E. J. Anthony, & C. Koupernik (Eds.), *The child in his family: The impact of disease and death.* New York: Wiley, 1973.

Gallant, D. M., & Simpson, G. M. (Eds.) *Depression: Behavioral, biochemical, diagnostic and treatment concepts.* New York: Halsted Press, 1975.

†Garfinkel, B. D., & Golombek, H. Suicide and depression in childhood and adolescence. *Canadian Medical Association Journal* (Toronto), 1974 *110(11),* 1278.

These authors, in contrast to others, state that "suicide is, however, considered as a leading cause of death in the (pediatric) age group." Like other authors, they emphasize the "immature comprehension of the state of death, combined with a wish to alter an intolerable living situation or to punish individuals significant in his environment." In discussing etiology, the authors refer to the concept of "depressive equivalent," and point out that, while "suicide is often linked to a trivial event which triggers a child's self-destructive behavior, a more careful analysis indicates that the seemingly meaningless event did produce an impulsive response in the child but there had been an ongoing depressive process that had surfaced only intermittantly and had been expressed episodically and behaviorally. There is often a history of appearing sad, withdrawn and inhibited. The child expresses an extremely poor self concept and has feelings of dissatisfaction, discontent and rejection." The author suggests a number of specific steps in the evaluation and management of the suicidal child.

Gauthier, Y. The mourning reaction of a ten-and-a-half-year-old boy. *Psychoanalytic Study of the Child,* 1965, *20,* 481.

Gay, M. J., & Tonge, W. L. The late effects of loss of parents in childhood. *British Journal of Psychiatry,* 1967, *113(500),* 753.

Geleerd, E. R. Clinical contribution to the problem of early mother-child relationship; some discussion of its influence on self-destructive tendencies and fugue states. *Psychoanalytic Study of the Child,* 1956, *11,* 336.

Gero, G. An equivalent of depression: Anorexia. In P. Greenacre (Ed.) *Affective disorders.* New York: International Universities Press, 1953. pp. 117–139.

Gittelman-Klein, R. Definitional and methodological issues concerning depressive illness in children. In J. G. Schulterbrandt, A. Raskin (Eds.), *Depression in childhood: Diagnosis, treatment, and conceptual models.* New York: Raven Press, 1977, pp. 69–80. (Discussion by Munroe M. Lefkowitz, pp. 81–85)

Dr. Gittelman-Klein presents the simple truth in a pithy manner: "a confluence of data (regarding depression in adults) of the disorder's natural course, response to pharmacologic intervention and genetics has made disorders of moods the best understood psychiatric state with clear therapeutic and prognostic implications . . . the study of childhood depression has not met, as yet, as happy a scientific fate as the study of adult disorders." Reviewing the problem of definition, Gittelman-Klein states that "the field of childhood depression is in a singular position of having an unspecified, undocumented disorder for which numerous equivalents are postulated." She then discusses the methodological issues that currently confront the investigator in this field, emphasizing the necessity of "necessary and sufficient clinical characteristics for the diagnosis of childhood depression." In his discussion of Gittelman-Klein's paper, Lefkowitz presents two epidemiological studies of deviant behavior in children "that treat some of the behaviors frequently classified as depressive symptoms." On the basis of a careful review of these two studies, Lefkowitz concludes that "they suggest that approximately twenty percent of the general childhood population has been reliably judged to posses the symptoms of depressive disorder observed in clinical samples."

Glaser, K. Suicide in children and adolescents. In L. E. Abt, & S. L. Weissman, (Eds.) *Acting Out.* New York: Grune and Stratton, 1965, pp. 87–99.

Glaser, K. Attempted suicide in children and adolescents: Psychodynamic observations. *American Journal of Psychotherapy,* 1965, *19,* 220.

Glaser, K. Masked depression in children and adolescents. *American Journal of Psychotherapy,* 1967, *21,* 565.

In this paper, Glaser begins with the commonly-expressed position that "depression in the adult is a well-known psychiatric condition ... in the child and adolescent depression is often not recognized as such because it may be associated with symptoms not readily identified with this condition." (I continue to question both aspects of this: On the one hand, I question whether depression in adults is as clear-cut and easily recognized a syndrome as these comments suggest, and I also question whether clinical expression of depression in children and adolescents really differs as greatly from those in adults as Glaser indicates.) Taking the position that "manifest behavior disturbances (reveal) underlying depressive reactions in children of different age levels," Glaser discusses deprivation reactions in infants and small children, behavioral problems and delinquent behavior in older children and adolescents, and delinquency, learning difficulties and psychophysiologic reactions, and masked depression in retarded children.

Glaser, K. Suicidal children—management. *American Journal of Psychotherapy,* 1971, *25(1),* 27.

Like other authors, Glaser emphasizes the frequency of casual expressions of suicidal intent in contrast to the infrequency of completed suicides in adolescence and their extreme rarity in children. Glaser divides potentially suicidal children into several categories: 1) casual expressions, 2) gesture, 3) threat, 4) attempt. In appraising the seriousness, Glaser recommends examining the depth of conflict in the child, the child's inner resources for coping, the available outer resources, and a realistic appraisal of the stressful situation.

Assessment of the psychodynamic background includes "... *intrafamily tensions,* with the mother often as the key person, or in conflicts within the child." The former conflicts within the child include sexual problems, low self-esteem, contagion and suggestion, as well as major psychiatric disorders. Glaser concludes that suicidal threats must be seen as an emergency and treated as such and that the psychiatrist should "... make himself available at all times."

†Goldie, L. The "Andorra" situation in childhood depressions. In A. Annell (Ed.), *Depressive states in childhood and adolescence.* Stockholm: Almqvist and Wiksell, 1972, pp. 104–110.

At the Fourth Congress of the Union of European Pedopsychiatrists in Stockholm, August 30–September 3, 1971, individual mental and family factors that produce a special situation leading to depression or persecutory feelings in the child patient were described. Case histories of nine patients are reviewed, giving the salient family features and stressing that in each case the family members have made use of the patient for their own projective identification. The theoretical basis for the analysis is Max Frisch's play "Andorra" which involves an illegitimate child incorrectly assumed to be a Jew and persecuted by the Nazis, who received no aid from his parents or the townspeople in establishing his own identity. Each case includes all of the traits of desperation and regression found in the play and each illustrates abnormal emotional and behavioral reactions of the child victim. When family situations are investigated, it is usually found that not only are the family members destructively using the patient as a scapegoat for their own guilt or frustration, but that the adults are exceptionally passive and noncommunicative themselves. Therapy in these cases is often difficult since the passive family members must admit their guilt and experience a depression on their own and the child must be aided in developing insight as to why he is being treated as he is.

Gould, R. E. Suicide problems in children and adolescents. *American Journal of Psychotherapy,* 1965, *19,* 228.

In this paper, Gould discusses the psychodynamic and sociological aspects of suicidal attempts in children and adolescents. In contrast to some of the prior literature in this field, Gould takes the position that depression is common in children and adolescents and is "almost always a part of the underlying psychodynamics of the 'suicidal personality' of children and adolescents as well as of adults." With respect to management, Gould advises that hospitalization may be indicated, that we should be cautious in attempting to reassure patients without understanding the dynamics involved since "to offer empty reassurance and superficial support . . . may be deadly . . . all that can result is that the patient will feel lowered in self-esteem for committing so stupid an act . . ." We are advised to pay attention to and listen to the patient, to avoid diminishing the patient's self-esteem and to recognize that we cannot in the final analysis prevent suicide from occurring.

Graham, P. Depression in pre-pubertal children. *Development Medicine and Child Neurology,* 1974, *16(3),* 340.

Grandis, S. V. Suicide in children and adolescents. *Medico-Legal Bulletin,* 1967, *172,* 1.

Gregory, I. Retrospective data concerning childhood loss of a parent. *Archives of General Psychiatry,* 1966, *15,* 354.

Green, R. G. Letter: Suicide and depression in childhood and adolescence. *Canadian Medical Association Journal,* 1974, *111(5),* 387.

†Gromska, J., & Tyszkiewics, M. Elementy psychodiagnostyki i psychoterapil w rysunkach mlodziezy z zespolami depresynjymi. (Elements of psychodiagnostics and psychotherapy in drawings by teenagers with depressive syndromes.) *Psychiatria Polska* (Warsaw), 1972, *6(4),* 417.

Paintings of 16 children aged 9 to 17 years with depressive syndromes were analyzed before, during, and after treatment with 200 mg per day thioridazine or 250 mg per day milipramine. Hereditary or environmental factors conducive to illness were found in all cases; 10 of these children showed depression in the course of cyclophrenia of several years duration, 7 showed depression for the first time. After overcoming initial reluctance they followed the physician's advice and started to paint, preferring to draw themes of their own choice rather than those which were assigned. During the acute stage of illness the paintings showed mutilations and monotony with lack of color and poor technique. With mental improvement islands of vivid color began to appear and with return to health the preillness color choice returned in almost all cases. Patients in whom graphic traits indicative of depression persisted in spite of clinical remission were prone to relapse and needed additional therapeutic care. 14 references. (Author abstract modified)

Haffter, C., Waage G., & Zumpe L. Suicide attempts of children and adolescents. *Psychologische Praxis,* 1966, *39,* 1.

Haider, I. Suicidal attempts in children and adolescents. *British Journal of Psychiatry,* 1968, *114(514),* 1133.

This paper describes suicidal children and adolescents seen over a 12-year span in a comprehensive psychiatric service serving a county in Scotland. Precise age breakdown is not given "sixty-four children in adolescence . . . between ages of six and nineteen." These youngsters were from large families and tended to be firstborn. The great majority of the families were "disturbed" and suicidal attempts seemed to be associated with family difficulties and adolescent crises. Haider states that "the largest diagnostic group was composed of character and behavior disorders. They were immature, impulsive children, and adolescents reacted strongly and excessively to stresses of a minor nature." They were "always in conflict with the environment . . ." Two were schizophrenic and 28 of the 61 studies were seen as depressed. Haider comments on the "erroneous impression that depression is rare in children . . . its presenting pictures may be different from those of depression in adults." Pure depression presented as restlessness, school refusal, crying without reason, sleep disturbance, isolation, boredom, antisocial activity, compulsive hyperactivity, running away from home and behavioral difficulties at home. It is important to recognize the symptoms as these symptoms represent an underlying depression.

†Haka-Ikse, K. Child development as an index of maternal mental illness. *Pediatrics,* 1975, *55(3),* 310.

It is maintained that the pediatrician's preoccupation with the health and welfare of children should not preclude his concern for the well-being of the mother when he encounters certain aberrations in the child's development. Children of mothers with severe depression usually present a common developmental pattern with delays or arrests in language, gross motor skills, and personal social skills. Once the developmental problems of the child are diagnosed as reactive to maternal mental illness, intervention aimed at reassigning the sick role from child to mother is recommended. 5 references.

Haldane, J. D., & Haider, I. Attempted suicide in children and adolescents. *British Journal of Clinical Practice,* 1967, *21(12),* 587.

This paper discusses 30 children and adolescents referred to the clinic because of attempted suicide. Five of these were 9 to 11 years of age, the remainder 12 to 15 years. The children are described as having been "abnormally intolerant of frustration, unusually dependent on one or both parents, aggressive and demanding in behavior and noticeably jealous of siblings ... The families included an aggressive, dominant father and anxious, submissive mother. The authors emphasize "a close association between attempted suicide, aggression, delinquency and family disorganization ..."

Hall, M. B. Our present knowledge about manic-depressive states in childhood. *Nervous Child*, 1951, *9*, 319.

On the basis of extensive personal clinical experience, Hall concludes that "major attacks of manic-depressive psychosis do not occur in childhood. Juvenile forms are encountered during adolescence, but are uncommon ... pronounced cyclothymic characteristics in childhood, combined with a family history of allied disorders, predispose to manic-depressive states in adult life."

Harlow, H. G., & Suomi, S. J. Production of depressive behaviors in young monkeys. *Journal of Autism and Childhood Schizophrenia*, 1971, *1*, 246.

Harms, E. Differential pattern of manic-depressive disease in childhood. *Nervous Child*, 1951, *9*, 326.

Harms vigorously advocates for the position that manic-depressive disease can exist in children and presents 10 case histories, the youngest of which was a 4-year-old girl. Harms argues that, while manic-depressive disorder in adults is classified as a psychosis, it is valid to diagnose manic-depressive disorder in children, even though the illness is not of psychotic severity. Reviewing the original concept of Emil Kraepelin, Harms conceptualizes "any manic-depressive ailment (as a disease of "des ganzen Gemuetslebens" (the total of the emotional sphere of the psyche) with various expressions in one or the other direction." Harms argues that appropriate treatment in childhood may "prevent their changing into a psychotic pattern later on."

Harrington, M., & Hassan, J. W. M. Depression in girls during latency. *British Journal of Medical Psychology*, 1958, *31*, 43.

Hersh, S. P. Epilogue: Future considerations and directions. In J. G. Schulterbrandt (Ed.), *Depression in childhood: Diagnosis, Treatment and Conceptual Models*. New York: Raven Press, 1977, pp. 147–149.

Most appropriately, Hersh ends this volume on depression in childhood with a resounding call for a developmental approach to the study of depression in adults: "for despite the impressive development over the last ten years, work on adult depression is not as precise as imagined and never will be until the ontogeny of affective states is better understood."

Hilgard, J. R. Depressive and psychotic states as anniversaries to sibling death in childhood. *International Psychiatric Clinics,* 1969, *6(2),* 175.

Hill, O. W. The association of childhood bereavement with suicidal attempt in depressive illness. *British Journal of Psychiatry,* 1969, *115(520),* 301.

Hill, O. W., & Price J. S. Childhood bereavement and adult depression. *British Journal of Psychiatry,* 1967, *113(500),* 743.

Hollon, T. H. Poor school performance as a symptom of masked depression in children and adolescents. *American Journal of Psychotherapy,* 1970, *24(2),* 258.

Howells, J. G. (Ed.), *Modern perspectives in child psychiatry.* Springfield, Illinois: C. C. Thomas, 1965.

Jacobs, J., & Teicher, J. D. Broken homes and social isolation in attempted suicides of adolescents. *International Journal of Social Psychiatry,* 1967, *13(2),* 139.

These authors compared the life histories of 50 adolescent suicide attempters with 32 controls, seeking to understand the importance of the "broken home" and the processes which progressively isolate the adolescent from meaningful social relationships.

By examining the biographies of these suicidal youths, the authors conclude that "the adolescent no longer seems to be attempting suicide over some trivial, isolated problem. *The findings also seriously call into question that adolescent suicide attempts are essentially unconscious irrational or impulsive in nature.*" The authors propose three stages beginning with a long-standing history of problems, an escalation of problems in adolescence and a final phase "characterized by the chain reaction disillusion of any meaningful social relationships in the weeks and days preceeding the suicide attempt." The authors engage the question of childhood depression as a predisposing factor and conclude that (in contrast to Bowlby and Zilboorg who propose that "parental loss in childhood predisposes to depression and suicide in later life") the authors' findings "do not tend to support this. Both the suicidal attempters and the adolescents had high rates of parental loss in childhood. One group attempted suicide, the other did not."

Jacobziner, H. Attempted suicides in children. *Journal of Pediatrics*, 1960, 56(4); 519.

Despite the title, this paper deals primarily with suicidal attempts by ingestion in adolescents rather than children. Of the total sample of 299, 5 percent were 9 to 12 years of age. Like other authors Jacobziner states that "many of the children in our series who attempted suicide came from broken, unstable and disorganized homes resulting from death, separation or divorce of parents."

†Jochmus, I. Reaktive depression bei legasthenikern. (Reactive depression in dyslexic children). In A. Annell (Ed.), *Depressive states in childhood and adolescence*. Stockholm: Almqvist and Wiksell, 1972, pp. 269–272.

At the Fourth Congress of the Union of European Pedopsychiatrists in Stockholm, August 30–September 3, 1971, the nature of reactive depression and its treatment in children with reading disability, or dyslexia, were described, with stress on the fact that constant excessive demands in school and environmental influences frequently lead to self-evaluation conflicts and psychoreactive disorders in normally or above-average gifted children who suffer from dyslexia. These disorders include reactive depression and are mostly accompanied by physical symptoms and therefore are easily overlooked. In some cases, psychopharmacologic drugs are given in support of psychotherapy. Somatic symptoms disappear almost invariably and, as a rule, even the depressive reaction is resolved within a few weeks. (Author abstract modified)

Joffe, W. G., & Sandler, J. Notes on pain, depression and individuation. *Psychoanalytic Study of the Child*, 1965, 20, 394.

†Jovanovic, N., & Radojicic, B. Kinderdepressionen. (Depression in children). In A. Annell (Ed.), *Depressive states in childhood and adolescence*. Stockholm: Almqvist and Wiksell, 1972, pp. 163–167.

At the Fourth Congress of the Union of European Pedopsychiatrists in Stockholm, August 30–September 3, 1971, depression in children separated from their mothers at an early age was described. The disturbance itself does not damage the personality but manifests itself mainly during the critical periods of life when psychological factors become particularly apparent. Experiences in early childhood are of special importance in the manifestation of depression, which often takes the form of anorexia, weepiness, or insomnia. Not every separation, however, causes depression. Feelings of guilt in the mother and the child are extremely critical in the development of the depression. The general constellation of the family, hereditary factors, and a number of other factors must also be considered when diagnosing such cases. 7 references. (Author abstract modified)

Kane, J., Coble, P., Conners, K., & Kupfer, D. J. EEG sleep in a child with severe depression. *American Journal of Psychiatry*, 1976, *137(7)*, 813.

This recent and exciting paper points out that "it is extremely difficult to diagnose depression in children because the clinical picture may vary depending on age and developmental level." In this paper, the authors report the psychiatric admission of an 11-year, 4-month-old girl "who had been referred for evaluation with withdrawn behavior and increasing school difficulties over the past years and suicidal threats over the previous several weeks." Utilizing methods for scoring EEG sleep records previously worked out by these authors, they studied this child's sleeping EEG. They found a variety of "sleep pattern (which was) characterized by a significant disturbance in sleep continuity." They report a very low value of mean sleep efficiency, and not an abnormally short REM latency.

Kasanin, J. The affective psychoses in children. *American Journal of Psychiatry*, 1931, *87*, 897.

Emphasizing the rarity of diagnosis of affective psychosis in childhood (in their experience, "only two or three children ... a year—of a total population of 1900") Kasanin presents a study of 10 cases, 6 boys and 4 girls, between the ages of 10 and 15 wherein the diagnosis of affective psychosis was made or considered. They found "serious physical anomolies and defects which differentiated them markedly from other children" in 5 of their 10 cases. The author was not able to divide the clinical material into homogeneous groups, did not find significant precipitating factors, and concluded that "the constitution of the child seems to be the most important single factor in the etiology and breakdowns."

Kaufman, I. Crimes of violence and delinquency in schizophrenic children. *Journal of the American Academy of Child Psychiatry*, 1962, *1*, 269.

†Kielholz, P. Aetiologische faktoren bei depressionen. (Etiological factors in depression). In A. Annell (Ed.), *Depressive states in childhood and adolescence*. Stockholm: Almqvist and Wiksell, 1972, pp. 63–73.

At the Fourth Congress of the Union of European Pedopsychiatrists in Stockholm, August 30–September 3, 1971, the etiological aspects of depression when treating and diagnosing the condition in children or adults were discussed. The suicidal risk must first be determined, and the choice of psychopharmacologic agent or therapy depends on this risk. An exact comprehensive diagnosis requires analyzing nosology based on etiological factors, such as heredity, personality, biographical data, social environment, and physical conditions. Organic and symptomatic depressions are often recognized too late, and very little is known about depressions caused by long-term medication and those occurring in drug addicts during abstinence, especially in the case of amphetamine addicts. In depression of organic or symptomatic origin, the basic illness must first be treated. Depressive schizophrenia must initially be treated with neuroleptics, while psychogenic depression mainly requires psychotherapy. In special cases, psychotherapy and drug therapy may be used in combination, such as with tranquilizers, to assist patients in relaxing and discussing their problems. The indication for and the choice of antidepressive drugs to be used in endogenous depression depend upon etiological factors, and upon phenomenological syndromal aspects of the condition. (Author abstract modified)

King, J. W. Depression and suicide in children and adolescents. *GP*, 1969, *39(3)*, 95.

In this paper King represents a general, clinically oriented overview of the field of depression, depression in children, and clinical management.

Klaus, M. H., Jerauld, R., Kreger, N. C., McAlpine, W., Steffa, M., and Kennell, J. H. Maternal attachment: Importance of the first postpartum days. *New England Journal of Medicine*, 1972, *286*, 460.

While this paper does not deal directly with depression in children, the issue of the mother-infant interaction in the earliest phase of life is of such importance that this clinical study is included in this bibliography. In order to "determine whether present hospital practices may affect later maternal behavior" the authors designed a control study to test the effect of sixteen hours of additional contact between mother and infant during the first postpartum days. The authors found that "extended-contact mothers were more reluctant to leave their infants with someone else, usually stood and watched during the examination, showed greater soothing behavior, and engaged in significantly more eye-to-eye contact and fondling" at 28 to 32 days.

Klein, M. The oedipus complex in the light of early anxieties. *International Journal of Psychoanalysis*, 1945, *26(1&2)*, 11.

†Kohler, C., & Beruard, F. Les etats depressifs chez l'enfant. (Depressive states in children.) In A. Annell (Ed.), *Depressive states in childhood and adolescence*. Stockholm: Almqvist and Wiksell, 1972, pp. 173–184.

At the Fourth Congress of the Union of European Pedopsychiatrists in Stockholm, August 30–September 3, 1971, the characteristics of depressive states in childhood were described based on observations of 17 children and adolescents between the ages of 10 and 16 years. Characteristics include feelings of tiredness, physical and mental heaviness, depressed mood, guilt feelings, fear of losing a loved one, suicidal thoughts and stupor and confusional anxiety, as well as problems at school and psychosomatic complaints. In addition, the relationship between these depressive states and the mourning neurosis and depersonalization found at the root of all depressions in children and in adults is described. The case material is classified as follows: melancholia (four cases), preschizophrenic conditions (two cases), reactive disturbances (three cases), neurotic disorders (two cases) and mixed or unclassifiable (five cases). Rorschach testing was the most frequently used diagnostic method, while psychopharmacological therapy was often used as treatment due to shortage of psychotherapists. In six cases, electroconvulsive therapy was used together with the other forms and is particularly important when treating dramatic reactions which often develop. It is concluded that depressive states are wrongly regarded as rare in children. Rather, the nature of the disorder is often concealed as the symptomatology is complex and atypical, making diagnosis difficult. 16 references. (Author abstract modified)

Kohler, C., & Beruard, F. *Les etates depressifs chez l'enfant*. (Depressive states in children) Brussels: Dessart., 1970, p. 118.

Seventeen cases of childhood depression are examined. Etiological problems are discussed including the exceptional character of depressive states before puberty, a tendency for vague yearnings during adolescence, the importance of similar familial antecedents, the effect of frequent moving in early childhood, problems of the structure or weakness of the ego, the psychoanalytical concept of the devouring mother as a bad object, scholastic relationship problems, somatic factors, and characterologic and biotypological considerations. The incidence of the different types of responses to the Rorschach Test are analyzed according to the groups of depression. The depressive states reveal the observation of indifferent forms, an absence of kinesthetic interpretations, a predominance of labile values, few animal interpretations, and banal responses.

The depressive preschizophrenic states are distinguished from the others by the reduction of forms, a much higher number of animal interpretations and the absence of human interpretations. Reactive depressions show a high percentage of good forms, more global interpretations, a slight number of animal responses, the constant presence of human responses, absence of responses about blood and the absence of perseveration.

Kohler, C. Suicide attempts in children and adolescents. *Pediatrics*, 1967, *22(7)*, 785.

Kosky, R. Severe depression in young adolescents: A report of five cases. *Medical Journal of Australia* (Sydney), 1975, *2(10)*, 387.

The clinical features of depressive illnesses in 5 boys aged 14 and 15 years are described. The early stages of the illnesses were not noticed by others and each boy made serious suicide attempts, which resulted in hospitalization. Subsequently, a depressive state was revealed in each case that was similar to major depressive illnesses of adults in depth and persistence. Elements of depression persisted for 6 months despite reasonably good functioning after six weeks. All received family and individual therapy. 16 references. (Author abstract modified).

*Kovacs, M., & Beck, A. T. An empirical clinical approach toward a definition of childhood depression. In J. G. Schulterbrandt, & A. Raskin (Eds.), *Depression in childhood: Diagnosis, treatment and conceptual models*. New York: Raven Press, 1977, pp. 1-25. Discussed by Nowels, pp. 27-31.

In this paper, Beck, widely known for his work in the systematic description of adult depression, and his coauthor present a very nice review of the literature defining depression in children. With respect to the concept of the "masked depression" the authors state that "the concept seems to have no clinical or heuristic significance and essentially signifies: (1) Events that initiate referral, or (2) Manifestations of a psychological disturbance acceptable or appropriate to that age category."

In the empirical portion of their paper, the authors, drawing upon Beck's well-known Beck Depression Inventory (BDI), administered a form of the BDI to children in the 7th and 8th grades. They note that "over fifty per cent of the sample apparently had concerns about self-dislike, work difficulty, dissatisfaction, and indecisiveness. Between twenty-nine percent and forty-nine percent of the sample had thoughts concerning sense of failure, fatigueability, self-image, change, guilt, anorexia, social withdrawal, self-harm, pessimism, and sadness." Turning to a population at the Philadelphia Child Guidance Clinic, the authors are currently seeking to validate a Childhood Depression Inventory.

I certainly agree with Nowels in his discussion of the paper that this paper is "a delight," representing beginnings of critical empirical research in this area. Further work by these two highly respected authors should be forthcoming soon and will undoubtedly provide a solid basis for research in this area for many years to come.

Krakowski, A. J. Depressive reactions of childhood and adolescence. *Psychosomatics*, 1970, *11(5)*, 429.

In this clinically-oriented discussion of depression, the author states that "in children practically all of (the symptoms of depression in adults) are in evidence but their character is somewhat different." He proposes that "depression in children can be diagnosed when the following conditions are in evidence: The child exposed to loss, as defined above, is unable to establish a compensatory defensive dependence; this results in a lowering of his self-esteem which he manifests by expressions of insecurity, inadequacy, helplessness and hopelessness whereby showing equivalent symptoms such as isolation, or other symptoms which create a vicious cycle leading to further rejection." Touching on the issue of the depressive equivalent, Krakowski states that "overdepressive feelings may be admitted, but also may be denied especially if the child uses a hostile tone or manifests aggressive behavior." The author then reviews the clinical manifestations of depressions in infancy, childhood, and adolescence, and discusses primary and secondary intervention. The use of antidepressive medication is discussed; in the author's experience "when the depressive symptomotology was in the foreground, antidepressants . . . were of little, if any, therapeutic benefit

... on the other hand, the greater the hyperkineticity and the hyperactivity as well as the behavior disturbances and somatizations the more positive were the effects ..."

Krevelen, A. Depression in children. *Acta Paedopsychiatria* (Basel), 1971, *38(7)*, 181.

Kuhn, R. Psychotherapie and pharmakotherapie. *Praxis der Psychotherapie,* 1967, *12*, 4, 145.

Kutschera, E. Treatment of restlessness and depressive conditions in children. *Medizinische Welt.,* 1972, *23(1)*, 39.

Labar, P. Depressive syndromes: The depressive syndrome in children and adolescents. *Revue Medicale de Liege*, 1972, *27(13)*, 432.

Labar, P. Suicide in children. *Revue Medicale de Liege*, 1973, *28(5)*, 142.

Langdell, J. Depressive reactions of childhood and adolescence. In S. A. Szurek, & I. N. Berlin (Eds.), *Clinical studies in childhood psychoses*. New York: Brunner/Mazel, 1973, pp. 127–148.

In this clearly written overview of depression in children and adolescents, Langdell presents a delightful review of the literature, both ancient and modern, and discusses depression in childhood, depression in adolescents, suicide in childhood, and proposes a diagnostic spectrum of depression in children: marasmic-anaclitic type, autistic type, marasmic type. Langdell briefly reviews, but does not discuss in depth, the "depressive equivalent" concept.

Landoni, G., & Ciompi, L. Statistical studies on the age of predilection of depressive disorders. *Evol. Psychiatr.* (Paris), 1971, *36(3)*, 583.

Langmeier, J., & Matejcek, Z. *Psychological deprivation in childhood*. New York: Brunner/Mazel, 1976.

Lawler, R. H., Nakielny, W., & Wright, N. A. Suicidal attempts in children. *Canadian Medical Association Journal*, 1963, *89*, 751.

The authors present a discussion of 22 suicidal attempts in children. The authors concur with many others in this field that family relationships were disturbed in the majority of cases, and state that "most patients demonstrated long-standing unrecognized disturbance of developmental states." In contrast to other writers, they note "superior intelligence in all but one patient." Their youngest patient was 8, the oldest 15.

†Lebovici, S. Contribution psychanalytique a la connaissance de la depression chez l'enfant et l'adolescent. (The contribution of psychoanalysis to the understanding of depression in children and

adolescents) In A. Annell (Ed.), *Depressive states in childhood and adolescence*. Stockholm: Almqvist and Wiksell, 1972, pp. 45–52.

At the Fourth Congress of the Union of European Pedopsychiatrists in Stockholm, August 30–September 3, 1971, Freud's psychoanalytical model for understanding depression as put forth in "Mourning and Melancholia" was used to analyze the nature of childhood and adolescent depression. The ego of the depressed person is possessed by the shadow of the lost object and the ambivalence formerly directed at the lost one turns to attack the ego. If the child is deprived of his mother, particularly at an early stage of development, depression may be explained as object loss. But the extensive interviews, drawing tasks and performance on the Thematic Apperception Test were the best methods of determining presence of depression. Different factors were then examined, including frequency, age at onset of depression, sex, role or cause of retardation, IQ, concomitant problems, and sociofamilial background. Depression in the severely retarded is apparently related to the depressive position described by Melanie Klein and the depressive reaction described by M.S. Mahler but a new dimension appears at adolescence which occasionally transforms subnormal reactions into grave pathological conditions. This is the dimension of time and the perception by the patient of expectations for the future: The illness is based primarily on anxiety about the future, the origin of which is as much familial and social as individual. (Author abstract modified)

Lempp, R. Depression in childhood and adolescence. *Landarzt*, 1965, *41(3)*, 94.

Lesse, S. Masked depression and depressive equivalents. *Psychopharmacology Bulletin*, 1977, *31(1)*, 68.

This brief clinical paper "calls attention to a broad spectrum of clinical patterns that may mask or hide a depressive illness," and includes a discussion of masked depression in infants and children. In this discussion, Lesse refers to developmental retardation, growth failure, impaired personality development, "acting out," hypochondriacal and psychosomatic problems and suicidal attempts.

Unfortunately, Lesse does not give us a rigorous definition of masked depression; his discussion covers so much ground as to raise the question as to what forms of abnormal behavior are in fact *not* masked depression.

Lester, D. Sibling position and suicidal behavior. *Journal of Individual Psychology*, 1966, *22(2)*, 204.

Lewin, B. D. Reflections on depression. *Psychoanalytic Study of The Child*, 1961, *16*, 321.

Liebermann, L. P. Three cases of attempted suicide in children. *British Journal of Medical Psychology*, 1953, *26*, 110.

Lindemann, E. Symptomatology and management of acute grief. *American Journal of Psychiatry*, 1944, *101*, 141.

Ling, W., Oftedal, G., & Weinberg, W. Depressive illness in childhood presenting as severe headache. *American Journal of Disturbed Child*, 1970, *120(2)*, 122.

Lipton, M. A. (reviewer of): Separation and depression. In J. P. Scott, & E. C. Jenay (Eds.), *AAAS* Publication 94, Washington, D.C., 1973.

Lordi, W. M. Suicide in children and adolescents. *Virginia Medical Monthly*, 1971, *98(4)*, 209.

> This is a brief clinical essay concerning suicide in children and adolescents. Lordi emphasizes "driving themes . . . are depression, despair, anger, retaliation, wishing to be reunited with lost loved ones and magical attempts to undo or resolve some of the world's conflicts and some of the families' conflicts." "The different sense of death and discontinuance of life," characteristic of children, is also a factor. Thus, the child may more readily entertain a fantasy of a return to life following death. (This is most elegantly outlined and presented in Mark Twain's novel, Tom Sawyer, wherein Tom repeatedly presents his wish to die and yet remain alive so that he may experience the greeting of his friends and family.) Lordi particularly brings to our attention factors, either biological or experiential, which reduce the child's capacity to handle impulse, and asserts that the "most grossly overlooked and neglected problem in the experience of the author is the presence of a brain dysfunction." In general, while suicidal attempts are "primarily an acting out of the child's omnipotence, even in a psychotic state" incidence of suicidal attempts in children are undoubtedly under-estimated and should be taken seriously.

Lourie, R. S. Suicide and attempted suicide in children and adolescents. *Texas Medicine*, 1967, *63*, 53.

> This paper is of particular interest, emphasizing that suicide in children, despite its statistical rarity, is in fact an important and growing problem. Lourie presents a delightful historical review. From 1880 to 1935, causality concerning suicide of the young was

blamed progressively on "trashy novels," "the educational system," and "constitutional factors," with the exception of a symposium at the Vienna Psychoanalytic Institute in 1910. Since the late 1930s, there has been an increasing interest on deeper underlying motives for children wanting to die. In this paper Lourie discusses impulsiveness, the absence of a clear precipitating cause, and the immature concept of death characteristic of children. Lourie presents case vignettes of 14 children, ranging in age from 7 to 12 and suffering from a wide range of problems. Depression is mentioned in one of these cases. In discussing determinants of the suicidal attempts, Lourie considers aggression and escape from an intolerable situation of reality as the two most frequent factors. In 10 cases, there was evidence of aggression turned against themselves. Several of the youngsters were psychotic or retarded. Lourie notes that "inevitably there was a pleasurable result which the child hoped to achieve by turning the aggression against himself." Escape motif was common, as was identification, particularly among the younger children. Lourie notes that "there were no depressions in the usual clinical sense unless one counted situational depressions growing out of the denial of an immediate satisfaction or as a response to a pattern of chronic deprivation of poor self image." Subsequently, Lourie notes that "it is interesting that chronic depression and superego problems were not major determinants in the children we studied. The depression we saw was situational."

Lourie, R. S. Clinical studies of attempted suicide in childhood. *Clinic Proc. Child Hosp. DC*, 1966, *22(6)*, 163.

Lukianowicz, N. Attempted suicide in children. *Acta Psychiatrica Scandinavica*, 1968, *44(4)*, 415.

This paper, one of the early extensive clinical discussions of attempted suicide in children, presents a review of the modest literature in this field, and reports on a number of children who made suicidal attempts of varying severity. The cases ranged in age from 9 to 13 years of age, and are described in rich, clinical vignettes. Lukianowicz divides the cases into four types: Attempted total suicide, attempted partial suicide, threatened suicide, and contemplated suicide. In his extensive discussion, Lukianowicz discusses the importance of the various factors leading to a suicidal attempt.

Masked depression and depressive equivalents: The Gutheil Memorial Conference. *American Journal of Psychotherapy*, 1967, *21(3)*, 565.

*Mahler, M. S. On sadness and grief in infancy and childhood. *Psychoanalytic Study of the Child*, 1961, *16*, 332.

In this paper, Mahler presents the point of view that "Bibring's definition of depression as the emotional expression of a state of helplessness is generally applicable" and argues that in infancy and childhood *grief as a basic ego reaction does prevail even though* ... the immature personality structure of the infant or older child is not capable of producing a state of depression such as that seen in the adult."

This paper nicely complements the work of Bibring and Anthony and stands in direct contrast to that of Rie.

Mahler, M. S. Development of basic moods. R. M. Lowenstein, L. M. Newman, M. Schur, & A. A. Solnit (Eds.), *Psychoanalysis—A general psychology*. New York: International Universities Press, 1966.

Elsewhere in this volume, we have discussed the importance of the "ego psychology school" of psychoanalysis for the development of a theory of depression in children. Reduced to its simplest terms, the issue here is whether or not a fully developed superego, i.e., the completion of the tasks of adolescence, is necessary before the diagnosis of depression is possible.

In this essay, Mahler discusses the complexity of the concept of loss and the importance of early mother-child interactions in affective development. She states that "in our studies, we came across unmistakable evidence for the belief that a basic mood is established during the separation-individuation process (which) is not due solely to innate factors but seems ... to be accentuated experientially and to counteract the constitutional characteristics of the individual child." Mahler and her group therefore "support Bibring's contention (1953) that the depressive response is also a 'basic affective reaction, very much as anxiety is' ... the depletion of 'confident expectation' and diminuation of self-esteem with concomitant deficiently neutralized aggression create the libido-economic basis for the depressive mood." Mahler points out that the depletion of basic trust, resulting from a "relatively great and sudden sense of helplessness" which underlie the depressive response can occur "*even before super-ego precursors are consolidated into a super-ego structure*" (Italics added).

Majluf, E. Sindromes depresivos en el nino (Depressive syndromes in the child). *Revista de Neuro-Psiquiatria*, (Peru), 1960, *23(3)*, 338.

†Makita, K. The rarity of "depression" in childhood. *Acta Paedopsychiatrica* (Basel), 1973, *40(1)*, 37.

The belief that childhood depression is a rarity is discussed. It is suggested that the number of depressed children that could be diagnosed as having depressive disease are few, and that other depressive conditions in children are more or less of a reactive nature. It is maintained that in any case the number of children who react with depressive features are still rare; this rarity is explained from three psychopathological interpretations. The adequacy of applying the term "depressive" to children to describe their so-called depressive moods is questioned and the tendency to apply the concept and the diagnostic criteria of adult depression retroactively on children is criticized. It is concluded that the study of childhood depression could be more rewarding when the manifestations of so-called depressive mood in children are studied in accordance with each developmental level independently of adult diagnostic criteria. 17 references. (Author abstract modified.)

*Malmquist, C. P. Depressions in childhood and adolescence. *New England Journal of Medicine*, 1971, *284(16)*, 887, 955.

This pair of papers, which appeared in the prestigious *New England Journal of Medicine*, represent a major landmark in this literature. Malmquist points out that "there are four primary ways in which the term (depression) is used: As an internal active affective state or symptom; as a set of physiological responses; as a clinical syndrome; or as a nosologic entity." Viewing the area of attachment behaviors, Malmquist points out that the "concept of loss has subsequently been extended to include more subtle variations of disruptions and distortions in parent-child relations. These have the possibility of being as devastating in their affects as gross maternal deprivation and separation." (See the paper by Sandler & Joffe concerning this point.) Depressive proneness is discussed in terms of the "varieties of pathologic self-esteem regulation." Malmquist discusses various family constellations which may predispose the child to depression, and presents a complex and comprehensive classification of childhood depressions of which the major types are: 1) those associated with organic diseases; 2) deprivation syndromes; 3) syndromes associated with difficulties in individuation; 4) latency types; and 5) adolescent types.

Malmquist presents a characteristic symptom list in the depressed child: appearance, withdrawal, physical and vegetative signs, a quality of discontent, a sense of feeling rejected, low frustration tolerance, reversal of affect, attempts to deny feelings of helplessness and hopelessness, provocative behavior, tendencies to passivity, sensitivity and high standards, obsessive-compulsive behavior, and episodic acting-out.

*Malmquist, C. P. Depression in childhood. F. F. Flach, & S. C. Draghi (Eds.), *The nature and treatment of depression*. New York: Wiley, 1975.

In this well-written comprehensive overview, Malmquist presents a review of the literature in this area, which is particularly useful for its review of the early psychoanalytic contributions of Abraham. Malmquist then reviews clinical work regarding infancy and middle childhood.

*Malmquist, C. P. Childhood depression: A clinical and behavioral perspective. In J. G. Schulterbrandt, & A. Raskin (Eds.), *Depression in childhood: Diagnosis, treatment and conceptual models*. New York: Raven Press, 1977, pp. 33–59. Discussion by E. James Anthony, pp. 61–63; discussion of Malmquist's paper by Leon Cytryn, pp. 64–68.

In this most recent of an impressive series of papers in this field, Malmquist first systematically reviews the major contributions to the prior literature in this field. Drawing on his own and prior work, he then presents "a composite picture of how a depressed child would appear based on our present state of knowledge"; in his composite, Malmquist includes an unhappy appearance, withdrawal and inhibition, somatizing, a quality of discontent, a feeling of rejection, negative self-concepts, low frustration tolerance, unusual response to reassurance, reversal of affect (i.e. clowning, etc.), blatant attempts to deny feelings of helplessness and hopelessness, provocative behavior, tendencies to passivity, sensitivity on high standards, obsessive-compulsive behavior, and episodic acting-out.

In his discussion of Malmquist's paper, Anthony points out that "we are now calling many things depressions which, in the past, we did not call depression and I think we may go over the top and label everything depression." Yet, the diagnosis of depression in children may be sufficiently difficult that "it is sometimes difficult to identify depression in children unless cases are followed carefully for extended periods."

Anthony here discusses what I consider to be a very central issue. "Depression in children," long an ugly duckling, may now become such a swan that it is ubiquitous and even useless. Yet, as we have sought to discuss the context of case reports elsewhere in this volume, the clinical use of "depression in children" may be a matter of considerable subtlety. That is, a "diagnosis" may be an easy, if relatively unimportant, exercise; appropriate clinical use of any concept challenges our best clinical resources.

Cytryn presents a very interesting discussion. Drawing on his own extensive well-known experience in this field, he reports the difficulty encountered in the assessment of depression in children. Very interestingly, in contrast to other authors, Cytryn here presents strong clinical evidence in support of the concept of the "masked depressive reaction" in childhood.

Mangold, B., & Seidl, J. E. Attempted suicide as a child psychiatric case of emergency. *Praxis der Kinderpsychologie und Kinderpsychiatrie,* 1974, *23(6),* 233.

Mattsson, A., Seese, L. R., & Hawkins, J. W. Suicidal behavior as a child psychiatric emergency. *Archives of General Psychiatry,* 1969, *20,* 100.

In this widely-quoted paper, the authors report "the results of a retrospective and follow-up study of seventy-five children and adolescents with suicidal behavior," and compared them to nonsuicidal acutely disturbed children. Eight-three percent of these were between the ages of 12 and 18 years all of the girls were older than 12 years, and 7 percent of the sample was younger than 11 years of age. The authors note "the abundant evidence of long-standing individual and family psychopathology. About seventy-five percent of both suicidal and non-suicidal children had a history of emotional disorder of more than one year's duration." Of considerable interest for the purposes of this volume, however, is the authors' observations that "the evidence of depression, however, separated the two groups of chronically disturbed children. Among the suicidal children, thirty patients—or forty percent—(eight boys and twenty-two girls) had for at least one month displayed signs of depressive illness (social withdrawal, loss of initiative and self-esteem, changing scholastic performance, sadness, crying spells, decreased appetite and motor activity, sleep disturbances); in only twelve (thirteen percent) of the non-suicidal patients had similar signs been observed." The hospitalization was triggered by an acute conflict between child and parents in 40 percent of both suicidal and nonsuicidal patients. There were no differences between primary diagnoses in the two groups. The authors divided their overall patient sample into six groups: Loss of love object followed by acute or prolonged grief; "the bad me," markedly self-depreciating patients; the final "cry for help" directed beyond the immediate family; the revengeful angry teenager; the psychotic adolescent; and the "suicidal game." With respect to management, the authors state that "the majority of young suicidal patients can be treated as outpatients provided the patient is no longer suicidal, seriously depressed, or psychotic. Of particular importance is whether the family's cooperation can be secured, in terms of re-establishing meaningful verbal communication with the patient. This is the sine qua non in preventing the intrapersonal and interpersonal conflicts from re-expressing themselves in self-destructive acts."

McAnarney, E. R. Suicidal behavior of children and youth. *Pediatric Clinics of North America,* 1975, *22(3),* 595.

Case reports are of adolescents and the discussion of the suicidal child is along familiar lines.

McConville, B. J., Boag, L. C., & Purohit, A. P. Mourning processes in children of varying ages. *Canadian Psychiatric Association Journal,* 1970, *15(3),* 253.

McConville, B. J., Boag, L. C., & Purohit, A. P. Three types of childhood depression. *Canadian Psychiatric Association Journal,* 1973, *18(2),* 133.

McConville, B. J., Boag, L. C., & Purohit, A. P. Mourning depressive responses in residence following sudden death of parent figures. *Journal of the American Academy of Child Psychiatry,* 1972, *11(2),* 341.

McDermott, J. F. Divorce and its psychiatric sequelae in children. *American Medical Association Archives of General Psychiatry,* 1970, *23(5),* 421.

McDermott, J. F., & Finch, S. M. Ulcerative colitis in children: Reassessment of a dilemma. *Journal of the American Academy of Child Psychiatry,* 1967, *6(3),* 512.

McHarg, J. F. Mania in childhood: Report of a case. *Archives of Neurological Psychiatry,* 1954, *72,* 531.

In this paper, McHarg reviews the literature concerning manic-depressive disorder in childhood and presents the case of an 11-year-old girl who demonstrated the onset of a manic phase two or three weeks before a major examination. Her manic phase lasted for approximately eight weeks and was then depressed, again for about eight weeks. She was subsequently stable.

McKinney, W. T., et al. Studies in depression. *Psychology Today,* 1971, *4(12),* 61.

†*McKnew, D., & Cytryn, L. Detection and treatment of childhood depression. *Scientific proceedings in summary form: 128th Annual Meeting, APA.* Washington, D.C.: American Psychiatric Association, 1975, pp. 87–88.

At the 128th Annual Meeting of the American Psychiatric Association, held in Anaheim, California, May 1975, a paper was presented in which studies on the beneficial effects of early detection and appropriate therapy in preventing permanent damage in cases of childhood depression were discussed. It was noted that the primary physician is in the most strategic position to detect early signs and may elect to investigate the case himself or refer the child to a psychiatrist. It was felt that the most important treatment modality is some variant of family intervention, which can vary from intensive family psychotherapy involving all family members to periodic counseling of the parents without direct contact with the child. When family and parental treatment are insufficient, individual treatment of the child becomes necessary. As a rule, the depressed child responds very favorably to psychotherapy. The therapist's interest in the child's successes both inside and outside the therapeutic setting provides an important avenue for increasing the patient's self-esteem and sense of mastery. In some cases brief hospitalization is an effective form of crisis intervention. (Journal abstract modified)

†*McKnew, D. H., Cytryn, L. Historical background in children with affective disorders. *American Journal of Psychiatry,* 1973, *130(11),* 1278.

In this interesting clinical paper, McKnew and Cytryn present the histories of "fifty children with affective disorders (and found that) certain environmental factors were present either singly or in combination in every case." They relate the categories of depression presented in their earlier paper (acute, chronic and masked), pointing out that "each category of depression could be linked with a characteristic cluster of environmental factors. . . ." These environmental factors were: frequent separations, sudden loss, depreciation and rejection, loss of involvement and depression of parents. They conclude that "the sine qua non in acute depressive reactions is the sudden loss of a love object and the sine qua non in chronic depressive reactions is depression in at least one parent. In masked depressive reactions, however, there does not appear to be a universal factor."

McKinney, W. T., Jr. Animal behavioral/biological models relevant to depressive and affective disorders in humans. In J. G. Schulterbrandt, & A. Raskin (Eds.), *Depression in childhood: Diagnosis, treatment, and conceptual models.* New York: Raven Press, 1977.

McKinney, whose exciting work in the use of nonhuman experimental models of human affective states has been appearing regularly in the psychiatric journals, is a most welcome addition to this volume. Following a brief review of the literature in this field, McKinney discusses fundamental experimental means whereby depression-like syndromes may be produced, including social and neurobiological methods. He concludes that "our work, as well as the work of others in different laboratories, has by now clearly demonstrated that the study of animal models can have relevance for our understanding of depression in the young developing organisms."

†Meierhofer, M. Depressive verstimmungen im fruhen kindesalter. (Depressions in infancy and childhood). In A. Annell (Ed.), *Depressive states in childhood and adolescence.* Stockholm: Almqvist and Wiksell, 1972, pp. 159–162.

At the Fourth Congress of the Union of European Pedopsychiatrists in Stockholm, August 30–September 3, 1971, the causes of depression in infants and toddlers, investigated in several cross-sectional and longitudinal studies, were considered. Observations of 400 young children living in residential nurseries revealed particularly severe depressive states, the main causes being loneliness and frustration resulting from collective care and frequent changes in environment. Resignation and depression caused retarded development, particularly in regard to language and intelligence. Frustration was also found in infants living with their families, as early as in the first few months of life, due to strict adherence to inflexible rules of general care and feeding. In longitudinal observations of more than 50 children followed from birth to school age, depressive states in infancy were found in about 25 percent. These states were usually due to conflict between mother and child or jealousy of a younger sibling. (Author abstract modified)

Mendelson, M. *Psychoanalytic concepts of depression.* New York: Spectrum Publications, 1974.

Meyendorf, R. Infant depression due to separation from siblings. Syndrome of depression, retardation, starvation, and neurological symptoms. A re-evaluation of the concept of maternal deprivation. *Psychiatria clinica* (Basel), 1971, *4(5)*, 321.

Milner, M. A suicidal symptom in a child of three. *International Journal of Psychoanalysis,* 1944, *25(3 and 4)*, 53.

Moch, M. Comparative study of suicide attempts by children and adolescents observed in three pediatric departments and those collected in a pedo-psychiatric department. *Reve de Neuropsychiatrie Infantile et d'Hygiene Mentale de L'Enfance,* 1969, *17(8)*, 513.

Morrison, G. C. Therapeutic intervention in a child psychiatry emergency service. *Journal of the American Academy of Child Psychiatry,* 1969, *8(3)*, 542.

Muller, H. Suicide in children and adolescents. *Deutsch Krankenpflegez,* 1975, *28(10)*, 571.

Muller, H. Suicide in children and adolescents. *Therapie der Gegenwart (Berlin),* 1975, *114(7)*, 1055, 1058, 1062.

Murphy, L. B. Coping, vulnerability and resilience in childhood. In G. V. Coelho, D. A. Hamburg, J. F. Adams (Eds.), *Coping and adaptation.* New York: Basic Books, 1974.

Murray, P. A. The clinical picture of depression in school children. *Journal of the Irish Medical Association,* 1970, *63(392)*, 53.

Nagera, H. Children's reaction to the death of important objects: A developmental approach. *Psychoanalytic Study of the Child,* 1970, *25*, 360.

Negri, M. Q. E., & Moretti, G. Some aspects of depression in children. *Acta Paedopsychiatrie* (Basel), 1971, *38(7)*, 182.

The Nervous Child, 1952, *9*(4). (The entire issue devoted to depressive and manic illness in childhood.)

Newman, C. J., Dember, C. F., & Krug, O. "He can but he won't"; . . . *Psychoanalytic Study of the Child,* 1973, *28*, 83.

†Nissen, G. *Depressive syndrome im kindes- und jugendalter: Beitrag zur symptomatologie, genese und prognose.* (Depressive syndromes in children and in adolescents: Contribution to symptomatology, origin and prognosis.) Berlin: Springer, 1971, p. 174.

A systematic investigation of the symptoms of depression in children and adolescents is presented, including a comprehensive representation and statistical evaluation of the multiform symptomatology and a summary according to diagnostic and nosological syndromes. A critical appraisal is presented of the case histories and the usefulness of an initial diagnosis and a consideration of the prognosis. The investigation is supported by 105 case histories of children and adolescents between 1942 and 1968 with moderate and severe symptoms of depression. These data are also analyzed from the sociological viewpoint and compared with widely distributed reports in the literature. It is of particular interest that none of the children, including those first diagnosed as endogenous depression cases, ultimately developed an endogenous depression. Less than half the patients developed a reactive depression and every 11th child developed a schizophrenic psychosis. Of the total number, 14 percent developed normally, 60 percent showed improvement or a complete cure. Because of the interpolation of the concepts applied to adult psychoses, this investigation marks an important step toward a new nosology which can be of use even in adult psychiatry.

Nissen, G. Depressice und hypochondrische storungen im kindesalter. *Praxis der Kinderpsychologie und Kinderpsychiatrie,* 1967, *16(1),* 6.
†Nissen, G. Lavierte depressionen bei kindern? (Disguised depressions in children?) *Acta Paedopsychiatrica* (Basel,) 1975, *41(6),* 235.

It is proposed that children's depressive conditions manifesting themselves in psychosomatic forms can be labeled as disguised depressions only from the viewpoint of adult psychiatry. It is suggested that in fact these manifestations are genuine primary depressions, albeit difficult to diagnose because of their childhood characteristic symptomatology. Retrospective and prospective investigations meant to identify behavior disorders in childhood as precursors or as first stages of affective psychoses are reported to have been unsuccessful. A considerable numerical discrepancy is noted between information derived from adult depressive patients and observations made by child psychiatrists with regard to frequency of endogenous stages in children. It is felt that early recognition of depressive syndromes in children is of prophylactic importance, since prognosis may be poor if treatment is not given at an early stage. 33 references. (Author abstract modified)

Nissen, G., & Spilimbergo, A. On the symptoms and therapy of depressive diseases diagnosed in early childhood. *Monatsschr Kinderheilkd,* 1970, *118(4),* 136.
Ockel, A. Clowning in childhood. *Praxis der Kinderpsychologie und Kinderpsychiatrie,* 1967, *16(2),* 41.
†Ossofsky, J. Endogenous depression in infancy and childhood. *Comprehensive Psychiatry,* 1974, *15(1),* 19.

Data obtained from 220 children between the ages of 1 and 12 treated with imipramine for a variety of disorders in which endogenous depression dominated the clinical picture are analyzed. Such depression can be diagnosed in infants and children and the pediatrician is in a better position than the psychiatrist to prevent disability by suspecting it in any hyperactive infant, especially the infant born following a precipitate labor, i.e., one considered to have the "minimal cerebral dysfunction" syndrome. Family history of depression, although often present, is almost never obtained during the initial psychiatric evaluation. As the parent begins to trust the therapist, a surprising amount of significant information in the family history is found to have been denied or ignored originally. The extent to which early treatment can reduce disability and alter the natural course of the disease is unknown. The possibility of defining more precise subtypes of depressive illness is most challenging and may serve to clarify some of the puzzling treatment problems encountered in treating endogenous depression in adults. 1 reference.

Ott, J., Geyer, M., & Schneemann, K. Multidimensional clinical psychotherapy of a group of children and adolescents following suicide attempt. *Psychiatrie, Neurologie und Medizinische Psychologie.* (Leipz), 1972, *24(2),* 104.

Otto, U. Suicidal attempts made by psychotic children and adolescents. *Acta Paediatrica Scandinavica,* 1967, *56(4),* 349.

Otto, U. Suicidal attempts in adolescence and childhood: States of mental illness and personality variables. *Acta Paedopsychiatrica,* 1964, *31,* 397.

In this paper of the series, Otto seeks to "give an account of observations concerning psychiatric illness and personality variables among children and adolescents attempting suicide." Following an extensive analysis of his own data and a careful and extensive review of the literature in this field, Otto concludes that "the analysis indicates that the most unusual personality variables are the infantile and the hysteroid. The most common psychiatric states of illness are: Neurosis and states of mental insufficiency on a neurotic basis with a depressively tainted syndrome."

Otto U. Suicidal acts by children and adolescents. A follow-up study. *Acta Paediatrica Scandinavia (Suppl.),* 1972, *233,* 7.

Otto, U. Changes in the behavior of children and adolescents preceding suicidal attempts. *Acta Psychiatrica Scandinavia,* 1964, *40,* 386.

In this member of a well-known series of papers, the author seeks to "elucidate the period preceding this suicidal attempt on the basis or the original material, for the primary purpose of endeavoring to arrive at a presuicidal syndrome of practical importance for appreciating the suicidal risk in children and adolescents." Otto reviews the earlier literature in the area and then proceeds to divide their own series of 1,727 Swedish children and adolescents under 21 years into five groups with respect to the kinds of changes in their behavior that occurred prior to the suicidal attempt: 1) changes which were conspicuous to the environment; 2) mental changes of an extrovert character, ambiguous to the environment; 3) symptoms of a more purely neurotic character; 4) depressive symptoms; 5) symptoms indicative of a psychosis.

The author concludes that "in spite of intensive efforts, it has not been possible to crystallize any specific presuicidal syndrome, which makes it possible to predict whether an individual will commit a suicidal act." He does note that "the most common change occurring in the period immediately preceding this suicidal attempt consists of the addition of depressive symptoms and of neurotic symptoms of the type anguish, unrest and sleep difficulties and of psychosomatic symptoms."

Palaszny, M., & McNabb, M. Therapy of a six-year-old who committed fratricide. *Journal of the American Academy of Child Psychiatry*, 1975, *14(2)*, 319.

Parnitzke, C., & Regel, H. Suicidal actions in childhood and adolescence. *Psychiatrie Neurologie und Medizinische Psychologie* (Leipzig) 1972, *24(9)*, 528.

Parquet, P. H. Child suicide and suicidal children. *Lille Medical*, 1974, *19(9)*, 980.

†Penot, B. Caracteristiques et devenir des depressions de la deuxieme enfance. (Characteristics and course of depressions in children aged five to eleven years.) In A. Annell (Ed.), *Depressive states in childhood and adolescence.* Stockholm: Almqvist and Wiksell, 1972, pp. 525–533.

At the Fourth Congress of the Union of European Pedopsychiatrists in Stockholm, August 30–September 3, 1971, characteristics and the course of depression in children between 5 and 11 years of age were described based on studies of 17 subjects with symptoms of severe depression. Clinical observations followed three methodological imperatives: A dynamic understanding of the whole personality and a psychotherapeutic approach of the psychoanalytic type; a protracted follow-up continued as long as possible into adolescence; and systematic family contact. It appears that: 1) severe depression in children may be manifested in different symptom pictures (affective psychosis, neurotic depression, and character changes) and does not constitute a particular clinical entity; 2) the favorable course observed in about 50 percent of the cases is determined by the capacity for secondary elaboration (adequate neurotic defense); 3) the family situation is sometimes characterized by temporary maternal deprivation but more frequently by traumatic separations. In all cases, the mothers had been subject to depression. Such cases should be followed in sufficient number from childhood to adulthood to better determine the role of early depression in subsequent development of pathological conditions. (Author abstract modified)

†Penot, B. On infantile depressions. *Psychiatrie de l'Enfant,* 1974, *16(2),* 301.

Pinneau, S. R. Infantile disorders of hospitalism and anaclitic depression. *Psychological Bulletin,* 1955, *52,* 429.

In this paper, Pinneau reviews extensive work of Rene Spitz and concludes that "some of the major vulnerabilities in Spitz's report of his studies may be summarized as follows: He fails to indicate the dates and places of the studies and neglects to indicate the composition and training of the research staff. He is inconsistant in his report of the number of children present in his studies, and his descriptions of their parents are contradictory. The groups which are compared as to mental and emotional development apparently differ in racial extraction, socioeconomic background and in heredity. He is inconsistent in his descriptions of their physical surroundings, of their care, and of their physical health." Pinneau concludes that while he "does not doubt the potential advantages of maternal as compared with institutional care," he concludes that "as yet ... we do not have convincing evidence based on scientifically controlled investigations, as to any of the major problems in this area."

Pinneau then discusses a study of infants in a Catholic home for unmarried mothers, carried out by Fischer. Pinneau concludes that there is "considerable doubt that Fischer's investigations support Spitz's conception of hospitalism."

*Poznanski, E., & Zrull, J. P. Childhood depression. *American Medical Association Archives of General Psychiatry*, 1970, *23(1)*, 8.

This widely quoted, now-classic paper in the literature on childhood depression presents clinical vignettes concerning 14 children ranging in age from 3 to 12 years, all of whom showed depressive symptoms. Negative self-image was the most frequent disturbance observed while some form of difficulty in handling aggression was the most frequent symptomatic behavior which initiated referral. Like other workers in the field, Poznanski and Zrull found long-standing difficulties in the families of these children, including: high incidence of parental depression, difficulties handling aggression and hostility, and overt parental rejection.

Provence, S. Bemerkungen uber entwicklungsphasen und psychosomatische symptome. *Psyche* (Stuttgart), 1967, *21*, 1, 44.

Putnam, C., Rank, B., & Kaplan, S. Notes on John I.: A case of primal depression in an infant. *Psychoanalytic Study of the Child*, 1951, *6*, 38.

Putnam, M. C. Case study of an atypical two-and-a-half-year-old. *American Journal of Orthopsychiatry*, 1948, *18*, 1.

Rajhkis, H. A. Depression as a manifestation of the family as an open system. *Archives of General Psychiatry*, 1963, *19(1)*, 57.

Rapaport, J. L. Report of subcommittee on the treatment of depression in children. Pediatric psychopharmacology in childhood depression. In J. G. Schulterbrandt, & A. Raskin (Eds.), *Depression in childhood: Diagnosis, treatment and conceptual models*. New York: Raven Press, 1977, pp. 87–100. Discussion by C. Keith Conners, pp. 101–104.

In this chapter, Rapaport, following the lead of Klein in work with adults, proposes that since some "creative uses of drug response have been proposed as a means of syndrome identification ... I would like to review some possible similar approaches to childhood depression..." She points to three major areas of focus: Difference between the "affective response of preadolescent children and that of adults to stimulant drugs and to steroids" secondly the "study of drug treatment of so-called masked depressions of depressive equivalents," and finally the use of pharmacotherapy "for 'depressed' children may suggest possible clinical subgroupings of these heterogeneous groups ..."

Rapaport then presents a nicely organized review of these areas, and summarizes that this survey "provides no conclusions about drug efficacy or about the validity of a concept of childhood depression."

In his discussion of Rapaport's paper, Conners reports the variability of response to stimulant medication, noting that "some children, in response to stimulant medication, are weepy, sad, and listless and they express feelings of mournfulness and hopelessness. They become quite retarded in their motor activity . . . I have never found anything that predicts that response. We looked for a history of family illnesses of various kinds including depression and that was not consistent either . . ." We are thus once again reminded of the complexity and variability of children's response to similar medication. Conners briefly touches on the issue of loss: "Every child experiences depressive affects in mourning after a loss, but only some children continue to experience such affects for a prolonged period and only some of those in later life have a depressive breakdown."

Raskin, A. Depression in children: Fact or fallacy? In J. G. Schulterbrandt, & A. Raskin (Eds.), *Depression in childhood: Diagnosis, treatment and conceptual models.* New York: Raven Press, 1977, pp. 141–146.

Herein we learn of important, but as yet unpublished work, directed toward defining diagnostic criteria of depression in children appropriate for research work. In contrast to his somewhat provocative title, Raskin concludes: "I am sure nobody questions that children are both capable of experiencing depression and do, in fact, become depressed. The unresolved issues are how children express or manifest depression: How pervasive, intense and long-lasting these feelings and associated behaviors are; and whether there are sub-groupings of depressed children with differing etiologies, patterns of symptoms, responses to treatment and susceptability for later adult depression."

Redlich, E., & Lazar, G. Uber kindliche selbstmorder. Berlin: Verlag von Julius Springer, 1914.

This hard-to-obtain book in German, is rarely mentioned in the literature on childhood depression but probably deserves mention as a classic in the field. Published in 1914, it includes a number of case reports concerning suicidal children. The youngest of these, a 5-year-old girl whose father "trinkt viel Rum" sprang through a window due to mishandling and hunger ("wegen Misshandlung und hunger feim Fenster hinaus-gesprungen").

Reichsman, F., Engle, G. L., Harway, V., & Escalona, S. K. Monica, an infant with gastric fistula and depression; an interim report on her development to the age four years. *Psychiatric Research Report,* 1957, *8,* 12.

Reinhart, J. B. Regional enteritis in pediatric patients: Psychiatric aspects. *Journal of the American Academy of Child Psychiatry,* 1968, *7(2),* 252.

†Renshaw, D. C. Depression in the young. *Journal of the American Medical Association,* 1963, *28(10),* 542.

†Renshaw, D. C. Sexuality and depression in infancy, childhood and adolescence. *Medical Aspects of Human Sexuality,* 1975, *9,* 24.

Renshaw, D. C. Depression in the 1970's. *Diseases of the Nervous System,* 1973, *34(5),* 241.

The increasing incidence of depression in the 1970s is discussed. Depression in infancy is described as a deviation from the expectable normal activity and responses to stimuli. Childhood depression is often acted out with angry outbursts and school avoidance. Depression is discussed in relation to the infant, the child, the adolescent, the adult, and the aged. Treatment procedures include: 1) ventilation of feelings; 2) informed reassurance and guidance; 3) medication and family involvement for the low suicide risk patient; and additional environmental assistance. The vulnerability of doctors and individuals in public office are considered. 13 references.

Renshaw, D. C. Suicide and depression in children. *Journal of School Health,* 1974, *44(9),* 487.

Depression is traced from infancy through childhood to adolescence to determine underlying causes and to prevent suicides. Infant depression is found to be related to absence of a mother figure and lack of proper fondling. Childhood depression may manifest itself indirectly through temper tantrums or games. The erratic behavior of adolescents is recognized and the use of drugs to treat adolescent depression is considered.

Rie, H. E. Depression in childhood; survey of some pertinent contributions. *Journal of the American Academy of Child Psychiatry,* 1966, *5(4),* 653.

Focusing on the "essential lack of definition of 'childhood depression,' " Rie states that "in the interest of clarity, the term 'depression,' when used in unqualified form, refers to those behavioral manifestations inferred or reported affects and inferred dynamics to which the term is typically applied in *adult* psychopathology (Italics original)." Rie thus discusses childhood depression "only with respect to the age of occurrence." Surveying the literature, Rie finds that "childhood depression and disorders which represented or emulated are rarely discussed." And that "it is generally agreed that the typical clinical manifestations of depression appear rarely, if at all, in childhood." After reviewing the literature concerning depression in adults, he discusses the implication of the classic formulation of depression for children. Reviewing the literature concerning depression in children, Rie summarizes that "an examination of the implications for child psychopathology of the dynamics of adult depression, including the roles of aggression, orality, and self-esteem, generate serious doubt about the wisdom of applying the concept of depression to children."

This paper clearly illustrates the power of theory and stands in interesting contrast to the papers by Sandler and Joffe, and Anthony.

Rosenberg, P. H., & Latimer, R. Suicide attempts in children. *Mental Hygiene,* 1966, *50(3),* 354.

Rosenbaum, M. Psychological effects on the child raised by an older sibling. *American Journal of Orthopsychiatry,* 1963, *33,* 515. (Discussion by Rudolph Ekstein)

Rutter, M., Lebovici, S., Sneznerski, A. V., Sadoun, R., Brooke, E., & Lin, Tsung-Yi. A tri-axial classification of mental disorders in childhood. *Journal of Child Psychology and Psychiatry,* 1969, *10,* 41.

Sabbath, J. C. The suicidal adolescent—the expendable child. *Journal of American Academy of Child Psychiatry,* 1969, *8,* 272.

*Sandler, J., & Joffe, W. Notes on childhood depression. *International Journal of Psychoanalysis,* 1965, *46,* 88.

This paper, clearly one of the finest in the literature on childhood depression, is a gem of clear writing and creative thinking. The authors present "the bridge, we believe, between the classical theory of melancholia (i.e. the theory proposed by Freud) and the views of depression expressed by Bibring (1953) and other writers." Comparing depression to anxiety, the authors deal with "the depressive reaction (which is) a specific mode of affective reaction rather than a syndrome or an illness in itself." Taking a line of thought subsequently developed at some length by Anthony, the authors propose that "if depression is viewed as an affect, if we allot to it the same conceptual status as the affect of anxiety, then much of the literature on depression in children ... can be integrated in a meaningful way." Elaborating the concept of loss, the authors point out that "while what is lost may be an object, it may equally well *be the loss of a previous state of self*" (Italics added). Indeed, we would place emphasis on the latter rather than on the fact of the object-loss *per se*. The authors therefore emphasize the "... state of well-being implicit, both psychologically and biologically, in the *relationship with* the object, rather than the simple presence or absence of an important individual." (Italics added) This emphasis on the relationship greatly enriches the concept of loss. The authors relate the "feeling of having been deprived of an ideal state" to depression by maintaining that "if his response is characterized by a feeling of helplessness and he shows passive resignation in his behavior, we can consider him to be depressed." In this state, there is inhibition both of drive discharge and ego functions. Reexamining from this perspective the classic view of depression as anger turned against self, the authors state that "it is an oversimplification to say, however, that this aggression has simply been turned against itself *via identification with the hated object*. It is our view that what is much more frequent in children is either the direct inhibition of aggression, or the direction of anger against the actual self, which is disliked or hated because it is unsatisfactory." (Italics original)

The authors propose that the superego functions in depression in two ways: First, through the presentation to the ego of ideal standards that are unrealistic and incapable of attainment and second, through the repression of aggression, which the depressive reaction may engender. The authors thus propose two necessary conditions for the development of the depressive reaction: An unattainable ideal state of the self and an attitude of helplessness in the face of frustrating internal or external circumstances.

The authors discuss "adaptive measures which can be taken in order to prevent either the arousal of depressive affect or its intrusion into consciousness." In this regard they discussed "reversal of affect, for example, in which depressive feelings are reversed and obscured by excitement and clowning ... " Psychosomatic states may be similarly conceptualized, as may identification with idealized objects. In all these maneuvers, the authors proposed that "what is crucial in all of this is the attempt to deny or prevent the passive experiencing of helplessness in the face of frustration or disappointment. Much of the behavior which is considered to be delinquent or anti-social in children can be fruitfully considered from this point of view." The authors thus provide a theoretical basis (the need to prevent the passive experience of helplessness in the face of frustration) for further discussion of the "depressive equivalent."

In discussing the relationship of depression to development, the authors refer briefly to the work of Klein, Winnicott, and Bowlby and conclude that "we do not subscribe to the view that the very experience of depression is *in itself* a valuable one. We would rather stress the importance of overcoming disappointment and mental pain in a healthy way." They conclude on the interesting point that individuation is not a phase which occurs only early in development, "but rather (is) a dimension of development which starts early and continues throughout life, a dimension which has to be considered in its place alongside many other important lines of development."

Sathavathi, K. Suicide among children in Bangalore. *Indian Journal of Pediatrics,* 1975, *42(329),* 149.

Schachter, M. Depression in and depressive episodes in children and adolescents. *Acta Paedopsychiatric* (Basel), 1971, *38(7),* 191.

Schachter, M. The cyclothymic states in the pre-pubescent child (A case report). *Nervous Child,* 1951, *9,* 357.

This is a care report concerning "several years of study of one case of a cyclothymic child." The author observed this child over a period of 5 years from age 4 to age 9 who "attracted the attention of his family to his behavior at the age of two by his comparative silence and his unwillingness to join other children." The author described rapid shift between active and inactive states.

Schaffer, D. Suicide in childhood and early adolescence. *Journal of Child Psychology and Psychiatry,* 1974, *15(4),* 275.

This paper is an epidemiological study concerning suicide in childhood and early adolescence and is remarkable for the thoroughness and care with which the study was carried out. Schaffer contrasts the frequency of suicidal threats and attempts in contrast to the very small number of completed suicides in children. The objective of their study was to "collect contemporaneous data on a total population of children who have committed suicide and to describe this as fully as possible." However, as is so often the case with papers concerning children and adolescents, the adolescents are more thoroughly represented. This study represents no persons below the age of 12; two 12-year-old males, ten 13-year-old children and eighteen 14-year-olds were a total sample of 31. Schaffer summarizes his study with "two common personality stereotypes: (a) children who, although they had one or more friends at school, seemed to lead a solitary isolated existence," (b) "Those who were ... impetuous and prone to aggressive or violent outbursts, to be unduly suspicious and sensitive to and resentful of criticism." In contrast to the first group, who are of superior intelligence, the second group frequently had trouble in school.

In summary, Schaffer proposes six factors that may predispose a child to a suicidal death: immaturity; disturbed family background; depressed mental state; precipitating incident, often of a humiliating kind; access to the means of suicide; close experience to suicidal behavior. Of particular interest in this study is the fact that Schaffer has specifically spoken to the criticism of underreporting suicides in children. He concludes, following a careful search of records for evidence of a large number of unnatural deaths, i.e., "undetermined whether accidental or purposely inflicted." As a result of this search, he concludes that "even if one were to assume that all 'open verdict' and a proportion of accidental deaths from hanging, gassing, falling and road traffic accidents were suicidally motivated, the phenomenon would remain an uncommon one in this age group and in particular among children under the age of twelve."

Schaffer's paper is remarkable for its apparent thoroughness. One might conclude that if we are permitted to use six variables with which to control our observations, there is much work yet to be done in determining what specifically would put a child at risk for suicidal behavior, particularly since Schaffer has wisely (concerning the preliminary status) chosen very general parameters such as "degree of conceptual maturity," or "disturbed family background." Schaffer's paper therefore provides a solid base for research seeking to more specifically delineate factors which are associated with a suicidal attempt. The small number of suicides in children, however, makes such definitive study unlikely.

Schechtman, J., & Gilpin, D. C. Symptomatic depression as seen in the clinic. In J. Noshpitz & I. N. Berlin (Eds.), *Basic textbook in child psychiatry*. New York: Basic Books, in press.

This paper reports a retrospective study of children diagnosed "psychoneurotic disorder depressive type." The goal of the study was "to look for trends which might help to differentiate these depressed children from other diagnostic labels (and) to determine which, if any, of the variables (thereby) identified could reliably and statistically differentiate between our target groups of children with a depressed diagnosis and a group of non-depressed children from the same clinic population." Thirty-three children were studied. Blacks were underrepresented and girls were overrepresented. Further, these children tended to be somewhat older than most of the children seen at the clinic. Diagnostic criteria were broad. The prevalence of loss and depression was noted in the histories of the families; "the mothers, in particular, had experienced losses themselves as they were growing up, many before the age of the twelve ... all but one mother had either suffered an early parent loss, were depressed or both." In an interesting corollary study, the authors took the opposite attack and looked at boys who were known to have experienced losses in their lives. Of the four boys who had experienced loss of a parent and were between the ages of 9 and 11, when seen in the clinic a diagnosis of personality disorder of sociopathic type was made in every case. Psychological testing and psychiatric evaluation were done and all but two of the children were seen as depressed by the psychologist and/or the psychiatrist. Depressed girls complained of friendlessness and somatic complaints; depression was more easily inferred in the girls than in the boys. The pattern of depression in the mothers, seen in the boys, was not seen in the girls, although they tended to view "females and femaleness as a negative." Developmental histories revealed "a striking history of early losses."

Statistical analysis of the depressed children as compared to a control group, using a 93-variable description of each child, revealed that only fearfulness, poor self-esteem and loneliness significantly differentiated between depressed and non-depressed. The authors note that "non-depressed children are seen by parents as having many more fears" and speculate that "because depressed children turn aggressive feelings inward upon themselves they have less need to project these impulses onto external objects."

Schechter, M. D. The recognition and treatment of suicide in children. In E. S. Schneidman & N. L. Farberow (Eds.), *Clues to Suicide.* New York, McGraw-Hill, 1957.

Following a brief theoretical discussion, Schechter presents case material (most of which, in fact, concerned the adolescent patients). He proposes that suicidal children may be divided into different diagnostic categories: Depressive reaction following death of a parent, hystical reactions, anxiety states and compulsion neurosis, character neurosis, perversions and psychosis.

He summarizes that "the handling of suicides or suicidal equivalences in children is based entirely on the concept of actual or threatened loss of a love object. The child's act is considered to be not just an attack on this object but also an attempt to regain it. The depressive elements in all cases are outstanding. Therefore, irrespective of the diagnostic category the case presents, treatment consists of strengthening the relationships."

Schmale, A. H., Jr. A genetic view of affects with special reference to the genesis of helplessness and hopelessness. *Psychoanalytic Study of the Child,* 1964, *19,* 287.

*Schmale, A. H., & Engel, G. L. The role of conservation—withdrawal and depressive reactions. In E. J. Anthony, & T. Benedek (Eds.), *Depression in human existence.* Boston: Little, Brown, 1975, pp. 183–198.

In these papers, the authors fully develop Engel's pioneering work with Engel's infant patient, Monica, and create a broad, biologically based frame of reference for our understanding of depressive phenomena.

†Schmidt, M. Reaktive depressionen bei hirngeschadigten kindern und ihre psychosozialen korrelate (Reactive depression in children with brain damage and its psychosocial correlates). In A. Annell (Ed.), *Depressive states in childhood and adolescence.* Stockholm: Almqvist and Wiksell, 1972, pp. 250–254.

At the Fourth Congress of the Union of European Pedopsychiatrists in Stockholm, August 30–September 3, 1971, the incidence and probable causes of reactive depression in children with brain damage were investigated, along with psychosocial correlates of such depression. Out of 76 clinically examined schoolchildren with brain damage and normal intelligence, 32 showed depressive symptoms classified as reactive. These symptoms showed positive correlation with fear of failure in children who were relatively gifted and capable of achievement but who had received a restrictive upbringing and overprotection from parents. Comparison of these subjects with physically handicapped and behaviorally disturbed children revealed that they had the highest incidence of reactive depression. In such patients, there is apparently a cumulative effect of two factors, both of which induce or predispose to depression: Achievement and adaptation problems that are typical of the handicapped group, and ego weakness, a factor ascribed to children with brain damage. A combined effect of both factors may well explain the high incidence of depression in these subjects. 10 references. (Author abstract modified)

†Schmitz, W. Nachlassen der schulleistungen als primarsymptom einer endogenen depression. (Impaired school performance as a primary symptom of an endogenous depression). In A. Annell (Ed.), *Depressive states in childhood and adolescence.* Stockholm: Almqvist and Wiksell, 1972, pp. 263–268.

At the Fourth Congress of the Union of European Pedopsychiatrists in Stockholm, August 30–September 3, 1971, the impaired school performance of 17 children as a primary symptom of an endogenous depression was reported. Subjects were from a population of 46,000 children and 14 of them were sent to treatment solely as a result of teacher observations. Gradual or sudden inexplicable reduction of school achievement connected with pensive or unconcerned behavior, timidity, and anxiety were characteristic behaviors. Short phases of illness combined with reduction of achievement appearing several weeks before any depressive symptoms could be stated were reported. It is suggested that laxity in school work with no discernible cause may be a primary symptom of depression in childhood. 8 references (Author abstract modified)

*Schulterbrandt, J. G., & Raskin, A. *Depression in childhood: Diagnosis, treatment and conceptual models.* New York: Raven Press, 1977.

To my knowledge, this is the first volume concerning depression in children published in the United States; it follows the Uppsala conference proceedings, edited by Annell, as the second such volume. In his foreword, Bertram S. Brown, Director of the National Institute of Mental Health, points out that tremendous progress has been made in research on adult depression and that we now "encroach on the once unquestioned phenomenon of a 'happy childhood.'"

The papers in this volume will be presented and annotated individually in this index.

Schuyler, D. When a child dies, accident or suicide? *RN,* 1975, *38(9),* 21.

Scott, J. P., & Senay, E. C. (Eds.), *Separation and depression: Clinical and research aspects.* Chicago: American Association for the Advancement of Science Symposium, 1970. American Association for the Advancement of Science, Location No. 94.

This is not a collection of papers concerning depression in children, but is included here as a basic reference work of interest to students of depression in general. As reviewed by Lipton (Science, August 23, 1974, page 689), it is described as a useful volume which "brings together the findings of many disciplines in both human and animal research."

Scott, J. P., & Jenay, E. C. *Separation and depression.* Washington, D.C.: American Association for the Advancement of Science Publication 94, 1973.

Seligman, M. E. P. Fall into helplessness. *Psychology Today*, 1973, 6, 43.

Senn, J. E., & Solnit, A. J. Problems in child behavior and development. Philadelphia: Lea and Febiger, 1968.

Sharma, D. B., Berry, A. M., & Ghosh, S. Childhood depression. Report of a case. *Indian Journal of Pediatrics*, 1973, *40(308)*, 332.

Shaw, C. R., & Selkun, R. F. Suicidal behavior in children, *Psychiatry*, 1965, *28:* 157. 1965.

Siegal, E., & Grund, H. Suicide in children and adolescents. *Psychiatrie Neurologie und Medizinische Psychologie.* (Leipzig) *25(1)*, 42.

Siggins, L. D. Mourning: A critical review of the literature. *International Journal of Psychiatry*, 1967, *3(5)*, 418.

†Sornmani, W., & Kupitak, P. Depressive feature in Thai children. *Journal of the Psychiatric Association of Thailand* (Bangkok), 1972, *17(1)*, 1.

The difference in depressive manifestations in Thai children and adults is discussed. Depression in children with masked clinical features may mimic symptoms of aggressiveness, hostility, abnormal psychomotor activity and delinquent behavior. This often results in misdiagnoses and inadequate treatment. 5 references (Journal abstract modified)

Sperling, M. Equivalents of depression in children. *Journal of Hillside Hospital,* 1959, *8,* 138.

Spiel, W. Studien uber den verlauf und die erscheinungsformen der kindlichen und juvenilen manisch-depressiven psychosen. (Studies on the course and manifestations of manic depressive psychoses in childhood and adolescence.) In A. Annell (Ed.), *Depressive states in childhood and adolescence.* Stockholm: Almqvist and Wiksell. 1972, pp. 517–524.

At the Fourth Congress of the Union of European Pedopsychiatrists in Stockholm, August 30–September 3, 1971, the course and manifestations of manic-depressive psychoses in children and adolescents were described based on data from children admitted to a university neuropsychiatric department for clinical treatment over a 20-year period. Thirty cases were followed up for more than 18 years. Findings were psychotic manifestations occurring occasionally and transition from a psychotic manifestation in childhood to cyclic fluctuation which were mostly unipolar depressive states with relapses. The high percentage of erroneous diagnoses, especially with manic children, is mentioned. Identifying symptomatology related to the age of the children involves projection of the basic process of "morbus depression" into the development phases. The syndrome of sad dejection and verbalization of existential needs should not be sought for in childhood. Psychosomatic illness with relapses, state of failure or inactivity, or marked changes in motor activity, along with states resembling neurasthenia, are found instead. Rarer symptoms include masking of depressive states by compulsive symptomatology, manic manifestations, physical feature and autistic withdrawal, as well as different forms of failure in school. (Author abstract modified)

Spitz, R. A. Hospitalism: An inquiry into the genesis of psychiatric conditions in early childhood. I. *Psychoanalytic Study of the Child,* 1945, *1,* 53. II. *Psychoanalytic Study of the Child,* 1946, *2,* 313.

These classic papers are discussed in the first chapter of this volume.

Spitz, R. A. Psychoanalytische begriffsbildung und physiologisches denkmodell. *Sch. z. Psychol. und Anwendungen,* 1953, *12(1),* 24.

Spitz, R. A. Infantile depression and the general adaptation syndrome. In P. H. Hoch, & J. Zugin (Eds.), *Depression.* (Proceedings of the 42nd Annual Meeting of the American Psychopathological Association.) New York: Grune and Stratton, 1954, pp. 93–108.

Stack, J. Chemotherapy in childhood depression. In A. Annell (Ed.), *Depressive states in childhood and adolescence.* Stockholm: Almqvist and Wiksell, 1972, pp. 460–466.

At the Fourth Congress of the Union of European Pedopsychiatrists in Stockholm, August 30–September 3, 1971, different types of childhood depression were analyzed as seen in a sample of patients in an outpatient clinic of a children's hospital. Out of 4,500 patients referred over a 5-year period, 490 cases of depression were identified. Treatment with psychotropic drugs is described and the reactions of different types of depressive illness to chemotherapy are tabulated. The necessity for evaluation of the total family situation and for concomitant psychotherapy is stressed. Classification of the depression was according to two groups: 1) Depression in preschool children, including hyperactivity, apathy, and somatic complaints; and 2) depressions in school age children, including simple depression, phobic or obsessional children with depressive reactions, mixed depressive states, and depressions associated with organic brain syndromes and psychotic states. Primary drugs used in treatment were the tricyclic antidepressants and monoamine oxidase inhibitors. 8 references (Author abstract modified)

Stanley, E. J., & Barter, J. T. Adolescent suicidal behavior. *American Journal of Orthopsychiatry*, 1970, *40(1)*, 87.

Stearns, A. W. Cases of probable suicide in young persons with obvious motivation. *Journal of the Maine Medication Association*, 1953.

Sterba, E. The schoolboy suicide in Andre Gide's novel, *The Counterfeiters*. *American Imago*, 1951, *8*, 307.

Stevens, H. A child is paralyzed: The neuroanatomy of melancholy. *Clinical Procedures in Child Hospitals D.C.*, 1968, *24(10)*, 330.

Szilard, J., Vargha, M., Farkasinszky, T., & Wagner, A. Depressionssyndrome im kindesalter. (Depressive syndromes in childhood.) In A. Annell (Ed.), *Depressive states in childhood and adolescence.* Stockholm: Almqvist and Wiksell, 1972, pp. 168–172.

At the Fourth Congress of the Union of European Pedopsychiatrists in Stockholm, August 30–September 3, 1971, depressive syndromes occurring in young children were described, based on case material. Six cases of obvious manic-depressive symptoms (psychopathology and phased development) are cited with primary states of hypothymia and anxiety and the manic phases, although pronounced, being of short duration, often lasting only a few hours. The earliest manifestations of typical phases were found at age 9. More frequently, reactive depressive syndromes, manifest as early as in preschool age, were noted. The releasing factors were very different in nature. Useful findings were found via psychological testing for diagnosis as well as for evaluation of therapeutic success in such cases. Antidepressant therapy was used with most patients and its success confirmed the correctness of the nosological classification of the disorder. (Author abstract modified)

Szurek, S. A. The child's needs for his emotional health. In J. Howells (Ed.), *Perspectives in international child psychiatry.* New York: Brunner/Mazel, 1971, pp. 157–199.

Taylor, R. W. Depression and recovery at nine weeks of age: Introduction and summary by Mollie S. Smart, Ph.D. *Journal of the American Academy of Child Psychiatry,* 1973, *12(3),* 506.

This paper concerns the recognition by a nurse of depression in a 9-week-old male infant whose relationship to his mother was disrupted due to the hospitalization of a 4-year-old sibling. The nurse made a diagnosis of depression on the basis of "his looking like a little waif, (and his) constant sucking unrelated to hunger." She suggested to the mother a diagnosis of "weaning shock" and recommended that the mother cuddle, sing to, and rock the baby, encouraging responses from him. She further hypothesized that the infant had been particularly responsive to a change in his relationship to his mother due to the *high* quality of mothering which he had previously experienced. The child responded well and was active and normal at 28 weeks of age.

Teicher, J. D. A solution to the chronic problem of living: Adolescent attempted suicide. In J. Schoolar (Ed.) *Current Issues in Adolescent Psychiatry.* New York: Brunner/Mazel, 1973, pp. 129–147.

Although this paper concerns attempted suicide in adolescents, it is of interest to us in that the author discusses the evolution of a life position such that the adolescent seeks to resolve his problems by suicide. First, these youngsters experience long-standing problems; like so many others that have written in this field, Teicher emphasizes the extensive disruption of the family relationships in these children. For example, "Eighty-four percent of those with stepparents felt they were contending with an unwanted step-parent" and seventy-two percent had one or both natural parents absent from the home (divorced, separated or deceased). This picture of family disorganization virtually echoes those described in the families of depressed children. The second phase described by Teicher is the escalation of problems due to the stresses of adolescence. In the third stage the "parents have been alienated and the adolescent seeks to re-establish the spontaneity, openness and intimacy that he feels characterized the earlier relationship with his parents." Difficulties develop with romances, school work, and peers. In those youngsters in whom failure in these areas leads to progressive isolation, a suicidal attempt may be made as an attempted resolution to the 'chronic' problem of living.

Teicher, J. D. Children and adolescents who attempt suicide. *Pediatric Clinics of North America,* 1970, *17(3),* 687.

This paper, which is primarily an essay concerning suicidal attempts by adolescents, contains a brief discussion of suicidal attempts in children, which Teicher argues "appear to be impulsive acts mostly motivated by poor treatment and desire to punish those with grief or death . . . in general, the child who threatens to kill himself is expressing his rage toward his parents, usually his mother. But death is not permanent to the young child and often means to him a better life . . ." In the case of those who seriously attempt to kill themselves, serious disturbance in both child and mother should be suspected.

Toolan, J. M. Depression in children and adolescents. *American Journal of Orthopsychiatry,* 1962, *32,* 404.
Toolan, J. M. Suicide and suicidal attempts in children and adolescents. *American Journal of Psychiatry,* 1962, *118,* 719.

In this paper, Toolan reviews statistics from Belleview Hospital for the year 1960. He takes the position that "contrary to popular opinion, suicide and suicidal attempts are not rare in childhood and adolescence," particularly above the age of 10. Like other authors, Toolan emphasizes the number of first children (see Haider) and the number of disorganized homes (see Tuckman & Youngman). Interestingly, however, few foster children were found in their study population. Toolan describes the suicidal youngsters as primarily suffering from "behavior and character disorders. They are immature, impulsive youngsters who react excessively to stress, often of a minor nature." When these patients are studied in more detail, however, they show many symptoms of depression, restlessness, boredom, compulsive hyperactivity, sexual promiscuity, truancy, behavioral difficulties at home and running away from home. Toolan takes the position that depression is an important etiological factor and that partly for this reason suicidal attempts have been overlooked in children and adolescents. Toolan points to several categories of difficulties: 1. Anger at another, internalized as guilt and depression; 2. attempts to manipulate; 3. a signal of distress; 4. reactions to feelings of inner disintegration; 5. a desire to join a dead relative. Toolan concludes that "if we can successfully recognize the signs by which depression is manifested in younger persons, we shall then be in a position to prevent many serious suicidal attempts."

Toolan, J. M. Depression in adolescents. *Modern Perspectives in Adolescent Psychiatry.* New York: Brunner/Mazel, 1971, pp. 358–378.

Toolan, J. M. Suicide in children and adolescents. *American Journal of Psychotherapy,* 1975, *29(3),* 339.

Trube-Becker, G. Suicide in children and adolescents. *Munchener Medizinische Wochenschrift,* 1970, *112(16),* 750.

This paper, in German with summary in English, reports 109 cases of "suicide committed by children and adolescents" although "adolescence" extends to the age of 21 years in this paper. Trube-Becker reports 35 cases between the ages of 10 and 17, presents brief clinical vignettes and concludes that "the motives—as far as identifiable at all—are multifactorial." She urges that "threats of suicide expressed by children and adolescents should be taken as a matter of serious concern."

Tuckman, J., & Youngman, W. F. Attempted suicide and family disorganization. *Journal of Genetic Psychology,* 1964, *105,* 187.

This frequently cited paper studies "the interrelation of attempted suicide, family disorganization and delinquency . . . in a sample of one hundred children and adolescents under eighteen years of age." Drawing from a sample of 223 suicidal individuals, the authors sought to determine the number of contacts with social agencies in the Philadelphia area. Fifty-one percent of the families had been known to one or more health and welfare agencies, and this the authors see as a low figure for the percentage of disorganized families. They conclude that "(the data) clearly indicates that family breakdown or family disorganization characterizes the life experiences of persons attempting suicide." More particularly, the breakdown was seen as "pervasive" due to the number of different agencies with which the families were involved. The authors note that "family breakdown, as measured by contacts with health and welfare agencies, was more prevalent among children and adolescents (75 percent of the families) than among adults (51 percent)."

†Ushakov, G. K., & Girich, Ya. P. Special features of psychogenic depressions in children and adolescents. In A. Annell (Ed.), *Depressive states in childhood and adolescence.* Stockholm: Almqvist and Wiksell, 1972, pp. 510–516.

At the Fourth Congress of the Union of European Pedopsychiatrists in Stockholm, August 30–September 3, 1971, special features of psychogenic depression in children and adolescents were described, based on observations of 84 cases with depression appearing for the first time and sixteen cases of the same age with recurring depressions. Depressive disorders were grouped as: 1) depressive inclusions in a diffuse symptomatologically indistinct picture in children under seven years of age; 2) depressive syndrome as a phase in the disease, in some cases also as the basic syndrome of the disorder without clearly pronounced basic symptomatology at the age of 7 to 10 years; 3) depressive syndrome, more frequently as the basic one, with a more pronounced symptomatology permitting classification in some cases as one of the clinical variants (hysterical, depression with excitation) at the age of 11 to 13 years; and 4) resistant, clinically heterogenous, frequently appearing as the basic syndrome, reactive depressions in the age group 14 to 17 years. In recurring depressive disorders, the symptoms were more pronounced, profound and massive, as is characteristic of persons of a more mature age. 9 references. (Author abstract modified)

Varley, J. E. Depression in pre-pubertal children. *Developmental Medicine and Child Neurology,* 1974, *16(5),* 689.
Varley, J. E. Depression in children. *Nursing Times,* 1974, *70(41),* 1568.
Vranjesevic, D., Radojicic, B., Bumbasirevic, S., & Todorovic, S. Depressive manifestations in children with intracranial tumors. In A. Annell (Ed.), *Depressive states in childhood and adolescence.* Stockholm: Almqvist and Wiksell, 1972, pp. 201–206.

At the Fourth Congress of the Union of European Pedopsychiatrists in Stockholm, August 30–September 3, 1971, depressive manifestations in children with intracranial tumors were described, based on observation of 80 such cases, mainly children between 5 and 12 years of age. Brain tumors are frequently followed by various psychological disturbances and mood alterations which result from increased intracranial pressure and damage to special brain structures. Discovery of the organic cause is sometimes difficult, due to the lack of a fully developed brain, limited possibility for the patients to express their problems, and problems in examination and interpretation of symptoms. In the sample, 32.5 percent of the patients had various psychic disturbances, more than half of which were depressive manifestations. Lesions of temporal lobe, frontal lobe, and hypothalamus were usually responsible for disturbances of temper, making diagnosis difficult. Alterations of sensation provoked directly (brain stem) or indirectly by increased intracranial pressure are also important factors in causing various psychic disturbances. Special attention should be paid to infratenorial tumors with psychic disturbances when intracranial pressure is not increased. 6 references. (Author abstract modified).

Waage, G. Suicide attempts in children and adolescents. *Praxris der Kinderpsychologie und Kinderpsychiatrie,* 1966, *15(1),* 3.

This paper, written in German with no English summary, reports suicidal attempts in 18 children ranging in age from 8½ to 14½ years. In an 8½ year old girl, they report alcoholism in a grandfather and uncle, a depressed mother, and a previous hospitalization for suicidal attempt in the father. In this child, Waage proposes a "depressive reaction." In a 9½-year-old boy, Waage reports pavor nocturnus somnambulism, nocturnal enuresis. In a 10-year-old boy, he reports reactive depression and anxiety. Waage finds the theory of Sigmund Freud relevant to the majority of the cases in terms of aggression turned inward. In a smaller group, he proposes a "hysterical demonstration" of suicidal impulse.

Watson, J. S. Depression and the perception of control in early childhood. In J. G. Schulterbrandt, & A. Raskin (Eds.), *Depression in childhood: Diagnosis, treatment and conceptual models.* New York: Raven Press, 1977, pp. 123–133.

If Malmquist's global and comprehensive discussion of the field of childhood depression stands at one end of a complexity spectrum, this paper by Watson certainly stands at the other end, as he summarizes in his initial statements: Within the past decade, there has arisen an impressive array of evidence which identifies a rather simple experiential variable as a fundamental cause of depression. *In both animals and humans, depression appears to be the direct consequence of exposure to significant events that are outside the subject's control* (Italics added). In this chapter, Watson reviewed the experimental research in the field of "non-contingent stimulation," considers implications of this research for our understanding of a child's perception of control, and outlines areas for future research.

McKinney's and Watson's papers are discussed by C. S. Dweck, pages 135–138. Dweck emphasizes that learned helplessness "refers to the *perception* of independence between one's responses and the onset or termination of aversive events" (Italics original). Citing her own research, Dweck reports "the striking consequences of such cognitions." While actively questioning the existence of depression in childhood, Dweck argues forcefully that although "learned helplessness may not result in true depression before adolescence because the necessity for control and expectations that one exert control are not as great as they are in later life, and the possible cognitive and emotional consequences of lack of control are not as far-reaching ... the tendency to react to adversity with helpless cognitions ... may predispose an individual to depression in post-adolescent period ... despite the absence of apparent problems earlier in life."

Weber, A. Depressive states in childhood and their treatment. *Therapeutische Umschau*, 1968, *25(12)*, 685.

Weinberg, W. A., Rutman, J., Sullivan, L., Perrick, E. C., & Dietz, S. G. Depression in children referred to an educational diagnostic center: Diagnosis and treatment. *Journal of Pediatrics*, 1973, *83(6)*, 1065.

WHO Chronicle: Suicide and the young. *WHO Chronicle*, 1975, *29(5)*, 193.

Winn, D., & Halla, R. Observations of children who threaten to kill themselves. *Canadian Psychiatric Association Journal*, 1966, (Suppl) *11*, 283.

Winograd, M. Pathological mourning. In E. J. Anthony (Ed.), *The child in his family*. 1973, pp. 233–243. New York: Wiley.

Wolfenstein, M. How is morning possible. *Psychoanalytic Study of the Child*, 1966, *21*, 93.

Wolff, S. Dimensions and clusters of symptoms in disturbed children. *British Journal of Psychiatry*, 1971, *118(545)*, 421.

Yacoubian, J. H., & Lourie, R. S. Suicide and attempted suicide in children and adolescents. *Clinical Procedures in Child Hospitals D.C.*, 1969, *25(11)*, 325.

†Yusin, A. S. Attempted suicide in an adolescent: The resolution of an anxiety state. *Adolescence*, 1973, *8(29)*, 17.

A case study of attempted suicide in an adolescent girl is presented, along with a review of literature on depression and suicide. The attempt was the seemingly logical resolution of an anxiety state produced by fantasies of destruction aroused by the loss of perceived life sustaining object (a boyfriend) and the lack of ability to cope with it. Since the loss could not be replaced, the girl, a 16 year old of Mexican-American descent, saw herself alone, at the mercy of a hostile environment and fantasized an annihilation more terrible than death. The fear of this annihilation led, in part, to the initiation of suicidal behavior. 12 references. (Author abstract modified).

Zetzel, E. R. The depressive position. In P. Greenacre (Ed.), *Affective disorders*. New York: International Universities Press, 1953, pp. 84–116.

Zetzel, E. R. Depression and the incapacity to bear it. In M. Schur (Ed.), *Drives, affects and behavior 2*. New York: International Universities Press, 1965, pp. 243–274.

INDEX

Abandonment, 35, 36
Abraham, K., 20, 21, 34, 219
Adolescence, 87–106
　adult models in, 90–91
　affectionless character in, 60
　depression in
　　diagnostic implications of developmental data for treatment programs, 100–105
　　and object removal, 109–127
　　varieties of, 97–100
　developmental tasks of, 87–88
　intimacy in, development of capacity for, 95–96
　need for challenge and learning to solve problems in, 91–93
　role of self-assertion in individuation in, 96–97
　sexuality in, 93–94
　talent development in, 93
Adult models in adolescence, 90–91
Affectionless character, 32, 60
Affective disorder, 38, 250, 264, 265
Affecto-motor storms, 117
Aggressive behavior, 30, 57, 77, 230–231
Ainsworth, M.D.S., 73
Aires, P., 93
Akiskal, H. S., 25, 37, 129, 138, 148, 220
American Psychiatric Association, 128th Annual Meeting of, 264
Anaclitic Depression (Spitz), 20
Anaclitic depression, 21, 32, 52–53, 80, 116, 226, 237, 270
Andorra (Frisch), 244

Anger, 57
Animal behavioral/biological models, 265
Annell, A. L., 24, 220, 222, 227, 232, 233, 236, 239, 249, 250, 252, 256, 265, 279, 280–283, 287
Anorexia, 242
Anthony, E. J., 18, 23–25, 38, 63, 74, 75, 89, 115, 138, 221
Antidepressant drugs, 40, 241
Atkins, Norman, 126
Attachment, 22, 23, 71–72, 80, 251–252
  normal vs. anxious, 73
Attachment deprivation, 37
Autistic withdrawal, 226

Bakwin, H., 140, 222
Bangalore, 276
Barger, B., 87, 89, 95, 98, 100
Bariskin, J. S., 188
Barker, J. T., 35
Basch, Michael Franz, 138
Battered child syndrome, 126
  (*See also* Child abuse syndrome)
Beck, A. J., 115, 223
Beck Depression Inventory (BDI), 254
Beigel, A., 64
Bemporad, J. R., 61
Bender, L., 141, 223
Benedek, Therese, 18, 22, 23, 221
Bereavement, 56–58, 219, 221–223, 226, 237, 248
  and psychiatric illness, 235
  and subsequent crime, 228–229
Bergstrand, C. G., 141, 224
Berlin, I. N., 88, 117

Bibring, E., 18, 34, 225, 274
Biochemical factors in childhood depression, 39–40, 41–42
Bipolar depression, 37–38, 55
Birch, H., 142
Blatt, Sidney, 116, 226
Block, J., 89
Blos, P., 88, 94, 112
Boarding school, 98, 100
Bowlby, John, 22–23, 32, 53, 57, 71, 72, 141, 218, 228
Brain tumors, 287–288
Brandes, N. S., 106, 228
Broeck, E. J., 187
Broken homes, 248
Bronfenbrenner, U., 93
Brumback, R. A., 63, 229
Burks, H. L., 30, 230–231

Caplan, G., 88
Caplan, M. G., 55, 231
Caretaker depression and childhood disorder, 77, 78–79
  (*See also* Parental depression)
Catastrophe theory, 25
Cathexis, 22
Chemotherapy, 282–283
Chess, S., 130, 142
Child abuse syndrome, 184–208
  case illustration, 196–205
  causes, 187–188
  child's role in, 188–190
  definition, 185–186
  environment, role in, 194–196
  epidemiology, 186–187
  parent's role in, 190–194
Childhood Depression (Anthony), 18
Childhood depression
  classification and typologies, 32–33

development of concept of, 46–48
diagnostic criteria, 29–31
studies on, 48–51
etiology, 33–40, 51–65
(*See also* Etiology of childhood depression)
in infancy, 80–82, *84*
in preschool child, 82, *84*
prevalence of, 31–32
psychopharmacological treatment of, 40
in school age child, 82–83, *84*
summary of, table, *84*
Children's rights, 125
Classification, 26
of childhood depression, 32–33
Classification: Purposes, Principles, Progress, Prospects (Sokal), 26
Clayton, P. J., 38
Cognitive deprivation, 37
Cohen, M. I., 187, 188, 190, 191, 195
Coles, R., 91
College students, 98, 100–101, 117
Concept of Developmental Lines (The) (Freud), 135
Connell, H. M., 49, 233
Conners, C. K., 40
Conservation, 279
Coping, 266
Criminality
and childhood bereavement, 228–229
and schizophrenic children, 250
Current and Past Psychopathology Scales (Endicott and Spitz), 38
Cyclothymic states, 276

Cytryn, L., 24, 32, 39, 48, 49, 138, 234, 264
Czechoslovakia, childhood suicide in, 232

Davidson, J., 142, 235
Deidealization in adolescence, 113, 114
D'Elia, G., 55
Dependency, 61–62
Depression and Human Existence (Anthony and Benedek), 18, 221
Depressive affect, 237, 275
Depressive core, 30
Depressive equivalent, 24, 30, 47, 57, 148, 206, 256, 258, 276
Deprivation, 36–37, 59–60
maternal, 236–237, 266
types of, 37
Derdyn, A., 124
Despair, 72
Despert, J. L., 141, 235–236
Detachment, 72
Development, 134–138
Developmental lines, 135–136
Developmental tasks of adolescence, 87–88
DeYoung, H., 97, 236
DiMascio, A., 36
Divorce, 58, 83
Douglas, V. I., 55, 231–232
Drugs
in treatment of depression, 40, 241
use of by adolescents, 99
Duncan, D. F., 195–196
Dyslexia, 249

Easson, W. M., 180, 237
Edinburgh, 106
Ego, 110–112, 115–116

Ego psychology, 22, 24, 227, 259
Elmer, E., 186–189, 194
Endicott, J., 26, 38
Engel, G. L., 23, 137, 143, 237–238, 279
Environment, role of in child abuse, 194–196
Epidemiology of child abuse, 186–187
Epigenesis, 134
Erikson, E., 87, 110, 114, 120, 124, 126
Erikson, G., 25
Etiology of childhood depression, 33–40, 51–65
  biochemical, 39–40, 41–42
  dependency, 61–62
  deprivation, 59–60
  genetic, 37–39
  loss, 51–58
  manic-depressive illness, 62–65
  organic factors, 62
  parental factors, 60–61
  psychological, 33–37

Farnsworth, D. L., 95
Fasman, J., 36
Feighner, J. P., 29
Feinstein, S. C., 65, 115, 239
Filicide, 126, 185
Fischhoff, J., 80
Fleis, J. C., 38
Fratricide, 269
Fraiberg, S., 80, 167
French, A. P., 23, 137, 239–240
Freud, Anna, 22–24, 73, 125, 129, 135, 136, 172, 228
Freud, S., 20, 21, 34, 51, 167, 240, 256, 274
Friedenberg, E. L., 126
Friedman, L. F., 26
Friedrich, W. N., 188

Frisch, Max, 244
Frommer, E. A., 31, 32, 38, 39, 49, 241
Furman, R. A., 57, 241

Gaines, R. W., 192
Gelles, R. J., 186–188, 192, 194, 196
Genetic factors in childhood depression, 37–39, 62
Ghosts in the Nursery (Fraiberg), 80
Gil, D. G., 185, 187, 188, 190–192, 194, 195
Gilpin, D. C., 277
Gladston, R., 186, 189–191, 194, 195
Glaser, K., 97, 149, 243–244
Goldstein, J., 125
Gould, R. W., 191, 194
Grandiosity, 64–65
Green, A. H., 188, 190, 192
Green, P. E., 187
Gregg, G., 187–189, 194
Grief, 51, 57, 228, 257, 259
Grossman, M., 187
Group for Advancement of Psychiatry, 24, 48
Guillain-Barré syndrome, 173
Gutman, D., 88
Guze, S. B., 38

Haan, N., 91
Halleck, S., 95
Hamburg, B. A., 87
Hamburg, D. A., 87
Hampstead Child Therapy Clinic, 34, 47, 48
Hamstead General Hospital, 229
Hardy, Thomas, 69
Harlow, H. G., 52, 247
Harrison, S., 30

Headache, 257
Heinicke, C., 53
Helfer, R. N., 192, 193
Henderson, A. S., 106
Homicide, 236
Homosexual feelings, 99
Hospitalism, 20, 21, 270, 282
Hospitalism - An Inquiry into the Genesis of Psychiatric Conditions in Childhood (Spitz), 20, 282
Hyperactivity, 64
Hyperarousal, 148

Indians, American, 98–100
Individuation, 112
  role of self-assertion in, 96–97
Infancy, 52–53, 59–60, 80–82, 111, 142, 143, 222, 228, 237, 238, 265, 270, 271, 273, 282, 284
Intimacy, development of capacity for, 95–96
Introjective depression, 116, 228
Intuitive stage of cognitive ability, 167
IQ tests, 60
Isle of Wight study (Rutter), 31
Israel, 220

Jacobson, Edith, 112, 113
Jacobson, S., 36
Joffee, W. G., 24, 34, 47, 48, 137, 249, 274–276
Jude the Obscure (Hardy), 69
Justice, B., 195–196

Kaufman, I., 30, 250
Kelly, J., 58, 83
Kempe, C. H., 185, 187
King, J. W., 142, 251
Klein, Melanie, 21, 252, 256

Kohler, Mary, 92
Kohut, H., 113, 136

Langley Porter Institute, 77, 81
Lauer, B., 187, 188, 190
Laufer, M., 34, 35
Law and children's rights, 125
Lebovici, S., 88, 255–256, 274
Levitt, M., 110
Levy, David, 182
Lewis, D. O., 30
Libido, 22
Loss, 36, 51–58, 74, 219, 221–222, 231, 237, 242, 245, 248, 263, 275
  perceived, 137, 138
Lourie, R. S., 141, 189, 194, 195, 257–258, 289
Lukianowicz, N., 140, 141, 258

McCulloch, J. W., 106
MacDonald, S. M., 63
McHarg, J. F., 65, 263
McKinney, W. T., 25, 37, 129, 138, 148, 220, 263, 265
McKnew, D. H., 24, 32, 39, 48, 49, 65, 138, 234, 264
Mahler, Margaret, 112, 113, 117, 118, 259
Malmquist, C. P., 24, 33, 47, 74, 83, 138, 142, 148, 260–262
Malnutrition, 81
Malone, C. A., 186
Mandell, A. J., 41
Manic State Rating Scale, 64
Manic-depressive illness, 38, 62–65, 211–212, 221, 222, 231, 239, 247, 263, 266, 281–283
Markland, L. D., 173
Martin, H., 188–190

Masked depression, 30, 47, 185, 234, 243, 248, 253, 256, 258
Masterson, J. R. Jr., 91, 94, 97
Maternal attachment, 251-252
  (*See also* Attachment)
Maternal depression, 77, 80
  (*See also* Parental depression)
Maternal deprivation, 236-237, 266
  (*See also* Deprivation)
Maternal mental illness, 246
Mattsson, A., 141, 172, 262-263
Melancholia, 21
Mendlewicz, J., 38
Milowe, I. D., 189, 194, 195
Mirroring process, 118
Monkeys, 52, 247
Morris, M. G., 191, 194
Morse, C. W., 186, 188-190, 192, 195
Mt. Saini Community Project, 93
Mourning, 21, 57, 74, 228, 240-242, 263, 281, 289-290
Mourning and Melancholia (Freud), 240, 258
Mulick, J. S., 137
Murphy, D., 64
Murphy, L. B., 137, 266
Mussen, P. H., 17, 25

Nagera, H., 130, 136, 266
Narcissism, 22, 23
National Commission for Youth, 92
National Institute of Mental Health, 218
Negative identity, 114, 120
Negativism in adolescence, 88, 113

Objective removal and adolescent depression, 109-127
Oedipus complex, 252
Offer, D., 87
Offer, J. L., 87
Organic factors in childhood depression, 62
Otto, U., 141, 224, 268-269

Panzetta, A., 26
Parental depression, 60-61, 69-70, *78-79*, 80
Parental factors in childhood depression, 60-61
Parental loss, 74, 219, 221-222, 231, 242, 245, 248, 263
Parents, role of in child abuse, 190-194
Perceived loss, 137, 138
Perris, C., 55
Perverse fantasy, 35
Phillip, A. E., 106
Piaget, J., 17, 25, 75, 91, 134, 135, 167
Play therapy, 182
Pollock, C. B., 186, 188, 190-192, 195, 206
Poznanski, E., 24, 29, 31, 47, 49, 61, 271
Preschool period, 82
Pribram, K. H., 19
Primal depression, 271
Primal papathymia, 21
Primary affective disorders, 38
Protest, 72
Pseudoretardation, 224-225
Psychoanalytic Study of the Child (Spitz), 20
Psychological causes of childhood depression, 33-37

Psychopharmacological treatment of depression, 40
Psychosocial dwarfs, 59
Psychotherapy, 42
Pumpian-Midlin, E., 124
Punishment vs. child abuse, 186

Raphling, D. L., 187
Rapaport, J., 40, 271–272
Rascovsky, A., 126
Ravenscroft, K. Jr., 88
Rawson, R. A., 137
Reading disability, 249
Regional enteritis, 273
Regression in adolescence, 88, 113
Reich, T., 38
Renshaw, D. C., 30, 273
Research Diagnostic Criteria, 51
Resnick, P. J., 185
Rie, Herbert, 18, 21–22, 25, 141, 273–274
Rigler, D., 190, 195
Riley, H. D. Jr., 173
Rinsley, D. B., 143
Rioch, D., 18
Robbins, E., 26
Robins, E., 38
Rubenstein, B. O., 110
Rutter, M., 31, 38, 274

Sabshin, M., 87
Sandgrund, A., 192
Sandler, J., 24, 34, 47, 48, 249, 274–276
Schizophrenic children, 250–251
Schmale, A. H., 23, 137, 279
School age period, 82–83
School performance, impaired, 248, 280
School phobia, 220
Schrut, A., 149

Schur, Max, 23, 228, 259
Scotland, 248
Scott, P., 38, 63, 221
Seese, L. R., 141, 262–263
Self-assertion, role of in individuation, 96–97
Self-esteem, 113
Seligman, M. E. P., 137, 281
Separation, 72, 73, 231, 249, 257, 280, 281
  through divorce, 83
  in early childhood, 53–55
  in infancy, 52–53
  from siblings, 265
Settlage, C. G., 90, 111, 112
Sexual molestation, 186
Sexuality in adolescence, 93–94
Shafer, R., 122, 126
Shore, J. H., 98–100
Sibling death, 226, 248
Sibling loss, 57
Sibling position, 257
Siblings, separation from, 265
Silber, E., 87
Sleep and depression, 250
Social deprivation, 27
Sokal, Robert, 26
Solnit, A., 125, 281
Solomon, T., 187
Spinetta, J. J., 190, 195
Spitz, R., 18, 20–21, 23, 26, 38, 52–53, 80, 141, 228, 237, 270, 282
Stanley, E. J., 35, 283
Steele, B. F., 185, 188, 190–192, 195, 206
Steward, M. S., 23, 137, 239–240
Stimulus deprivation, 37
Strauss, J. S., 26
Suicide, 140–141, 143, 219, 220, 222–224, 228, 233, 235–249, 251, 253, 255, 257–258, 262–263, 266,

268–269, 272–274, 276–277
  in adolescence, 34–35, 105–106
  in American Indians, 98–100
  in college students, 98, 117
  in Czechoslovakia, 232
Superego, 21, 35, 111, 112, 275
Sweden, 220
Symptomatology of Childhood (The) (Freud), 24
Symptoms of childhood depression, 29–31, 48–51
Szurek, S. A., 73, 81, 284

Tajfel, H., 18
Teicher, J. D., 105, 248, 284–285
Thai children, 281
Thom, Rene, 25, 26
Thomas, A., 130, 142
Toolan, J. M., 25, 30, 141, 285–286
Transitional object play, 111
Trilling, Lionel, 111
Tuckman, J., 141, 286
Turkish children, depression in, 232

Ulcerative colitis, 263
Union of European Pedopsychiatrists, Fourth Congress of, 48, 222, 224, 226, 227, 232, 233, 236, 239, 244, 249, 251, 252, 256, 265, 269, 279, 280, 282, 283, 287

Unipolar depression, 55
University of California at San Francisco, 77
University of Michigan Medical Center, 31

Vaillant, G. E., 26
Vanishing Adolescent (The) (Friedenberg), 126
Varsamus, J., 63

Waelder, R., 182
Wallerstein, J., 58, 83
Waters, D., 124
Watson, J. S., 137, 288–289
Weinberg, W. A., 29, 31, 50, 64, 65, 229, 257, 289
Weiner, M., 135
Westheimer, I., 53
White, I., 39
White, R. T., 91
White, R. W., 89
Wilson, E., 19
Winnicott, D. W., 111, 115
Winokur, G., 38
Wolfenstein, M., 55, 56, 289
Wolpert, E. A., 65, 239

Young, L. R., 186, 189, 190, 192, 194
Youngman, W. F., 141, 286

Zeeman, E. C., 25
Zilback, J., 30
Zrull, J. P., 24, 29, 31, 47, 49, 271